Housing the Homeless and Poor
New Partnerships among the Private,
Public, and Third Sectors

Housing is fast becoming the most critical issue facing North American cities today. In Canada a quarter of a million people a year find themselves, at some time, on the streets without permanent shelter. For some individuals, and a growing number of families, housing is simply beyond reach altogether, and the numbers of homeless have become legion, even in our wealthiest cities.

The first four essays in this volume explore the housing problem as a social, economic, and political issue. They present an overview of the problem, with an analysis of who the homeless are and how great are their numbers; a study of how the housing market is structured; a review of policy developments in various levels of government; and an examination of the breakdown of consensus for housing policy.

The essays in the second part discuss the possibilities of new roles for municipalities, the private sector, and non-profit groups (the third sector). Although most homeless people and those with severe housing problems live in privately owned rental housing, this sector has been little involved in developing housing programs. Experience in other countries suggests there are other ways in which the strengths of the private sector can be effectively combined with public and third-sector programs.

A final chapter draws out the central themes and conclusions, suggesting that the most promising solutions lie in partnerships among government at one or more levels, private, and non-profit sectors. It also considers the role of those least often included in the debate: the poor themselves.

GEORGE FALLIS teaches in the Department of Economics at York University.
ALEX MURRAY teaches in the Faculty of Environmental Studies, York University.

Housing the Homeless and Poor

New Partnerships among the Private, Public, and Third Sectors

Edited by

George Fallis
Alex Murray

UNIVERSITY OF TORONTO PRESS
Toronto Buffalo London

© University of Toronto Press 1990
Toronto Buffalo London
Printed in Canada

ISBN 0-8020-2689-3 (cloth)
ISBN 0-8020-6722-0 (paper)

Printed on acid-free paper

Canadian Cataloguing in Publication Data

Main entry under title:
Housing the homeless and poor

Papers originally presented at a symposium sponsored
by the Canadian Real Estate Association and the
Central Mortgage and Housing Corporation.
ISBN 0-8020-2689-3 (bound). – ISBN 0-8020-6722-0 (pbk.)

1. Homeless persons – Housing – Canada – Congresses.
2. Poor – Housing – Canada – Congresses. I. Fallis,
George, 1947–   . II. Murray, Alex L.

HD7287.96.C3H68 1990   363.5'96942'0971   C90-093048-9

Contents

Acknowledgments

The research that led to this book was generously supported by the Canadian Real Estate Association and Canada Mortgage and Housing Corporation. Their contribution also included encouragement to focus on real policy problems and to adhere to deadlines. The views expressed in this book, are, of course, those of the editors and authors and do not represent the views of either the association or the corporation. Having set the basic agenda, both sponsors let the authors follow their research where it led. The participants at the symposium where the papers were first presented greatly enriched the development of the research. Numerous secretarial and administrative members of staff at York University, in the Faculty of Environmental Studies and the Department of Economics, gave generously of their time and goodwill in seeing a lengthy and complicated project to its conclusion. Finally, we owe a great debt to Lydia Burton who not only copy edited the book, but also patiently advised and encouraged us throughout.

Housing the Homeless and Poor

GEORGE FALLIS AND ALEX MURRAY

1 Introduction

All member countries of the United Nations designated 1987 as the International Year of Shelter for the Homeless (IYSH). When the UN resolution designating the IYSH was adopted in 1982, most people believed that the focus of the year would be on developing nations. But although it is true that homelessness is still mainly a developing-nation phenomenon, hardly a day passes without new evidence that, however one defines it, there are significant numbers of homeless in developed countries. Canada is no exception.

How one defines homelessness is, of course, of profound importance – philosophically, socially, statistically, and politically. If homelessness is narrowly defined as lacking a roof over one's head, the number of homeless in Canada is quite low. Even the most stereotypical street person can usually find shelter at night if he or she chooses. But almost everybody would find this definition too narrow; emergency shelters are nobody's idea of 'home.' At the same time, how does one put reasonable limits on or establish consistent parameters for a definition of homelessness?

The UN chose a very broad definition of homelessness that included two kinds of people: (1) those who have no home and who live either outdoors or in emergency shelters or hostels and (2) people whose homes do not meet UN basic standards. These standards include adequate protection from the elements, access to safe water and sanitation, affordable prices, secure tenure and personal safety, and accessibility to employment, education, and health care (Cox 1986).

This is a very encompassing definition indeed and surely contrary to normal usage of the word 'homeless.' For example, those who have adequate and affordable housing with security of tenure would be classified as homeless if their housing was not accessible to their employment. The common use of the word 'homeless' would include only the first kind of people: those without a roof over their heads. But the spirit of the UN definition is clear: if you do not have decent housing, then your home is incomplete and therefore you are 'homeless.' The UN definition of the homelessness problem becomes the same as what we in Canada have often termed the social housing problem. A problem exists if people don't have decent housing, comprehensively defined.

It may seem pedantic to devote the introductory chapter in a book to a discussion of definitions and semantics. But the discussion is critical to understanding the nature of this book, and it recurred time and time again as the authors prepared their chapters. It has also been part of the literature that emerged as a result of the IYSH.

Both 'homelessness' and the 'social housing problem' encompass 'a continuum of uncertainty' regarding housing. The total absence of shelter is merely the extreme end of that continuum (Schwab 1986). We can include within the continuum living on the street, sleeping in doorways and over hot-air grates, and squatting in empty buildings or on unused land in self-constructed huts; hostel dormitory accommodation on a night-by-night basis; emergency-shelter accommodation on a fixed short-term basis; rooming-house accommodation on a weekly or monthly lease; permanent housing that is physically inadequate or overcrowded or that has no lease or other security of tenure; rent that is barely affordable even when a person is working full time; housing located with poor access to employment, education, and health care. Emerging from this continuum is not a single idea of the social housing problem but several levels of jeopardy in which individuals can find themselves.

And people do not remain at one level of jeopardy, especially those people at the extreme end of the continuum. An essential part of their existence is change and instability. Many drift from the street to doubling up with a friend, to emergency hostel, to rooming-house, and back to the street. They can be grouped into one of three categories, depending on how much time and how frequently they are without shelter: the chronic, who are without shelter for more than thirty consecutive days (most chronic homeless have been in that state for months or years); the episodic, who tend to alternate for varying periods of time between being and not being domiciled; and the situational, for whom homelessness is the temporary result of a life crisis (Greer 1986). Another approach is to use a less-fine distinction and characterize those at the extreme end of the continuum as persons of no fixed address.

As the International Year of Shelter for the Homeless approached, public attention was focused increasingly on people at the bottom: those without a roof over their heads or in emergency shelters. They were becoming more numerous in Canada and more visible. We had always had hoboes and panhandlers, but something had changed. There were young people and young families without housing. Despite the broad definitions adopted by the United Nations, the focus was on those without shelter and those with no fixed address.

BACKGROUND TO THE BOOK

It was in this context that the Canadian Real Estate Association (CREA), with the financial assistance of the Canada Mortgage and Housing Corporation (CMHC), developed its contribution to marking the IYSH. CREA had long had an interest in Canada's housing policy and had extended its interest into the international sphere as a result of the UN Habitat Conference held in Vancouver in 1976. After that, the CREA president was the private-sector representative on the Canadian delegation to the United Nations Commission on Human Settlements. CREA led up to the IYSH by helping to sponsor, with other private-sector groups around the world, two international shelter conferences. The second conference produced a document called the Vienna Recommendations, which were offered as a basis for a partnership between the public and private sectors in addressing shelter problems (see appendix 1). To mark the IYSH in Canada, CREA approached us with a proposal. What emerged is, we believe, a unique and creative collaboration.

CREA wanted a serious and non-ideological examination of the private-sector's capacity to meet the needs of the most disadvantaged households in Canada. CREA was also looking for a set of specific recommendations that were relevant, practical, and capable of being implemented. We are academics. Academics are leery of sponsorship by agencies with a particular point of view. The reflective and analytical perspective of academics often makes it difficult for them to have enough familiarity with the details of the situation and political context to make recommendations that are immediately implementable. Nevertheless, we were absolutely convinced that social science had a vital contribution to make in understanding and solving housing problems.

We were able to establish a trusting but arm's length relationship with CREA. After stating its basic objectives, CREA neither directly nor indirectly exercised any control over the contents of the project – a truly remarkable sponsorship. The project had two outcomes. The first was a set of specific recommendations regarding the private-sector role in meeting the needs of the most disadvantaged households. These were delivered to CREA and presented at the Canadian Conference to Observe IYSH held in Ottawa in September 1987 (see appendix 2). The second outcome was this book. The first outcome was specific and immediate; the second outcome is more abstract and analytic.

To produce these two results, seven papers were commissioned from across the country as contributions to this book. All authors had previously published extensively on housing matters or related issues. Each brought the perspective of a certain background and a social-science discipline that were necessary for a comprehensive, interdisciplinary analysis of homelessness. The first drafts of these papers were presented by the authors at a symposium held in August 1987. Ten people were invited to the symposium to criticize and discuss the papers (see list of symposium participants). They were selected to complement the background of the authors: they came from universities, the private, public, and third sectors; some were researchers, some had written government reports on homelessness, some had administered housing assistance programs, and some had worked directly on the street with homeless people. The quality of each paper and of the entire book owes a great deal to the thoughtful contributions of the participants. (It is equally true that the thoughtful contributions of the University of Toronto Press readers substantially improved the book.)

The lengthy discussion of the background to this book serves two purposes. First, it details a unique collaboration. The private sector and public sector together sponsored a group of university professors to write papers and hold a symposium. Symposium participants came from all sectors. The project produced specific recommendations that are useful today and a book that is useful today and, we hope, will also be worth reading five years from today. One of the themes of the IYSH was new partnerships. The latter half of the book is organized around the roles of the private, local-government, and third sectors in such partnerships. We believe that this collaboration is itself an example of the sort of creative initiative – the sort of new partnership – that will help us to understand and solve the problem of homelessness.

Second, discussion also serves to explain the environment surrounding the book and therefore helps to understand its focus. The IYSH adopted a broad definition of homelessness, synonymous with the social housing problem, but public attention and concern were fixed on people without a roof over their heads or with no fixed address. Our investigations quickly revealed that there was almost no scholarly research published on this topic of public concern. Therefore, the task was to commission authors to write papers that focused, to the extent possible, on the truly shelterless and those with no fixed address but within the larger context of the social housing problem. For example chapter 2, which seeks to understand the dimensions of homelessness, begins from a comprehensive definition of the social housing problem, then looks at what data are available about people without shelter and in hostels, and finally tries to convey something of what it means to be a person with no address. Some chapters focus more on the extreme end of the continuum, others deal more with the broad context. Throughout, the authors use the word 'homeless' to refer to those at the extreme end – those without a roof or with no fixed address. This follows conventional usage, rather than UN usage.

The papers are written by social scientists and thus are analytic and synoptic, endeavouring to understand the history and causes of the homelessness problem that has emerged in the 1980s. This is what social scientists are equipped to do and how they can best contribute. In no sense, however, can this book provide a complete understanding. The authors were acutely aware of how far they were from the pain and distress of those on the street. Social activists, government administrators, private landlords, and real-estate developers all have their contribution to make as well. This book complements the other activities and other publications, often by people and agencies more directly involved with the homeless, that were part of IYSH.[1] Also the book complements the existing literature on social housing policies and problems in Canada. Most of that literature has concentrated on the housing assistance programs of the federal and provincial governments. This book provides both a wider context for understanding housing policy, and a greater emphasis on the most disadvantaged: the homeless.

UNDERSTANDING HOMELESSNESS

There are many ways in which the study of homelessness could be approached and many ways in which a book could be organized. For example, a book could be organized around studies of people at each level in the continuum of housing problems – from those living outside, to those in emergency shelters, and so on. Or the book could study different types of homeless people – released psychiatric patients, single men, street kids, etc. Or it could focus on causal factors such as poverty, mental illness, government restraint, or the lack of affordable housing. Or it could be organized around types of solutions: income assistance, more permanent assisted housing, or community development.

This book is organized in still another way. In seeking to understand the history and causes of homelessness and the response of Canadian society to it, the book situates homelessness in a broad context. Homelessness cannot be understood simply through an examination of who the homeless are and through an analysis of the number of available hostel beds and how more beds can be provided. Nor can sound policy be developed from such a narrow focus. The causes of and reasons for our current policy response and the understanding needed to provoke a stronger response lie beyond limited analyses. This book examines broad contributing factors such as the recession of the early 1980s, disillusionment with the welfare state, and struggles between the federal and provincial governments, as well as more directly contributing factors such as family breakup, the deinstitutionalization of psychiatric patients, the gentrification of old inner-city housing, and the shift in social housing policy away from helping the very poorest households. Most housing literature in Canada has focused on the activities of the federal government. This book explores also the roles of the homeless themselves, the private sector, the third sector, and local government. The theme of IYSH was 'New Partnerships – Building for the Future,' and the later chapters of the book explore the promising solutions that can be found in partnership arrangements among one or more levels of government, non-profit groups, and profit-motivated institutions in the private sector.

Like all studies of homelessness, the book begins by asking, in chapter 2, who are the homeless? how many are they? where do they live? Not surprisingly, data are rather sparse. In any event, data could never represent the human side of the problem and it is surely at the human level that one must begin. The chapter tries to convey something of the personal situation of homeless people and in so doing suggests some of the social and psychological causes of their problems. It also analyses the possibilities for self-help approaches to solving those problems.

Chapter 3 provides contextual data for the analysis of homelessness and also analyses the urban housing market, using throughout the approach of an economist. The chapter supplies further analysis about the causes of homelessness. It identifies three groups of causes: those relating to income and employment, those relating to the shrinkage of the affordable rental housing stock in cities, and those preventing an increase in affordable rental units.

The IYSH provoked much study of housing problems but the time would have been opportune for other reasons as well. Despite Canada's long experience of government housing policy, its housing problems have continued and are becoming especially acute for the neediest. Also, the social consensus that had permitted the development of the welfare state seems to have broken down. Governments have been restraining expenditure growth. Perhaps Canadian society's commitment to solving the social housing problem has fundamentally eroded. Chapter 4 examines the evolution of the welfare-state consensus and considers its implications for how we can respond to homelessness.

Another major political force shaping our response to homelessness is constitutional: the very structure of our federal and provincial political institutions moulds the programs that we choose. Albert Rose (1980) observed that 'the most important background fact in the Canadian housing experience is that Canada is a federal state.' Early chapters in the book note the multiple causes of homelessness: any solution involves not only housing policy but also social-services policy and income-security policy. Our federal state shapes our political responses in these policy areas. Chapter 5 considers this relationship between our federal/provincial institutions and social policies, and its consequences for the poor and homeless.

The traditional response to social housing problems has been to call on the federal or provincial government for a housing program; no doubt these levels of government must continue to play a major, even dominant, role in this arena. However, because of the weakened welfare consensus and because people are increasingly sceptical about the ability of senior levels of government to solve the housing problem, there has developed a recognition that other parts of society must play a greater role: new partnerships must emerge in the welfare state. It is likely that the private sector, the third sector, and municipalities will play more important roles. Chapters 6, 7, and 8 examine the past and future roles of these three sectors in dealing with homelessness. These chapters supply a more detailed look at the situation of the homeless and poor within the larger context developed in the preceding four chapters. They provide specific examples of creative collaboration among the private, public, and third sectors and tend to be more normative, suggesting other promising collaborations that should be tried.

Chapter 6 examines the private-sector role. It is often forgotten that most people at risk of becoming homeless live in private-sector housing, and that private-sector developers, builders, mortgage lenders, realtors, and lawyers play a major part in all housing matters. The chapter deals with homelessness and the private-sector role in the United States, most examples being drawn from the experience of Massachusetts. The private sector is much more involved in addressing the problem of homelessness in the United States than in Canada – both as a participant in delivering assistance and in thinking about what the private sector can and cannot do. The United States has many more examples of innovative partnerships among the private, public, and third sectors. It is true that the United States has a more severe homelessness problem than does Canada, and a much different attitude to the role of government; but the homeless situation and the willingness of government to intervene in Massachusetts, which is the focus of chapter 6, are not that different from Canada's problems. We can learn from the US experience. As one reader noted: 'I trust Canadians are open to free trade in ideas.'

Chapter 7 examines the third-sector role. During the late nineteenth and early twentieth century, religious and voluntary benevolent associations were the channels of society's assistance to the poor, the sick, and the homeless. Homelessness is not something new; it is not a product of the 1980s; it was often a severe problem in the nineteenth century, particularly after major fires. By the middle of the twentieth century the welfare state was well established and the major issue for the third sector was what supplementary or complementary functions it might perform. Its functions are now many: supporting agencies that do not receive government aid, lobbying to improve government services, championing the causes of those still in need, responding rapidly to new problems, and in the housing area becoming a major agency developing and managing assisted housing. There can be little doubt that the third sector will play an increasing role in housing issues and that it will require increased, and regular, public funding. But this process creates the dilemma of how to preserve the autonomy of groups in the third sector. How can they strike the appropriate balance between providing service to the needy and being an effective source of criticism of statutory welfare services? 'When in practice does a watchdog become a lapdog?'

Chapter 8 studies the past and current role of local government in housing policy and in its assistance to the lowest-income households. Like the third sector, local government is keenly aware of housing needs. When problems arise, pressure is placed on local politicians and officials. They feel intensely the need for new initiatives and also neighbourhood resistance to assisted housing: the not-in-my-backyard (NIMBY) syndrome. And municipalities do tackle housing problems, but their mandate is unclear, and often their tools are inappropriate and their funds inadequate. Their activities range from land-use regulation to cost sharing of welfare and social housing programs with senior levels of government; in some cases they implement their own housing programs. Within Canada, the local level seems to be taking on a larger role in social housing policy, almost by default. There will be required a clearer delineation of these growing local responsibilities as well as local leadership in addressing the NIMBY problem.

A BASIC FRAMEWORK

A basic framework, implicit and explicit in varying degrees throughout, emerges from this book. It provides a template to further organize thinking about how to house the homeless and the poor. This framework has three components: causes, solutions, and actors.

The homeless are diverse and their situation dynamic. The causes of homelessness are many: the problem is general but also specifically affects the plight of single individuals. The multiplicity of causes of homelessness can be usefully sorted into three parts. One part relates to the operation of the housing market, especially the shrinking stock of affordable rental housing. The second part may be labelled as poverty. Many people have bad housing because they are poor, and they are poor because they don't have a job and because government assistance gives them very little to live on. The third part includes psychological causes such as family breakdown and the deinstitutionalization of psychiatric patients. Many of the diverse causes of homelessness are unrelated to traditional housing matters. We could ask, for example, whether the social housing problem might be better considered an income problem, or if homelessness is better considered as a psychological problem.

In any event, just as the causes are multiple and go beyond the housing issue, so also are the solutions multiple and go beyond the housing issue. Solutions can also be usefully sorted into three parallel parts: those related to housing markets, those dealing with poverty, and those dealing with psychological issues. The need for a holistic approach seems obvious; but it remains an open question whether housing policy, income-security policy, and social-services policy can be fully co-ordinated, or whether they even should be.

In thinking about both causes and solutions, it is clear that all society is involved. For analytical purposes, however, there are four major actors to consider: individuals, the private sector, the third sector, and the public sector. And each of these can be further partitioned: individuals may be partitioned into the homeless themselves, those at risk of being homeless, and the general public; the private sector is made up of builders, developers, realtors, lawyers, financial institutions, and landlords; the third sector may be divided into private social-service agencies, self-help groups, charitable organizations, religious organizations, non-profit groups, and co-operatives; and the public sector consists of the federal, provincial, regional, and local levels of government. In thinking about solutions to homelessness, it is important to ask what role each of these actors must play.

RECURRING THEMES AND QUESTIONS

Each author in this book contributes to understanding some recurring themes and questions and to formulating responses and answers to them. Many of these issues will be taken up again in the concluding chapter.

A cynic – or a person with a strong historical sense – might well ask if homelessness is just the 1980s' word for poverty. Once we called for the war on poverty; now we call for the war on homelessness. The general consensus seems to answer no. Things are not the same; things are qualitatively different. A whole contingent of forces has conspired to make this housing problem different. These diverse forces include increased divorce rates and the decline of the nuclear family, the baby boom, a huge economic recession and uneven recovery, a challenge to the basic assumptions of the welfare state, government restraint, gentrification, and rent control.

Is there now the social commitment, the social will, to make the effort and sacrifice necessary to solve the problem? As the welfare state emerged, we developed a commitment to universal education, health care, and an income-security system, all financed by progressive taxation. The commitment to this basic state structure seems to be wavering and there is no move to guarantee everyone basic shelter. But even if tax money could be raised, housing presents special problems related to the essence of cities: scarce space. We know that the solution cannot be to confine the poor in one area, in a ghetto; the poor must be integrated into the community. The poor shall not only be with us, but among us. Most agree, but 'not in my backyard.' This NIMBY syndrome is a major barrier to solutions. Social commitment is needed not just to finance housing and related assistance; equally important is commitment to permit assisted housing in our neighbourhoods.

Homelessness is both an individual problem and the result of complex social and economic forces. Solutions are to be found within individuals themselves; in housing policy, economic- and income-security policy, and social policy from all levels of government; and in private- and third-sector contributions. The problem is multi-causal and solutions must be multi-faceted. Yet the question keeps arising about how to cut into the individual's cycle of housing, employment, and psychological problems; and about how to co-ordinate the multi-dimensional solution. It is clear that both an immediate emergency response is needed as well as long-term preventive measures. But the first step for the literally homeless and those without fixed address must be permanent, assisted housing. If individuals do not have a place to live, then all the other programs may ameliorate individuals' problems but cannot break the cycle of homelessness.

The new-partnerships theme of the national Canadian Conference to Observe IYSH is also a central theme of this book. In preparing the papers and throughout the symposium, many examples of collaboration among individuals, community groups, non-profit groups, and the private and the public sectors emerged. There was enormous creativity, vitality, and diversity across the country; indeed, researchers were far behind what was actually happening. However, least recognized was the involvement of the private sector in the social housing situation, and least understood and appreciated was the potential for a private-sector role in a solution.

We know that the majority of the poor live in private-sector housing. Most of it is decent, liveable housing; and most of it is, of course, not new housing. Both rich and poor alike do not live primarily in new housing. Over 45 per cent of Canadian housing stock was built before 1961, and 25 per cent before 1945. Some of the required affordable housing units must come from new housing, that is, from new government and third-sector housing; but the majority of such affordable units will come from private-sector landlords, including the large real-estate corporations, owners of small apartment buildings, and individuals renting a portion of their homes. Recognition of the existing private-sector supply and encouraging its expansion are part of any solution to the social housing problem. More debatable is what role private landlords can play in providing permanent housing for those on the street and in emergency shelters.

But the private-sector role goes well beyond the provision of rental housing. The private sector builds and renovates all housing – whether government, third-sector, or private-sector projects. The private sector assembles and develops almost all land; realtors and lawyers organize the purchase and sale of land and housing; and financial institutions supply the mortgages to permit construction, renovation, and purchase. The private sector has tremendous expertise that is being used somewhat by governments and non-profit groups; but it can be much more exploited with goodwill on all sides. And finally, the private sector is a major political force shaping our society. It can participate with governments, the non-profit sector, and the homeless in identifying problems, analysing their causes, developing a social commitment to respond, and designing solutions. On occasion, it should take the lead.

There can be little doubt that the public sector will remain the dominant agent – whatever partnerships develop and however the traditional roles of the four groups of actors are shifted. Even the most aggressive neo-conservative regimes in Western countries have only marginally curtailed the role of the public sector in social policy. There is even belated recognition of the inevitability and necessity of the public sector. However, within the public sector the roles are shifting and the outcome remains unclear. Throughout the post-war era, the federal government, through CMHC, has led in fostering a commitment to social housing, designing programs, and paying for them. In the late 1960s and into the 1970s, the provinces began to take a more active role – sometimes mounting programs to complement federal initiatives, sometimes creating independent programs. By the early 1980s, both federal and provincial governments were restraining their expenditure growth, but municipalities were emerging as major players. This was in part by default, in part because it was recognized that national or provincial solutions could not cope with the diversity of local housing markets, and in part because the urban reform movement had impressed on local government the recognition of how important local decisions were in shaping urban problems and created a commitment to developing independent local solutions.

This shift to the local level is not without difficulties. Local governments must rely on property taxes to raise revenue, and most believe these cannot be a major source of new revenue. Higher levels of government have a greater ability to pay, but it is a fundamental principle of democracy that the government which raises the revenue takes responsibility for how it is spent. The balance between federal/

provincial ability to pay and the need for local control and initiative remains to be struck.

Although municipalities are sometimes a progressive force in building social consensus, they can also be a force preventing the development of housing assistance. The NIMBY syndrome blocks projects at the neighbourhood level: a counterbalancing, strong regional government is needed. Often individual municipalities leave it to other municipalities to develop assisted housing: a strong, counterbalancing provincial or federal government is needed.

The authors in this book speak most eloquently to all these issues. Each has a slightly different emphasis and shading on the problem; each offers aspects of diagnosis and suggestions for solutions. Together they provide a coherent discussion of homelessness and some potential for improving a problem that diminishes the stature of all societies.

NOTES

1 Some flavour of the various activities as part of IYSH in Canada can be gained by reading CAHRO and ICSWC 1988, various issues of *Canadian Housing* magazine, especially Summer 1986 and Fall 1987, and Ontario Ministry of Housing 1988.

REFERENCES

CAHRO (Canadian Association of Housing and Renewal Officials) and ICSWC (International Council on Social Welfare Canada). 1988. *New Partnerships – Building for the Future.* Ottawa: CAHRO/ICSWC
CAHRO. Various issues. *Canadian Housing/Habitation canadienne.* Ottawa: Canadian Association of Housing and Renewal Officials
Cox, John E. 1986. '1987 International Year of Shelter for the Homeless.' *Canadian Housing* 3, no. 2: 14–16
Greer, Nora R. 1986. 'Homelessness: Demographics, Causes and Cures in a Nutshell.' *Urban Land* (May): 32
Ontario Ministry of Housing. 1988. *More than Just a Roof.* Final Report of the Minister's Advisory Committee on IYSH. Toronto: Ministry of Housing
Rose, Albert. 1980. *Canadian Housing Policies: 1936–1980.* Toronto: Butterworths
Schwab, Jim. 1986. 'Sheltering the Homeless.' *Planning* 2, no. 4: 24–7

ALEX MURRAY

2 Homelessness: The People

Even though homelessness can be observed and analysed as an economic, governmental, and institutional phenomenon, it is also a disturbing reality involving human beings with expectations, hopes, fears, longings, and passions. This chapter draws a profile of these people by first inquiring into the nature of homelessness through consideration of its opposite, 'homefulness,' or what it means to have a home. Next, an examination of the numbers of the homeless is organized within a demographic, life-style, and social-condition typology. An attempt is made to determine who the homeless are and how many categories of homeless there are in various parts of the country, despite scarce data, which are also uneven from one agency and one region to another. Finally, the chapter explores the psychological and social implications of being homeless by presenting qualitative descriptions of the lives and environments of various types of homeless people.

'HOMEFULNESS' AND HOMELESSNESS: REVERSE CONCEPTS

Semantically, psychologically, and spatially, the word *homelessness* implies the absence of a home in a person's life. What this absence means qualitatively and subjectively can, perhaps, be felt through a reverse process of contemplating 'homefulness.' A helpful conceptual framework is one developed by psychologist Jerome Tognoli as an ideal concept of 'six aspects of home' (Tognoli 1987: 657–65). One can only be deeply moved by the almost total absence of these six aspects in the daily lives of the homeless.

Centrality, rootedness, and place attachments. Home is seen as rootedness and the central place of human existence. It is a pivotal place around which human activity revolves, yet it is a place from which to reach out and to which to return. Home is seen as a place wherein one can achieve a balance among privacy, territoriality, and personal space, elements that are essential in achieving some sense of belonging and identification and some degree of personalization of dwelling space.

Continuity, unity, and order. Home can represent the continuity of life from one generation to the next. It gives a person a context through which to comprehend a more complete and complex sense of self. Home can have an almost sacred quality that symbolizes the unity of the family even in the face of non-ordered domestic lives.

Privacy, refuge, security, and ownership. Home is a place where one feels comfortable and at ease, which feels familiar and warm, and which one loves. It can serve as a retreat from the more public world of work. It is place for restoration, re-energizing, and regeneration.

Self-identity and gender differences. Home can be a source of personalization, individualism, identification as belonging, feeling in control, feeling habituated or adapted, and feeling that one has the freedom to do as one chooses. Home has also been viewed as a concept of self. For most (but not all) women, home is an especially powerful source of self-identity.

Home as a context of social and family relations. Home is the place where many of life's most intense, highly personal, and intimate interactions occur. It is the locus of much social intercourse, particularly with relatives.

Home as a socio-cultural context. Home and the house itself are both an expression of the residents' culture and a determinant of it. Thus, it reinforces inherited values at the same time that it serves as a medium for gradual adaptive change.

These six aspects of home, so powerful in their positive appeal to our emotions, are not present in the lives of the homeless. As we consider their numbers and scan their lives, we should be aware of this profound absence.

NUMBERS

The National Scene
The United Nations chose a very broad definition of homelessness that included two kinds of people: (1) those who have no homes and who live either outdoors or in emergency shelters or hostels and (2) people whose homes do not meet UN basic standards. These standards include

adequate protection from the elements, access to safe water and sanitation, affordable prices, secure tenure and personal safety, and accessibility to employment, education, and health care (Cox 1986: 14). We in Canada use these same standards to identify what we term the social housing problem, which develops when market forces cannot provide environments that meet these standards, thus creating a demand for government intervention.

Central to this social housing approach – and not all that remote from the UN definition of homelessness – is the concept of core housing need, a recently developed measure of housing problems. People are assessed as being in core need according to a two-step process. First, it is established whether the household has one of the three basic housing problems: housing that is physically inadequate, unsuitable (crowded), or unaffordable. These categories are defined as follows:

1 Adequacy: the dwelling unit lacks basic plumbing facilities (inside hot and cold running water, inside toilet [including chemical], and bath and shower) or the dwelling unit is in need of major repair (occupant assessment).
2 Suitability: the dwelling is crowded according to the National Occupancy Standard.
3 Affordability: the household is spending 30 per cent or more of household income for the dwelling unit (CMHC Research Division 1988a).

In the second step, if a household suffers from an adequacy and/or a suitability problem, there is a determination of whether the household has enough income to 'solve' its housing problems itself. If the household could not rent the average unit of suitable size and adequate condition in its community without spending more that 30 per cent of its income, then the household cannot solve its problem and is defined as being in core need. If the household can find an adequate and suitable unit for 30 per cent of its income, it would be defined as not being in core need.

Using these indicators and data from 1985, CMHC developed a profile of the extent to which Canadian households experienced one or more of the three housing problems and the incidence of core housing need among these households. CMHC estimated that of 8.75 million private households, housing problems were experienced by 33.8 per cent of all households, 28 per cent of owning households, and 44 per cent of renter households. Of those households with problems, affordability was the most common for over half the owning households and almost 60 per cent of the renter households. (The implications of this pattern of housing problems are further discussed in chapter 3.) Of all households experiencing problems, 44 per cent met CMHC's criteria for core need, of which 28 per cent were owning households and 61 per cent were renter households. This means that, in 1985, 14.8 per cent of all private households, 7.8 per cent of owning households, and 27 per cent of renter households were in core housing need, as defined by CMHC.

The demography of households in core housing need was distributed almost equally among four types: non-senior unattached individuals, 29.4 per cent; seniors, 27.8 per cent; families, 22.5 per cent; and single parents, 18.1 per cent. But the likelihood of falling into core need was very unevenly distributed among household types, particularly when they were renting: 31.5 per cent of non-senior unattached individuals, 38 per cent of seniors, 14 per cent of couples with children, and 50 per cent of single parents.

Variation among the provinces was also quite considerable, particularly between renters and owners. Newfoundland had the lowest incidence of core need among renters (22.5 per cent), while it had the highest among owners (13.7 per cent). British Columbia had the highest incidence among renters (37.2 per cent) but ranked seventh for owners (9.6 per cent). Manitoba had a similar pattern for renters (33.2 per cent) and owners (9.8 per cent). Quebec's 25.4 per cent for renters and 5.4 per cent for owners and Ontario's 25.2 per cent for renters and 7.1 per cent for owners represented the lowest incidence of core need. The rest of the provinces hovered around the Canadian average of 27 per cent for renters and 7.8 per cent for owners (CMHC, Research Division 1988b: 6, 11, 14–17).

All these households may have had serious housing problems, but they did have housing. They are at the medium level of jeopardy; they are not at the bottom end of the continuum of uncertainty (see chapter 1). Thus, these households do not represent the focus of this book – those without shelter and those with no fixed address – but they are the households from which the homeless are most likely to be drawn. They are the 'at-risk' group: households that may, with the slightest deterioration in income or family circumstances, be pushed along the continuum towards its bottom end of no fixed address and no shelter. This 'at-risk' group constitutes almost one-third of Canadian rental households, suggesting a looming social problem of great potential. In Ontario, for example, a 'Minister's Advisory Committee … for the Homeless' estimated that of 'the households in core need … about

100,000 are at substantial risk of becoming homeless should their economic or personal living situation worsen, even temporarily' (Ontario,
Ministry of Housing 1988: 37). This number represents approximately
9 per cent of the rental households in Canada's richest province!

It is hard to establish the numbers of people who find themselves at
the lower end of the continuum of jeopardy, those without shelter
and/or a fixed address. By the very nature of their cycle of homelessness,
such people are transient, elusive, and hard to count. The most
ambitious and large-scale attempt at counting was carried out by the
Canadian Council on Social Development (CCSD) in 1987 as a contribution to the International Year of Shelter for the Homeless. On 22
January, the same day that the preliminary estimates of the 1986 Census
were released, the CCSD conducted a 'snapshot' survey of agencies
providing service to people in need of temporary and emergency
shelter. These data were merged with others derived from interviews
with service providers and police and from consultations held in every
province and territory to create the only nationally based overview we
have of homelessness in Canada. The survey results were flawed by
some methodological limitations that are discussed below, but some
interesting insights emerged nevertheless.

The survey identified 472 shelters that exist primarily to serve the
homeless and destitute. Shelter nightly capacity was estimated at 13,797.
The overall occupancy rate of the 283 shelters that provided data was 77
per cent. However, in Ontario the men's shelter occupancy rate was 96
per cent and the general shelter rate was 101.5 per cent. As expected, the
largest group using shelters was men staying in men-only hostels: 61 per
cent. Women constituted 27.5 per cent, and 11.5 per cent were children
under age 15. Shelters for battered women and children held 16.4 per
cent of the reported residents.

In total, 259,384 different individuals spent at least one night in a
shelter in 1986 and the average length of stay was 19.4 days. But it has to
be assumed that some persons stayed in more than one shelter over the
course of the year. Therefore, the CCSD estimates that about 130,000
people used the 283 shelters that reported. The Council report concludes that 'since the options available to the homeless are few, and
since many homeless people do not use shelters an estimated range of
130,000 to 250,000 homeless people during the year remains conservative.' This estimate represents 0.5 to 1.0 per cent of the Canadian
population.

People who need night shelter also need food, clothing, and a safe place during the day. Some will also need medical attention, legal assistance, and counselling on employment and other matters. The CCSD survey, however, was able to get national data only on the provision of food. Of the reporting shelters, 78 per cent provided meals but there was great variation. Some served light breakfasts to those who had stayed overnight; others served meals to these and to drop-ins; some handed out vouchers to be redeemed at other agencies or restaurants. The CCSD report estimated that, in 1987, 3,210,947 meals would be provided: 2,829,115 by the shelters and 381,832 by the soup kitchens (CCSD 1987: 3–6).

Many of the numbers in the CCSD report probably are underestimates of the reality of homelessness in Canada because of the way in which the survey was conducted. The 22 January 1987 snapshot survey of homelessness across Canada asked 1000 agencies to complete a questionnaire regarding their services to homeless people. Although CCSD was able to identify 472 facilities 'that exist primarily to serve the homeless and destitute,' only 283 shelters provided data to the survey. This number clearly did not include all facilities and thus omitted many homeless persons. The CCSD executive director wrote on 6 April 1987: 'The fact that 8,000 persons were identified as homeless on January 22nd is serious in itself, but it represents only the tip of the iceberg.' For example, the CCSD survey did not include four categories of persons: (a) persons who slept in shelters that did not participate in the survey, including about half the emergency homes for battered women and children in Canada; (b) persons who were out on the streets or slept in abandoned buildings, restaurants, stairwells, parking garages, and public buildings or doubled up with friends or acquaintances; (c) persons in detoxification centres, maternity homes, or other special-needs centres that frequently assist people who have nowhere else to go; and (d) persons sent to hotels or motels by social-service providers or accommodated in local jails because no other shelter beds were available (CCSD 1987: 2).

The omission of these four categories of persons from the survey leads to the conclusion that the report probably underestimates the numbers of at least some types of homeless persons and that it never overestimates them.

The Provincial and Municipal Scenes
Data gathered at the provincial and municipal levels are equally problematic and vary widely from one jurisdiction to another. Three provinces and their capital cities for which there are some dependable

but varied data were selected for analysis. The same demographic, life-style, and social-condition typology of the homeless has been used for each example.

Manitoba and Winnipeg

The demographic, housing-market, attitudinal, and political changes outlined in chapter 1 and throughout the book have had an impact on Manitoba and Winnipeg more than on many other parts of Canada. Furthermore, homelessness in this area has its own special characteristics.

During the late 1980s, Manitoba had the second highest incidence of core need among rental households (33.2 per cent) and the incidence among owning households also was slightly higher than the Canadian average (CMHC, Research Division 1988: 17). It is from this pool of 64,000 'at-risk' households that the homeless men, women, and children emerge, especially in Winnipeg. Although the city, at 625,000, constitutes 58 per cent of the Manitoba population, 65 per cent of core-need family households and 79 per cent of core-need single households live there (Bairstow 1987a: 47).

On 22 January 1987, 728 people were estimated to be in Winnipeg's shelters by the CCSD survey (CCSD 1987). This means that on a per capita basis Winnipeg had one of the highest proportions of homeless people: over twice that of Edmonton or Toronto. But the CCSD survey did not cover all the shelters. A telephone survey of shelters in Winnipeg and other Manitoba communities, done nine months later, is probably more accurate. For 28 October 1987 it estimates an accommodation capacity of 1338 with an occupancy rate of well over 90 per cent, almost twice the estimate of the CCSD survey (see Bairstow 1987b: 88–9).

Shelters in Winnipeg are organized to focus on the shelter needs of the situational and episodic homeless persons, not the chronically homeless. In this they appear to be successful. For example, of 3,553 individuals admitted to the emergency shelter of the Main Street Project in 1985–6, only 198 (6 per cent) were admitted more than ten times. Even in the hostel the average length of stay was 22.3 days and only 10 per cent of clients were admitted more than twice; 51 per cent stayed in the hostel two weeks or less; 31 per cent remained for two to six weeks. There was approximately an even chance of the clients establishing at least short-term stability: 45.4 per cent left the hostel because of 'abandonment of goals (drinking, disruptive behaviour, etc.),' while 49.3 per cent moved on to 'alternative accommodation' or were 'referred to treatment.' The 'chronically homeless' were estimated at 718 individuals and 87 families (Brundrige 1987: 15).

Persons of native ancestry probably were a significant percentage of the episodic and of the chronically homeless. Although exact figures are elusive, Winnipeg appears to have a larger native population (4.7 per cent) than other western cities, such as Edmonton with 1.5 per cent (Edmonton Coalition 1987: 28; Bairstow 1987b: 50). Estimates of the native population in Winnipeg range from 20,000 to 30,000, which translates into 11,000 households of which 8769 (79 per cent) are renters. Of these, 3101 (35 per cent) have affordability problems when afford- ability is defined as 'payments greater than 35% of income for rent' (Bairstow 1987b: 50). This figure is 9 per cent higher than the national average for renting households with affordability problems as measured by CMHC, even though CMHC uses 30 per cent as the rent-to-income threshold (CMHC, Research Division 1988: 14). Thus, the true incidence of affordability problems among native households is probably some- what higher. This assumption is confirmed by an examination of the rent-to-income ratios of 202 Winnipeg native households searching for housing. Those who reported spending more than 30 per cent on shelter were single women (93 per cent), single men (50 per cent), and couples (77 per cent). Overall, the rent-to-income ratio for these 202 native households was 47 per cent (Bairstow 1987b: 52). Similar high ratios were reported for native singles in a survey of 209 clients of ten social agencies. The survey also revealed that 'native households appear to be living in the worst housing in terms of housing conditions' (ibid.: 78, 79).

Another factor affecting homelessness among natives is alcohol abuse. The extent of this problem can be measured by admissions to the treatment program of the Alcohol Foundation of Manitoba: in the mid 1980s, 40 per cent were clients of native ancestry (ibid.: 67). The executive director of the Main Street Project observed that, over time, the ratio of native people to Caucasians using its services steadily increased until by the mid 1980s it was 65 per cent native people (Brundrige 1987: 14).

Single men are still the largest group among the homeless on the streets and in the shelters of Manitoba. And they are a substantial part (possibly the largest) of that population that is in core need and 'at risk' of losing its shelter. On 22 January 1987 approximately 70 per cent of shelter residents in Manitoba were men (CCSD 1987: 4; McLaughlin 1987: 3); Brundrige (1987: 14) reported that in the Main Street Project hostel 78 per cent of the residents were male. Singles households in Winnipeg represent 19 per cent of the population but constitute 28 per cent of the households in core need (Bairstow 1987b: 47), perhaps because for singles on welfare the shelter component is about 30 per cent less than the average rent they pay (ibid.: 76). Thus, the average rent-to-income ratio of one group of agency clients was 46 per cent, with native singles paying 49 percent (ibid.: 78). Single low-income men were not eligible for shelter allowance benefits or for social housing if they were attempting to be independent by working (ibid.: 91).

The data from the ccsd, Brundrige, and Bairstow surveys suggest that at any one time there are at least 930 to 950 single men homeless on the streets of Winnipeg. Half of them are between 18 and 33 years old; over half are of native ancestry; about 45 per cent have less than Grade 10 education; about 37 per cent have some high school; approximately 45 per cent have not worked in the last twelve months; and 20 per cent have worked less than 40 per cent of the past twelve months. Although many have given up the search for work, some still persist. At the extreme end of the homelessness continuum is a group of hard-to-house clients, most (but not all) single men who have mental health problems and/or suffer from chronic alcohol and chemical dependencies. Bairstow and Associates' best estimate in 1987 was 500 such people, of which at least 200–300 could benefit from some long-term and supervised housing (ibid.: 92). 'Winnipeg has sufficient short-term hostel accommodation for single men, but ... this kind of facility is not that desirable and does little to foster stability in order to turn one's life around and get back on one's feet' (ibid.).

Homeless *single women* are less numerous than homeless single men in Manitoba; the ratio is about 3:7 (Brundrige 1987: 14; ccsd 1987; 4; McLaughlin 1987: 3). Even so, they share much the same environment: they make up a disproportionate percentage of core-need households; the shelter component of their welfare payments falls far short of rent levels; their rent-to-income ratios are well over 30 per cent; and they are ineligible for social housing and, if employed, for shelter-allowance benefits.

No data exist to suggest significant differences between homeless single men and women except that the women are on average three years younger than the men and are less likely to experience chronic homelessness in younger years. Often they are taken in by a male. As they grow older the incidence of chronic homelessness increases (Brundrige 1987: 14–15).

One factor affecting single-woman homelessness in Manitoba is that spousal abuse or wife-battering has been increasing for several years. Among the provinces, Manitoba in 1986 had the highest rate of charges for spousal abuse, exceeded only by Yukon and the Northwest

Territories (Bairstow 1987a: 20). Consequently, from 1985 to 1986 there was a dramatic increase in battered women seeking shelter: 12.3 per cent in Manitoba and 22.4 per cent in Winnipeg (Bairstow 1987b: 48). Some of these women had children with them; some did not. The data do not permit an estimate of how many of them were single women. The data do suggest that the total number of women in Manitoba who became homeless as a result of battering is approximately 1000 per year; 52 per cent or 537 of them were in Winnipeg (ibid.: 49).

The data from the Bairstow, CCSD, and Brundrige surveys suggest that approximately 375 homeless single women are on the streets of Winnipeg at any one time. But this estimate may err on the low side because the occupancy rate for women's shelters in Manitoba is virtually 100 per cent (ibid.: 48, 88). As a result, there are probably many women who do not even bother to apply for admission.

Youth homelessness is a matter of growing concern in Manitoba. Sister Lesley Sacouman, a nun with over eleven years' experience working with homeless youth, said in 1987 that 'the number of homeless children in Winnipeg is growing and the victims are getting younger.' She was 'unwavering about the major cause of homelessness among children in Winnipeg – family poverty. "Any attempt to call it something else is mistaking the symptom for the cause."' The economic pressures on families are so great, she thinks that they '"just buckle under the hopelessness of ever changing their lives." Thus home becomes "a dangerous place or a very unhappy place." Quite rationally, some children "feel they have no choice but to get out and fend for themselves"' (Bainbridge 1987: 49).

One symptom of families buckling under economic pressure is increasing physical and sexual abuse of children. Manitoba Child and Family Services reports that from 1982 to the late 1980s there has been a 27 per cent annual increase in the incidence of this kind of reported abuse (Bairstow 1987b: 70). Some of these children are among the 520 who each day come through the doors of Sister Sacouman's Rossbrook House, a 'safe house' for homeless street children. About 800 children, who would otherwise be on the street, use the House on a regular basis. But the Sister claims that they 'are only a drop in the bucket of the number roaming around on the street ... There are children out there literally sleeping under garages, in doorways and in empty houses' (Bainbridge 1987: 49).

Many of the girls increasingly turn to prostitution. Back in 1985, the YWCA and the Elizabeth Fry Society estimated that close to 30 per cent of

Winnipeg prostitutes were less than 18 years old (Bairstow 1987b: 27). But in 1987 a spokesperson for Prostitutes and Other Women for Equal Rights (POWER) claimed that '60% of the girls hooking in the area are under 16 and homeless' (Bainbridge 1987: 49). Other estimates are that there are 250 girls working the streets of Winnipeg, of which at least 80 per cent or 200 have no permanent house (Bairstow 1987b: 49).

Although there were eleven agencies providing shelter for children or youths in crisis in 1987 their facilities were very limited and directed towards clients with special problems (ibid.: 72). Shelter occupancy rates tell us little about the total number of homeless youths. '"It is impossible to estimate the number of homeless children in Winnipeg," Inspector Bill Heintz of the Winnipeg police youth division said.' Of the 5817 runaways reported to the division, 25 per cent or 1500 do not return home in a few days. In addition, the figures do not account for the many children not reported missing by their families, sometimes because they do not want to lose the child portion of their welfare money. '"It makes it really difficult to get a handle on the number of children out there"' (Bainbridge 1987: 49). However, Bob Knight, the director of Winnipeg Receiving Resources Inc., which has six community-based residences, cautiously suggests 'that there are between 250–300 homeless youth in Winnipeg at any one time' (Bairstow 1987b: 70).

Most of these youths are not served very well by the system. Sister Sacouman reports that on a typical weekend there are 50–60 youths sleeping on the floor of Rossbrook House because they had nowhere to go (Bainbridge 1987: 49). Bairstow and Associates concluded, late in 1987, that 'there appears to be an adequate number of special purpose facilities for youth with special problems but there are few residential options for runaway youths who do not have ... problems that fit them into a medical or clinical category' (Bairstow 1987b: 73).

Family homelessness in Manitoba is difficult to assess because families are shattered and dispersed by the very processes that create home-lessness and because few data have been collected on those that may survive. The exception is single parents (some of whom may be battered wives) and their children. A 1988 CMHC study concluded that Manitoba had the second highest incidence of core need among renters and that 50 per cent of renting single parents were in core need nationally (CMHC 1988b: 15). Therefore, it is not reckless to assume that at least 50 per cent of Manitoba's renting single parents were in core need; and their numbers were increasing fast: 52.3 per cent in the decade from 1976 to 1986, during which all household types increased by 16.6 per cent. It is understandable why 68 per cent of family households in Winnipeg public housing are female single-parent families (Bairstow 1987b: 32).

Even for two-parent families, finding affordable housing can be very difficult. Of one group of 202 native couples applying for housing to non-profit agencies, 77 per cent reported spending more than 30 per cent of their income for rent (Bairstow 1987b: 52). This percentage is much higher than the Canadian average of 26.1 per cent of renting households spending more than 30 per cent or 37 per cent of renting family households with children in core need (CMHC 1988b: 14).

Spousal violence or wife-battering contributes greatly to the creation of single-parent families and their homelessness. After fleeing the violence of her husband, a mother finds it difficult to get suitable shelter quickly and cheaply on her own. Increasingly, she has to turn to shelters for battered women and children. The annual rate of such admissions in Winnipeg increased 22.4 per cent in 1986. This meant that the number of battered women and children seeking shelter in Manitoba that might have become homeless as a result was 2559 per year, 49 per cent (1251) in the City of Winnipeg (Bairstow 1987b: 48–9).

People with mental disabilities have long been closely linked with homelessness, both in the literature and in the public's mind. Manitoba is no exception. Like the rest of North America, beginning in the early 1960s, Manitoba deinstitutionalized its mental health services without transferring adequate resources to the community in terms of qualified mental health workers and sufficient and varied residential settings. One result is that 'no one, not even the mental health practitioners, have [sic] a very good handle on the number of people in Manitoba who need specialized or supportive housing' (Bairstow 1987b: 92).

Estimates of the number with mental disability in Manitoba range from 8000 to 50,000, though Bairstow (1987b: 53) reports that the 'general feeling given by agencies in Manitoba is that there are 26,000 Manitobans with some form of need for mental health services and of this group, 6–8,000 have more severe problems.' In 1987, the current case-load of Community Mental Health was over 1600, of which fewer than 25 per cent (429) were being served in establishing mental health residential settings. A majority of those with problems lived in personal-care homes where they received only off-site treatment and counselling, except for some on-site supervision of medication. About 25 per cent lived in 3–5-person apartments scattered across the community, but were backed up by a range of staff and volunteer support (ibid.: 53–6). Although Winnipeg appears to have an appropriate range of types of supportive residential facilities, the number is small in proportion to the need (ibid.: 58).

Even though the Manitoba and Winnipeg data are incomplete, we conclude cautiously that well over 100 people with mental disabilities in Winnipeg must struggle with their problem in environments that are themselves sanity-threatening, whether on the street or in an emergency hostel.

Alberta and Edmonton
The impact of demographic, housing-market, attitudinal, and political changes on Alberta and Edmonton is the same as the average for Canada as a whole. But homelessness in this province has its own special characteristics.

During the late 1980s the incidence of Alberta *households in core need* ranked eighth among the provinces at 14.1 per cent – slightly lower than the national average of 14.8 per cent. But among those households that were in core need, Alberta's ratio of renting households to owning households (70:30) ranked second among the provinces. This means that, more so than in eight other provinces, a renting household is more likely to be a core-need household than an owning one (CMHC 1988b: 17). Also, affordability was more likely to be the reason for renting households in Alberta being in core need than for those households in other provinces (Statistics Canada 1985). We can surmise that although some of the 33,000 owning households in core need were probably at risk, it is from the pool of 78,000 core-need renting households that the homeless men, women, and children of Alberta emerge.

The CCSD snapshot survey of 22 January 1987 estimated that the shelter bed count for Alberta was 1118 (McLaughlin 1987: 4), but we know that the CCSD survey did not cover all shelters. The survey of the Edmonton Coalition on Homelessness (ECOH) is probably more accurate: it 'identified the existence of over 1,500 sheltered homeless households per month' in Edmonton (ECOH 1987: 59). Accompanying the survey was an estimate of between 785 and 1570 'persons who have no housing alternatives and little or no income ... the absolutely homeless' (ibid.: 10).

Native homelessness in Edmonton is more difficult to estimate than in Winnipeg, partly because agencies are reluctant to categorize clients under 'native and non-native.' Also, our major source, the ECOH survey, received a limited response from native organization (ibid.: 27). Edmonton's overall native community was, in the mid 1980s, estimated to be

12,000; one-fifth of the households expressed dissatisfaction with their housing. Studies suggest that by every measure of housing quality, native households must endure vastly inferior conditions (ibid.: 28). Perhaps the major reason is that the 1985 average income of native households in Edmonton was $9900, less than one-third of the $31,000 average for all families (ibid.: 52).

The ECOH research group, through surveys and personal interviews with sixteen agencies, assembled the following profile of homeless native people: 218 single men constituted 60 per cent of the homeless; 74 single women (sometimes with young children) constituted 20 per cent of the homeless; 70 families, mostly with fewer than four children, constituted another 20 per cent of the homeless. Including dwellers in substandard units and the sheltered homeless, ECOH estimated the homeless native community to be approximately 292 singles and 70 families (ibid.: 28–9).

Single men and women have to be counted together because some of the agencies house both and do not distinguish between them. The ECOH estimate for both was 483 (ECOH 1987: 19). I would guess that the ratio of men to women was about 4:1. Both groups had access to temporary and second-stage/longer-term housing. Temporary housing had a capacity of 411 men and 80 women per night, and occupancy rates varied considerably. For second-stage housing, capacity was 228, including a few families; occupancy rates were virtually 100 per cent.

Although no precise data are available, it is clear that in 1987 almost no long-term permanent housing was accessible to single men or women. This situation was aggravated in 1987 when the provincial government reduced the shelter-allowance component by 30 per cent for single employable social-allowance recipients to $118–215. This amount would not even permit a single person to live in the YMCA Hostel, let alone in a single room (ibid.: 59, 65).

Homeless persons with alcohol/drug abuse problems who were seeking shelter and one of several treatment modes were faced with nine agencies with 256 beds and an occupancy rate of over 90 per cent. ECOH concludes that the total number of sheltered homeless with alcohol or drug problems was 225 (ibid.: 22).

The number of *elderly* homeless in Edmonton is unknown. 'No studies have been effective in determining the incidence rate of elder abuse or elder homelessness' (ibid.: 40). But one surprising and disturbing insight was circumstantial evidence suggesting that there might be 100 or more old people who 'live in garages, or sheds, in cellars or in old cars. But they show an address.' It is, of course, that of a relative or a friend and is used once a month to pick up a pension cheque (ibid.: 41).

Ex-offenders were offered shelter and services by three agencies, who estimated them to number eighty-five at any one time (ibid.: 35).

The number of homeless *youth* is difficult to establish because it is such a transient and isolated group. Between the ages of 16 and 18, these youths have an ambiguous status; they exist in a legal limbo. They are allowed to leave home, quit school, and get a job, but they do not have full access to adult services. They are denied both the legal protection of children and the legal rights of adults.

In 1985, Alberta Social Services estimated that there were 70–130 homeless youths on the streets of Edmonton without stable accommodation: 64 per cent were between 16 and 18 years old; 25 per cent were native. Because economic circumstances in Alberta worsened after 1985, both for many families and for social agencies, it can be assumed that things have got worse. One respondent to the ECOH survey estimated that in 1987 'the numbers might be 200 kids on a busy night like Friday or Saturday within defined areas such as the Jasper Avenue corridor and the Boyle Street strip' (ibid.: 30).

Youths had access to four emergency, two transitional, and five residential facilities with a total of 241 beds, but the occupancy rates were very high; often there were waiting lists (ibid.: 30–1). The average length of stay at Youth Emergency shelter was two months, a rather extended emergency (Callwood 1987). The total number of sheltered homeless youths was estimated to be 348 (ECOH 1987: 31).

Family homelessness in Edmonton was in the majority of cases precipitated by spousal violence/wife battering (ibid.: 37). Families fleeing the danger of physical abuse might have found shelter in WIN House with its fifty-bed capacity or they might equally have been turned away; in 1986 WIN House turned away 441 families, nearly as many as they served. About half that many families were referred to appropriate accommodation by Emergency Social Services. It is unclear what happened to the 200-plus other families. In total, the system could handle 143 persons in families at any one time (ibid.: 16–19, 37). The Edmonton data make no distinction between single-parent and two-parent families. Therefore, it is not possible to make any generalizations about the Edmonton situation for homeless single-parent households, a group we know is rapidly increasing in North America.

Homeless *persons with mental disabilities* are found in both treatment-focused and emergency shelters. The former can be counted, the latter only guessed at. Like the rest of North American, Alberta deinstitution- alized its mental health services from the early 1960s onwards. Now, Alberta has 30–40 per cent of the psychiatric beds it had in the 1960s, despite a 50 per cent increase in population (ECOH 1987: 42). The Alberta Hospital (Edmonton), in 1986, discharged almost 1500 persons with mental disabilities into the community. Experts estimate that between 53 per cent and 62 per cent of these discharged patients require supportive housing but the majority are returned to their families. Unfortunately, 'over time family breakdowns result in a significant number of these people being turned out on the street' where their illness can only be aggravated by the stresses of marginal living. The ECOH survey estimated that 'between 17% and 40% of hostel residents had either "known or probable" psychiatric histories' and that 'approxi- mately 68% of persons on hostel "barred" or "caution-alert" lists had psychiatric histories' (ibid.: 24).

In 1987, at any one time, Edmonton was able to shelter an average of 295 persons with mental disabilities in eleven facilities. The largest percentage were in approved homes where usually the least amount of care and attention can be given to the residents (ibid.: 25).

A final significant insight from the Edmonton data further erodes the myth that the typical homeless person is a single, middle-aged, un- employable male. Even among persons in shelters, fewer than one-third met those criteria (ibid.: 60).

Ontario and Toronto
All the factors contributing to homelessness have been experienced to the extreme in Ontario, and in Toronto in particular. The increase in the number of homeless in the past decade has been huge and, for most people, unexpected. In response, private-, public-, and third-sector groups have steadily increased the number of emergency shelter facilities, but little has been done to provide longer-term or permanent housing.

Relative to most other provinces, Ontario has a smaller at-risk population. It has the lowest incidence of households in core need and the third-lowest incidence of renters in core need. But it does have the third-highest ratio of renter-to-owner households in core need (CMHC 1988b: 17). This means that more so than in seven other provinces, a renting household in Ontario is more likely to be in core need than an owning household. In Canada's richest province, 429,000 households, including 284,000 renting households (25.2 per cent of all renters) are in core need (ibid.: 17). Unfortunately, at the time of writing, accurate data focusing on core need in Metropolitan Toronto were not available, but there are indications that the incidence of core need is higher there than in the rest of the province.

Rent-to-income ratios of social-assistance recipients in Ontario and in Toronto can provide further insights into the degree to which low-income people are 'at risk.' A 1986 study of four Ontario cities concluded that at least 70 per cent of General Welfare Assistance recipients were devoting 40 per cent or more of their monthly income to rent. In Toronto, 77 per cent were paying 40 per cent or more; 87 per cent of singles were paying 50 per cent or more. Family Benefits Assistance recipients were better off, because of the shelter subsidy, but even then *Transitions* comments that in 'higher cost housing markets, many recipients are paying amounts at least twice as high as they really can afford to pay' (Ontario, Ministry of Community and Social Services 1988: 59–60). As a result, some households have to double up. The chair of the Toronto Metropolitan Housing Authority estimated, in 1987, that 25,000 people were living illegally in his organization's 32,000 subsidized units. Similarly, an experienced housing advocate claimed that 20,000 Metro Toronto families were doubled up (Fine 1987).

The CCSD snapshot survey of 22 January 1987 (p. 5) estimated 1853 people sleeping in nineteen Toronto shelters, but a few months later the Metro Commissioner of Community Services reported that there were 2328 beds in thirty-one shelters (Metropolitan Toronto 1987: 1). A later and more accurate CCSD report identified ninety-five Ontario shelters housing 3268 people, and an 88.8 per cent occupancy rate (McLaughlin 1987: 4).

In the course of a year, the shelters of Metropolitan Toronto make 45,060 admissions that translate into 25,316 different individuals/ families. They do not stay long: 62.3 per cent stay 1–5 days; 93 per cent stay fewer than 31 days (Metropolitan Toronto 1988: 3). The reasons for seeking shelter are complex and multiple, and the data are largely unhelpful. However, a few reasons do emerge. For single parents, the incidence of 'spousal abuse' was 48.8 per cent; for females under 25, the incidence of 'family breakdown' was 18.5 per cent. 'Moving to the city' and 'stranded in the city' were significant to singles and families as was eviction for couples and families. But otherwise the reasons remain buried in vague terms like 'transient' and 'other reason' (ibid.: 15).

As the number of homeless persons and the demand for shelter increased, private-, public-, and third-sector organizations responded. Between 1982 and 1987, 953 beds were added, most of them for women, families, and youths; the same groups are to be focused on with 503 additional beds planned for the next five years (Metropolitan Toronto 1987: 2).

Single men are a very large part of the Toronto homeless population. Their 35,580 admissions constitute 78.9 per cent of all admissions to Toronto shelters. The actual number of individuals involved is 15,194, indicating a high level of repeat admissions; 30 per cent of the individuals were under 25 years old (Metropolitan Toronto 1988: 2–3). The most cited reasons for homelessness were 'moving to the city,' 'stranded in the city,' and the catch-all phrase 'transient,' even though over half the men listed Metro Toronto when asked their 'permanent address one year prior to admission' (ibid.: 6, 15). When asked their next destination, upon leaving the shelter, a very large majority responded, 'destination unknown': under 25, 78.6 per cent; 25 and over, 86 per cent (ibid.: 15). Although the shelters are usually occupied close to capacity, there are no plans to increase the number of beds for single men. In fact, two facilities have been converted from emergency shelters to longer-term housing (Metropolitan Toronto 1987: appendix A).

Single-women admissions were 7157 but because of a fairly high rate of repeats, that figure represents 3648 individuals. The single-women population was 43 per cent under 25, 13 per cent greater than the men (Metropolitan Toronto 1988: 3). Family breakdown was given as the reason for being homeless by 18.5 per cent of single women under 25 and the catch-all phrase 'transient' covered the reason for 31.3 per cent (ibid.: 15). The occupancy rate was very high; the YWCA, for example, was forced to turn away twelve women daily from its emergency shelter (Fine 1988). The Metro Toronto Commissioner of Community Services was baffled by this pressure and – the basic shortage of affordable housing for singles aside – could not understand why the demand for shelter for single women had grown (Metropolitan Toronto 1987: 5). Whatever the reason, Metro Toronto and the third sector responded to the demand. From 1982 to 1987, shelter facilities for single women increased 170 per cent. Another 30 per cent increase is projected for 1987 to 1992 to give a total of 335 beds (ibid.: appendix A).

Youth homelessness in Toronto is not easily understood; it is not known who the youths are and how many there are. The number of shelter beds is so small (185) that their use gives no clues to what the size of the homeless youth population really is (Metropolitan Toronto 1988: appendix XI). A frequently repeated but unsubstantiated number is

10,000. The Salvation Army street ministry estimates that 12,000 kids come and go from the streets of Metro at various times in the course of a year (*Toronto Star* 1989). Some singles shelters will accept people 16–18 years old (Metropolitan Toronto 1987: 7). Growth of shelters for youth from 1987 to 1992 is projected to be almost 90 per cent, to 350 beds (ibid.).

The number of *single-parent families* seeking shelter increased by at least 240 per cent between 1982 and 1987 and the increase continues (ibid.: appendix A). Approximately 2900 children from single-parent families were given shelter in the year ending July 1988 (Metropolitan Toronto 1988: 3). Of the reasons given for homelessness, 50.1 per cent was some type of abuse (physical, psychological, or sexual; only 15.6 per cent was 'eviction' (ibid.: 15). Despite the increase in capacity, the hostels are crowded. For example, the director of the Women's Habitat in Etobicoke said: 'The Hostel was forced to turn away more than 2,000 homeless women and children last year. When they get in they stay for too long. Unfortunately we have trouble moving women on because they can't find anywhere to go' (*Toronto Star* 1987). In response to anticipated need, a 42 per cent increase in accommodation is projected between 1987 and 1992 (Metropolitan Toronto 1987: appendix A).

Two-parent families (538) constituted 28 per cent of all families and had approximately 1000 children: 37 per cent reported an address outside Canada one year before their admission, and 37 per cent a Metro address (Metropolitan Toronto 1988: 3, 5). The Metro Toronto Commissioner of Community Services noted in 1987 that there had been 'tremendous pressure for shelter from couples, two-parent families and single father-led families over the past two years' (Metropolitan Toronto 1987: 7). Despite a 260 per cent increase in beds from 1982 to 1987, existing shelters became filled and as many as fifty families at a time were housed in commercial hotels and motels (ibid.: appendix A and 7). The Community Services Department plans a 47 per cent increase in beds for these types of families to make a total of 356 by 1992 (ibid.: appendix A).

The number of homeless *people with mental disabilities* in Toronto is no easier to establish than in other Canadian cities. A 1985 estimate of 1200 by the Gerstein Task Force (Gerstein 1984) is still accepted by workers in the field as the most realistic.

Habitat Services has twenty-five boarding-houses providing accommodation for 500 people with psychiatric histories. They are run by private operators under very comprehensive contracts. Approximately 400 more people live in independently managed buildings, while another 100–200 live in very low-quality housing shared with drug and alcohol abusers (interview 1989a). A pilot project providing counselling and treatment services to 100 people living in Metro Toronto hostels was begun early in 1989 (interview 1989b).

This overview of some of the numbers associated with homelessness can affect our intellects but not our hearts and feelings. Numbers give us only a hint of how it feels to become homeless, to be homeless, and to have been homeless. The discussion following attempts to convey some qualitative sense of how people become homeless and what kind of world they live in.

Typologies of homeless people can be based on several different approaches. One can look at their current situation or ask what caused them to be homeless. One can study the agencies and programs aiding the homeless and look for solutions to homelessness. Here, I have chosen to focus on the current condition and the demography of the homeless (see Baxter and Hopper 1982; Bingham, Green, and White 1987; Hope and Young 1986; Sub-Committee on Housing Needs 1986).

THE PEOPLE

Persons at Risk of Losing Their Housing
Although not literally homeless, these are people who are never more than a step away from losing their shelter and crossing the line between the haves and have-nots that distinguishes the merely poor and the desperate. They are the population from which come the increasing number of homeless people. Even if people at risk never actually become homeless, the stress of living with such a threat and with continual uncertainty can erode self-esteem and make people touchy and thin-skinned in personal and social relationships.

Most people at risk cannot find appropriate housing that is affordable and offers security of tenure. Because so few units of this kind are vacant, tenants feel they must accept poor conditions like dirty halls, broken screens, and uneven heat without complaint to, or about, their landlords. With or without rent control many single persons and families pay such a high percentage of their income into rent that they cannot buy other necessities such as food, transportation, and clothing. When a household has absolutely no discretionary income or savings, one mistake or a few weeks of illness or unemployment can result in its being out on the street. Even if the rent is affordable, a household can be evicted because the owner wants to sell, renovate, or convert to condominiums. Finding another affordable unit is almost impossible because, as described in chapter 3, traditional low-income housing is disappearing: the rooming-house, the single-room occupancy hotel, the small apartment in the converted inner-city old house.

Some evicted individuals and families have relatives or friends with whom they can move in and 'double up.' Doubling up is difficult for everyone involved. The dwelling unit is usually appropriate for just one household. Privacy and any sense of independence becomes impossible. An individual or a family is entirely dependent on the goodwill of another individual or family – an unhealthy and volatile situation. After a short time this dependency produces tensions, and bad feelings begin to boil up. Then, in an atmosphere of anger and hurt feelings, the dependent individual or family has to move out and start the search again in an almost zero-vacancy market. Sometimes, yet another relative or friend will take them in and the cycle resumes. Or they cross that dividing line into homelessness.

Without regular employment, people run into trouble fairly quickly. If there are well-established networks of family and friends, ethnic or religious groups, professional or social agencies, people may be able to weather long periods of irregular employment. but if some of these networks are not present, it is easy to slip into a deteriorating situation. Usually the most crucial loss is access to secure, permanent shelter (Alternative Housing Sub-Committee 1985; Kristolaitis 1982; Social Planning Council 1983; Metropolitan Toronto 1983).

Single Men
The single, disaffiliated man is the traditional stereotype of the homeless person. Hobo, bum, wino, transient, panhandler are the familiar labels for the figure sleeping under the park bushes or dozing in the library reference room or the bus terminal and for the four guys in the alley weaving about as they share a bottle of cheap sherry. The stereotype is reinforced by the groups of defeated-looking men standing in a queue outside a hostel or a mission soup kitchen. These are the inhabitants of Skid Row. In the popular mind, most of them are there because they choose to be or because of some defects in their characters that prevent them from planning for the future, disciplining themselves, and taking responsibility for other people. The abuse of alcohol and drugs is seen as the main factor in keeping such men poor and homeless.

This image of the homeless and hostel-sheltered man has been both supported and challenged by the research and writing of psychologists, political economists, anthropologists, and sociologists. Terms such as 'escape from the larger society,' 'deviant life-style,' 'radically present-oriented,' 'immediate gratification,' and 'de-socialized' are used to explain both the causes of these men's homelessness and the reasons for its continuation. Most homeless men are seen as avoiding work unless it is absolutely necessary (Bahr 1970, 1973; Banfield 1968; Liebow 1967; Merton 1963; Wallace 1965).

Other research suggests that this characterization of homeless men, whether valid or not in the past, is not consistent with recent and present realities. In some American and Canadian studies the majority of homeless men are found to regard work favourably; usually they moved to find work and would move elsewhere if work was available. Casual-labour offices, exploitative as they may be, provide significant if uneven income. They may give some men exposure to potential full-time employment, which is much desired but not often achieved (Blumberg et al. 1973; Single Displaced Persons' Project 1972, 1981, 1983a, 1983b; Sub-Committee on Housing Needs 1986).

Escaping the casual-labour syndrome is next to impossible. Because of the men's general lack of saleable skills and experience, federal employment services often refer them to core-area day-labour purchasers. Social workers rarely offer a hostel referral long enough for a man to find and settle into a full-time job. 'No matter where he turns, then, the Skid Row man is directed to the casual labour office. This is always his starting point, and while there he is reduced to complete poverty' (Hauch 1985: 39). His impoverishment is caused not so much by the smallness of his payment as by the manner in which he receives it – one day at a time, with deductions for coffee, transportation, and lunch. With less than $40 at the end of the day, he cannot afford the usurious daily rates at even the sleaziest of hotels. If he wants accommodation, he must go to the men's hostel where any money remaining may be stolen from him.

Through different styles of robbery, neither the hotels nor the hostel enable the men to save money. Unable to afford non-Skid Row hotel rooms, or accumulate one month's rent plus damage deposit for apartments, the men are effectively circumscribed within the Skid Row business district. There they are worked, as a group (consequently denied welfare benefits) policed, and drained of their disposable income. Under these circumstances 'present time orientation' seems much more a consequence of high powered coercion than choice (at least if 'they who benefit' in any way suggests the direction of causality).

Clearly, no one wishes to be homeless, so businesses of the area – afforded literally a captive market – utilize homelessness, or rather the daily possibility of it as a threat. The message is 'you can't work full time, so if you don't work here ...' or 'if you don't rent here ... you'll have to sleep outside.' [Hauch 1985: 4]

An often-observed characteristic of homeless and hostel-sheltered men is 'binge spending.' To the outside world, this is conclusive evidence of the present time orientation and desire for immediate gratification of many homeless men. But looked at from the inside, from the perspective of the men themselves, and given Skid Row's economic customs and organization, binge spending begins to make some sense. It is difficult for a hostel resident to save money because he may be robbed and in any case it can never accumulate to an amount he can do anything with. Furthermore, the very immediacy of the hazards of homelessness creates a virtue of philanthropy. 'When it is known that a literal consequence of privation may be death by exposure, the secretive hoarding of even small sums is seen as both hostile and isolationist in the extreme' (Hauch 1985: 40). When all residents are equally poor, it is not unnatural that there develops a parallel expectation that even small surpluses should be shared.

Some of the cohesiveness of hostel or Skid Row culture is more apparent than real. The population is fluid, with people moving in and out of the area, the institutions, and the culture. Consequently, support networks for any purpose beyond the sharing of surplus wealth never have evolved. This characteristic has probably been strengthened by a change in the age and level of education and training of homeless men and hostel residents. There is clear evidence that, right across Canada, hostel residents are younger and have more years of education and training than such residents did a decade ago. Consequently, contemporary homeless men do not identify with and are scornful of Skid Row mores.

Many hostel and drop-in day-centre users dream of a place of their own. If only they could find an inexpensive, clean room or a small apartment in an inner-city area, close to the services they are accustomed to using, they might stand a chance of getting their lives in order. They would find dignity. They would have a space they could control beyond the perimeter of their bed. They would be spared the line-ups, the enforced showers, and being put out on the street at an early hour in order to seek work. They would have an address to which cheques could be sent and a phone number where messages could be left.

Single Women
A single woman is particularly vulnerable to the degrading experiences inherent in having no fixed address. She knows that the homeless are not only the lowest rank in our social system but that homeless women in particular are 'the total failures, total rejects ... perhaps because of our concept of womanhood there is no room for anything as shockingly deviant as the picture they represent' (Ross 1982: 95). The possibility of being raped has to be added to the fear of being robbed and mugged. If she is on the street, the homeless woman tries not to sleep at night or learns to sleep in snatches or with her eyes open. Keeping clean and decent looking is impossible. For food she is dependent on hand-outs or picking through other people's garbage.

In most cities a woman looking for emergency shelter has many fewer options than does a man. There are relatively fewer beds available; the admission and residency rules are often more restrictive; there is less counselling. These conditions are particularly true if she is young and without any identifiable problem other than that she needs housing and some money. In some provinces, it is difficult to get welfare cheques without a fixed address; and in several provinces, singles cannot even apply to get on the waiting list for public or non-profit housing.

A young woman's only choice may be to move in with the most acceptable (or the least objectionable) man she can find. If she rejects that option she may spend some time in a hostel, some time in shared accommodation, or some time outside under a bridge or in an abandoned car. Or perhaps she will stay up all night in doughnut shops, sleeping in libraries during the day.

Aside from the basic shortage of affordable housing, it is not clear why the demand of single women for emergency shelter has grown so dramatically. For some women, access to affordable and secure housing is all they need; they can handle their other problems by themselves or with the help of friends and relatives. But many other women have multiple problems and no family or other kind of network to support them. What appears to be especially crucial for women is the lack of opportunity to become self-sufficient. For example, young women leave group or foster homes at 18 and cannot find jobs, even low-paying ones, unless they move to where housing is unaffordable. The same is true for ex-psychiatric patients, women who have been serving time, women struggling with substance abuse, and victims of domestic violence. Whether their problems are multiple or singular, affordable permanent housing is a necessary first step (Morissette 1987; Ross 1982; Rousseau 1981; Winnipeg YWCA 1983).

Youths

Most homeless youths see themselves as escaping from intolerable family environments, which may involve physical or sexual abuse, emotional neglect, or a gross indifference towards the welfare of the child on the part of any responsible adult. In a few cases the youth is attracted by the glamour of the street in contrast to the perceived indifference or oppression at home. But this celebration of freedom often does not last long as the realities of street living make themselves felt. For some, home begins to looks better and better. Those who remain on the street do so not because they want to but because they feel they have no choice.

Many street youths start out with unrealistic expectations about how well and fast they are going 'to make it' once they are free of their unsatisfactory life at home. But soon they become enmeshed in the painful realities of unemployment, alcohol and drug abuse, prostitution, pregnancy, sexually transmitted and other diseases, malnutrition, theft, violence, exploitation, isolation, and depression.

Homeless youths can be grouped into two main categories: runaways – those who feel they have to escape abuse and neglect at home – and throwaways – those who, because of blended families, family breakdowns, or extreme behavioural problems, are no longer tolerated at home. In some parts of the country, poverty puts such economic pressure on families that they just buckle under the hopelessness of ever changing their lives. In such circumstances, some parents lash out at those who are closest and most vulnerable. But poverty alone – and the crises it engenders – is not a sufficient explanation for youth homelessness. In Toronto, runaways and throwaways do not come from any particular socio-economic group, or from any particular ethnic group.

What homeless youth do have in common is that they 'labour under an almost unimaginable deficit of resources, skills and information. Many of them are functionally illiterate, unable to fill out job application forms or write a resume' (ECOH 1987: 55). They are also trapped in homelessness by poor health, ignorance about available programs and services, substance abuse, lack of social skills, lack of family or other network support. But even in situations where young people are able to confront these obstacles successfully, they can't find a place to live.

Families
Family homelessness is increasing in most Canadian cities. Families lose their homes for several reasons. Women and children finally flee physical, sexual, and psychological abuse that they have been putting up with because they had nowhere to go. Eviction forces families into hostels unless they can double up with relatives or friends. But sooner or later landlords (both private and public) force them to leave; or the stress of two households occupying one unit becomes intolerable. This routine can be followed by a sequence of short-term subleasing, staying with friends, or resorting to family hostels. In some cities, refugee families add to the numbers seeking low-cost housing. Even in cities where units are vacant and affordable, landlords resist renting to tenants with children and dependent on welfare, especially if they are single parents.

The need for family hostel accommodation greatly exceeds the supply. This means that a family seeking even temporary shelter may be forced to live in a tent or a trailer; in a crowded hostel room with rollaway beds, mattresses on the floor, and two kids to a bed; in a cattle-exhibition dormitory or an armoury. None of these 'accommodations' provides any privacy or any sense of belonging. Some municipalities have to turn away families every day from their hostels. Some of the luckier ones are put in hotels and motels where it is very difficult to counsel or monitor families who need more than just shelter.

Families that live in hostels or welfare hotels/motels experience fracturing strains on their relationships. Parents lose their sense of self-worth and the respect of their kids because staff take over and run the lives of the family. They are told when to get up, when to go to bed, where the children can play, and where they can't. The children either withdraw from their parents or assert: 'Who are you to tell me what to do; you don't even run your own life.' Some families, especially those headed by single parents, make several moves a year, effectively destroying any classroom continuity for their children. At school, children are labelled as those who live in a shelter, a lower status than kids in public housing.

An increasing number of parents have given up their children to relatives, to foster homes, or to adoption agencies because of their inability to find decent housing. In those families that eventually do find decent accommodation, the emotional damage stays with the children and the parents for a long time.

Those with Mental Disabilities

It is widely believed that mental illness is pervasive among the homeless. We have all been startled on the street by the scruffily dressed woman shouting at invisible enemies, or the glassy-eyed dirty young man deeply engaged in an inner-directed conversation as he looks right through us. Such people are so visible that we tend to assume that they are what most of the homeless are like. Then we read in the newspaper about how deinstitutionalization has for years discharged hundreds of ex-psychiatric patients into the community. No wonder, we conclude, that there are so many with mental problems among the homeless. The stereotype slips from 'wino' to 'weirdo.'

A search of the North American and British literature produces a wide range of opinions and estimates about the percentage of homeless people who have been or are psychiatrically disabled; depending on the criteria used and the populations studied, the range encountered is 40 per cent to 17 per cent. On balance, I think that the percentage has been exaggerated, perhaps because people are viewed as members of the deserving poor if the cause of their homelessness is mental disability. Mixing up the processes of cause and effect obscures the fact that mental disabilities and deviant behaviours are as much symptoms of homelessness as causes of it. Some homeless people intentionally adopt bizarre behaviours or present a bizarre appearance as a protective tactic. Women in particular may use filth and foul odours as a defence against attack, sexual or otherwise. Such behaviour may also be a last-ditch way of getting back at a genteel world that labels them the worst of the losers.

Life on the street or living constantly at risk can create or aggravate emotional disturbances, so that disorientation, for example, may be as much an effect of homelessness as its cause. The day-to-day search for a toilet, food, and a refuge from the police and the weather is a draining experience and leads to permanent exhaustion. Sleep deprivation can produce disorientation in the healthiest of persons. Add to sleep deprivation other factors such as poor nutrition, exposure to the elements, physical infirmities, and the fear of robbing and mugging and we have a recipe for total collapse of body and spirit.

There are homeless persons whose mental disabilities certainly preceded and contributed to their homelessness, and their experiences have been frightening. If they have been institutionalized, they lived lives of child-like dependency in which their sense of self-worth was sucked out of them. First, they were judged to be crazy. Second, they often were rejected or shunned by their family and friends. Although they may have experienced the disorientation of their disability and of the drugs used to treat them, they probably – and gradually – began to feel 'at home' in the institution.

Even when deemed ready for a return to the community, persons with mental disorders often have problems that make them likely candidates for homelessness. First, the unpredictability of their behaviour because of their illness and their medication may result in their being barred from their family home, their friends' homes, or rented accommodation. Most shelters and hostels have lists of persons whose behaviour prevents them from being admitted or places them on a 'caution list,' which gives them low admission priority. Second, a diminished ability to cope with stress of any kind, such as dissatisfaction with living arrangements or with neighbours, may cause their illness to recur. Third, mental illness may cause people to have few if any of the social and interpersonal skills needed to live in the community. Thus, they may resist living in programmed housing; at the same time, their appearance and behaviour restricts their access to private accommodation. Fourth, they have low and irregular incomes because they lack training and have poor job records. The money they receive from government income programs and shelter allowances is too little to permit acquiring suitable housing. Finally, people with such problems discover the ultimate 'Catch 22': most ex-patients are eligible for General Welfare Assistance to help them get re-established in the community. But, in some provinces, to be eligible for welfare, one must have an address to which the cheque can be sent; one cannot get money without an address. But without money, one cannot get an address – particularly when many landlords require the first and last week's or month's rent as a deposit. In many institutions, patient departures have to be delayed for weeks because no housing is available.

Even if they are able to find affordable housing, most deinstitutionalized mental patients require several different services to varying degrees of intensity and comprehensiveness. Such services include income maintenance, vocational/educational training, social recreational programs, and treatment for illness. Although individual needs differ, this group as a whole needs a wide spectrum of institutional arrangements from 24-hour supervision to a weekly support session or an on-call supervisor.

The ex-patient faces an uncoordinated tangle of complex application forms, searches for documents, appointments at different agencies, all understaffed and overworked. Even when an ex-patient needs help and knows it, he or she is confronted with hospitals and other agencies that do not communicate or co-operate with each other. Thus, each sporadic crisis is treated as a separate event; there is little accumulation of insight into the context and nature of the person's problem. To the person in crisis, nobody really cares; the system sees her or him not as a whole person but as a medical problem to be dealt with. As one workshop participant put it: 'If he doesn't meet kind people, his life is likely to be hell.'

In a few places in Canada, particularly where vacancy rates are not low, a discharged patient may be lucky enough to get into a contract lodging-house where he or she can find an affordable room with 24-hour supervision, monitoring of medication, and experienced and caring staff. Although the number of such settings is increasing, there are still too few of them (Gerstein 1984; Snow, Baker, Anderson, and Martin 1986).

This examination of homeless people in Canada raises many philosophical, societal, and policy implications. The obvious question arising from these implications is whether such an examination results in our feeling overwhelmed by the magnitude and the complexity of homelessness in Canada. The answer is no, if we focus on numbers. We are not faced with a socio-economic epidemic in homelessness. At a maximum, 1 per cent of the Canadian population is on the streets or in emergency shelters and hostels. The low level of repeat shelter admissions, especially for families, means that most hostel users solve or adapt to the problems that made them homeless. The small percentage of hostel residents who stay over twenty days means that the hostel is a way of life for only a very small number of people (mostly single men).

At the same time, we do feel overwhelmed at how disruptive, frightening, and soul-destroying the experience of homelessness can be: at least one-quarter of a million people are denied any of the six aspects of home discussed at the beginning of this chapter. It is overwhelming that 875,000 households or 1,750,000 people cannot afford minimally suitable housing and are always at risk of losing what housing they do have. We may be further overwhelmed at learning that in emergency shelters the average cost per bed per year is almost $11,000, enough to rent a one- or two-bedroom apartment, even in low-vacancy Toronto (Metropolitan Toronto 1987: 8). Surely, we wonder, with that much money available, could we not provide something better for homeless people than smelly barracks-like dormitories with no privacy or security?

Certain kinds of homelessness seem to be particularly appalling. For example, single-parent households are especially significant because children are involved and because half these households are in core need. Their increasing dependence on food banks and their need for hostel shelter are a shrill warning of social disintegration, present and future.

Increasing homelessness resulting from violence is very disturbing in itself, but it is even more significant as an indicator of both a growing incidence of violence and the unwillingness of women to submit to it. Although there is an immediate housing need to be met, there are decisions to be made about how to deal with violent husbands or partners.

Youth homelessness remains baffling to all who study it, but it clearly is associated with some complex social, attitudinal, and economic changes in Canadian society. Those who make decisions about youth-oriented laws, programs, and institutions are finding it difficult to respond effectively.

At first glance the homeless seem to lack networks and connectedness with other people, but a closer examination reveals how much their lives are linked with other people who help or who hinder their search for a satisfactory life. Creating effective and more integrated networks and services is an arena to explore.

Although the supply of cheap rental housing has been declining for two decades everywhere in Canada, the poor and the homeless depend more on private landlords for shelter than on public- or third-sector landlords. This interdependence often may be tense and adversarial but, like it or not, tenant and landlord need each other. Public policies, especially provincial and municipal ones, need to recognize this interdependence and develop programs that enhance the interests of both. Examples of such programs are discussed in chapter 8.

Public- and third-sector shelter operators can deeply affect the quality of people's lives by their programs, regulations, and implementation of these elements. Shelter operators are faced with a diverse clientele that dislikes its dependency on shelters but has no options. These operators, at best, attempt to apply a balance of fairness to all and firmness with the few disruptive residents, avoiding attitudes of condescension. It is not an easy task. Many shelter operators agree with many of their clients that transitional and permanent housing would create a stable environment in which clients could begin to deal with whatever other problems, if any, pushed them into homelessness. Chapters 7 and 8 discuss the current trend towards transitional and permanent housing.

Some homeless people have links with police officers, social workers, and health- and medical-care workers. These workers usually have well-formed social and ethical systems that are largely accepting of middle-class and middle-of-the-road values and criteria. These values and criteria impel them to try to ameliorate the condition of the homeless and also to seek to understand and reconstruct the reasons for homelessness. Many of those who work with the homeless try to gain understanding by measuring the degree to which a person is a victim of a system that failed and the degree to which a person is the author of his or her own fate.

Any careful observer of the homeless soon learns that, because of their diversity, very few homeless people fall into one or the other of these categories. In most cases, homelessness is the result of some mix of forces outside the control of the homeless, or of decisions they have made and behaviours they have chosen. However, we should avoid slipping into a 1990s version of the Victorian/Edwardian view of the 'deserving and undeserving poor.' A homeless person cannot be scored on a responsibility scale, like a court attributing responsibility for an automobile accident: the system failed, 60 per cent; the individual made some bad decision, 40 per cent. It is more important to understand the diversity among homeless people: the many causes of their homelessness and the variety of the conditions in which they find themselves. Logically, society also needs to explore the diversity of the policies, programs, and practices that must be developed if the numbers of homeless and the damaging intensity of their experiences are to be reduced.

REFERENCES

Alternative Housing Sub-Committee. 1985. *Off the Streets; A Case for Long-Term Housing.* September. City of Toronto

Bahr, Howard M. 1970. *Disaffiliated Men.* Toronto: University of Toronto Press

– 1973. *Skid Row; An Introduction to Disaffiliation.* New York: Oxford University Press

Bainbridge, Catherine. 1987. 'Homeless and on the Run.' *Winnipeg Free Press.* 21 February, 49

Bairstow and Associates Consulting Ltd. 1987a. *Manitoba Directions for the International Year of Shelter for the Homeless.* Winnipeg

– 1987b. *Reaching Out for Help: Manitoba's Homeless in 1987.* Winnipeg: Manitoba Department of Housing

Banfield, Edward C. 1968. *The Unheavenly City.* Boston: Little, Brown and Company

Baxter, Ellen, and Hopper, Kim. 1982. 'The New Mendicancy: Homeless in New York City.' *American Journal of Orthopsychiatry* 52: 395

Bingham, Richard D.; Green, Roy E.; and White, Sammis B., eds. 1987. *The Homeless in Contemporary Society*. Newbury Park, CA: Sage Publications

Blumberg, Leonard, et al. 1973. *Skid Row and Its Alternatives*. Philadelphia: Temple University Press

Brundrige, Rick. 1987. 'Homelessness: Bleakness and Poverty in a Day to Day Existence.' *City Magazine*. April: 10–18

Callwood, June. 1987. 'The Homeless.' *The Globe and Mail*. 16 November: A1. Toronto

CCSD (Canadian Council on Social Development). 1987. 'Homelessness in Canada a Grim Reality for 100,000 in 1986.' Communiqué. 6 April. Ottawa

CMHC (Canada Mortgage and Housing Corporation). Research Division. 1988a. *The Core Need Housing Model*. Ottawa

– 1988b. *1985 Estimates of Canadian Households in Core Housing Need*. Ottawa

Cox, John E. 1986. '1987 International Year of Shelter for the Homeless.' *Canadian Housing* 3, no. 2: 14–16

ECOH (Edmonton Coalition on Homelessness). 1987. *Homelessness in Edmonton: No Place Like Home*. May. Edmonton.

Fine, Sean. 1987. 'No Vacancy.' *The Globe and Mail*. 3 September: A8. Toronto

– 1988. 'Housing Puts Squeeze on United Way Funds.' *The Globe and Mail*. 8 March: A16. Toronto

Gerstein, Riva. 1984. *The Final Report of the Mayor's Task Force on Discharged Psychiatric Patients*. Toronto: Office of the Mayor

Hauch, Christopher. 1985. *Coping Strategies and Street Life: The Ethnography of Winnipeg's Skid Row*. Report 11. Winnipeg: University of Winnipeg, Institute of Urban Studies

Hope, Marjorie; and Young, James. 1986. *The Faces of Homelessness*. Toronto: Lexington Books

Interview. 1989a. Conversation with Mary Ellen Polak, executive director, Mental Health Program Services, Habitat Services. 10 August

– 1989b. Conversation with Sherril Lindsay, Community Resource Consultants. 11 August

Kristolaitis, George. 1982. 'Skid Row Demography and Housing Preferences.' MA thesis, University of Waterloo

Liebow, Elliot. *Tally's Corner*. 1967. Boston: Little, Brown and Company

McLaughlin, MaryAnn. 1987. *Homelessness in Canada: The Report of the National Enquiry*. Ottawa: Canadian Council on Social Development

Merton, Robert K. 1963. 'Social Structure and Anomie.' In *Varieties of Modern Social Theory*, ed. Hendrick M. Ruitenbeek. New York: E.P. Dutton

Metropolitan Toronto. Community Services Department. 1987. *Emergency Shelters for the Homeless*. Memorandum from Commissioner of Community

Services to Community and Housing Committee, 25 September. Municipality of Metropolitan Toronto
- Hostels Operation Unit. 1988. *Statistical Package, July 1, 1987 – June 30, 1988.* Municipality of Metropolitan Toronto
- Policy and Planning Division. 1983. *No Place to Go – A Study of Homelessness in Metropolitan Toronto: Characteristics, Trends and Potential Solutions.* Municipality of Metropolitan Toronto
Morissette, Diane. 1987. *Housing for Canadian Women: An Everyday Concern.* Ottawa: Canadian Advisory Council on the Status of Women
Ontario Ministry of Community and Social Services. 1988. *Transitions: A Report of the Social Assistance Review Committee.* Toronto
- Ministry of Housing. 1988. *More than Just a Roof: Action to End Homelessness in Ontario.* Final report of the Minister's Advisory Committee on the International Year of Shelter for the Homeless. Toronto
Ross, Aileen D. 1982. *The Lost and the Lonely: Homeless Women in Montreal.* Montreal: Canadian Human Rights Foundation
Rousseau, Ann Marie. 1981. *Shopping Bag Ladies.* New York: Pilgrim Press
Single Displaced Persons' Project. 1972. *Single Displaced Persons in Downtown Toronto.* Toronto
- 1981. *Effects of the Diagnostic Process on the Men.* Toronto
- 1983a. *The Case for Long-Term Supportive Housing.* Toronto
- 1983b. *Action Research on 'Younger Men' Demographic Survey.* Toronto
Snow, David; Baker, Susan G.; Anderson, Leon; and Martin, Michael. 1986. 'The Myth of Pervasive Mental Illness among the Homeless.' *Social Problems* 33, no. 5: 407–23
Social Planning Council of Metropolitan Toronto. 1983. *People without Homes: A Permanent Emergency.* Toronto
Statistics Canada. 1985. *Household Income, Facilities and Equipment* (HIFE) *Micro-Data File for 1985; with Calculations by Canada Mortgage and Housing Corporation, Research Division.* Ottawa
Sub-Committee on the Housing Needs of the Homeless Population. 1986. *Final Report.* November. Toronto: Metropolitan Toronto Council
Tognoli, Jerome. 1987. 'Residential Environments.' In *Handbook of Environmental Psychology*, eds. D. Stokols and I. Altman. New York: Wiley Interscience Publishers
Toronto Star. 1987. 10 July: A6
- 1989. 14 April: F10
Wallace, Samuel E. 1965. *Skid Row as a Way of Life.* Totawa, NJ: Bedminster Press
Winnipeg YWCA Task Force on Homeless Women. 1983. *Of No Fixed Address.* Winnipeg

GEORGE FALLIS

3 The Urban Housing Market

This chapter provides contextual data for the analysis of the housing problems of the homeless and poor that will be useful throughout the book. It also analyses the urban housing market to identify certain causes of housing problems and discusses some programs that hold promise as solutions.[1] The title of this chapter might be 'An Economist Looks at Homelessness and the Social Housing Problem' because the chapter also provides an economic analysis of the issues.

I deal here with the operation of the housing market in cities. (Of course, there are households in towns and rural areas suffering similar housing problems, but they are a small percentage of the total problem.) Within the urban housing market, the emphasis is on rental housing for low-income households and on the influence of government on the price and availability of low-rental housing, because it is to the rental market that the very poor and homeless look for shelter.

This chapter first explores broad context, examining how the average housing conditions of Canadians have changed over the last twenty-five years. Housing conditions are usually measured according to the adequacy, crowding, and affordability of rental housing. There proves to have been no significant decline in average housing conditions and, therefore, attention shifts to forces that might make worse the housing situation of the very poor. Second, the process of gentrification and, more generally, the changing internal structure of the city are considered; both these changes have adversely affected the poor. Third, the barriers to increasing the amount of rental housing are considered. And finally, the chapter concludes with some suggested solutions for housing problems and homelessness.

HOUSING CONDITIONS

We know that some Canadians are homeless, others live in inadequate housing, and the numbers with severe housing problems are rising. We might ask whether this deterioration is the most severe and obvious case of a more general problem for all households. The housing literature usually measures the situation of households according to the adequacy of the housing that they occupy, whether the housing is crowded, and its affordability. These measures are not simply descriptive, but are implicitly normative, for they are taken as indicators of housing problems.

Housing Adequacy
Clearly, the housing of Canadians has not become less adequate on average. There has been continuous improvement over the post-war era, even over the last fifteen years when housing problems have commanded so much attention. Between 1972 and 1982 the proportion of households living in dwellings without basic plumbing facilities, such as piped hot and cold water, inside toilet, and installed bath or shower, declined from 9.4 to 1.6 per cent (Canada 1985). Indeed, because virtually all households now have basic plumbing, these data are no longer very useful proxies for housing adequacy. An alternative indicator of adequacy is whether a dwelling needs major repairs. Data on the physical quality of dwellings are notoriously hard to interpret, but they also show improvement. In 1982, about 13 per cent of occupants assessed their dwellings as needing major repairs; in 1985 this figure had fallen to 12.5 per cent; and in 1987 it stood at 10.6 per cent (Statistics Canada 1987). These assessments are based on such indicators as damp walls, crumbling foundations, rotting porches and steps, and corroded pipes. There can be no doubt that Canadians are very well housed on average and the quality of housing they occupy has continuously improved.

Crowding
A household is usually deemed to live in crowded housing if there is more than one person per room. From 1972 to 1982, the percentage of dwellings with more than one person per room declined from 7.8 to 2.3 (Canada 1985). The pattern of declining crowding is also supported by other data: from 1978 to 1988 the average number of persons per

TABLE 3.1
Distribution of non-farm tenants by cash rent as a percentage of household income (by year)

Cash rent as percentage of household income	1988	1986	1982
less than 25 per cent	62	62	69
25–29	11	10	8
30–34	6	7	6
35–39	5	5	3
40–49	6	6	5
50 +	10	10	9
	100	100	100
30 or more per cent (affordability problem)	27	28	23

SOURCE: Statistics Canada 1982, 1986, 1988a

household declined from 3.0 to 2.7, while the average number of rooms per dwelling rose from 5.5 to 5.8 (Statistics Canada 1988a). Again, because almost all households have less than one person per room, this factor is no longer a very useful indicator of crowding. During the 1980s, the federal and provincial governments developed the concept of 'suitability' to replace the idea of crowding. The suitability measure is set out in the National Occupancy Standard (NOS), which determines the number of bedrooms suitable for different household types according to certain prescriptions. There is a maximum of two persons per bedroom and a minimum of one; parents have a separate bedroom from their children; persons over 18 have a separate bedroom unless married; and dependents age 5 or over of the opposite sex do not share a bedroom. The NOS measure showed 7 per cent of households in 1985 lived in unsuitable housing (CMHC 1988). The research to see how the incidence of suitability problems has changed over time has not yet been completed.

Affordability
The last commonly used measure of the housing conditions of Canadians is whether their housing is affordable: a household is said to live in unaffordable housing if it spends more than 30 per cent of its income on

housing. About 27 per cent of tenants spent 30 per cent or more of their income on housing in 1988 in Canada (table 3.1) – a slight decline from 1986 but well above the level of 1982. (The 1982 data report the situation just before the large recession of the early 1980s.) The median rent-to-income percentage in 1988 was 22, a slight rise over 1982. Clearly, the most significant housing problem for tenants is affordability; and the incidence of the problem has risen since the beginning of the 1980s. Affordability problems are most severe for those with low incomes: in 1988, 76 per cent of those earning less than $10,000 a year spent more than 30 per cent of income on housing, compared to 59 per cent of those earning between $10,000 and $15,000, and 29 per cent of those between $15,000 and $20,000.

Chapter 2 discussed the concept of core need, which considers all those households with adequacy, crowding/suitability, and affordability problems and asks whether they could afford to solve their problems themselves. If they could not, they are said to be in core need. In 1985, 27 per cent of renters and 8 per cent of owners were in core need (CMHC 1988). However, the concept of core need is relatively new and has not yet been used to examine whether there is an increasing percentage of households in core need in the 1980s.

Relative Price of Rental Housing

Examining the changes in the percentage of households spending more than 30 per cent of income on housing is one way to detect changes in housing affordability. But rent-to-income ratios are the outcome of many factors, including the price of housing, income, and household tastes. An alternative way to measure changes in affordability is to see whether the price of rental housing has risen faster than other prices. Housing is a very heterogeneous commodity, and the quality of each dwelling unit changes over time because of depreciation, maintenance, and renovation. In order to measure price change over time, one must measure a change in the price of a standard commodity; one must measure the price of the same thing at two points in time. Thus, if the monthly rent on an apartment were to fall between 1988 and 1989, the price of housing to the tenant would not necessarily have fallen. The apartment may have so depreciated that the price per unit of housing service has actually risen, even though the monthly rent has fallen. Similarly an increase in rent if there has been renovation may not indicate a rise in the price of housing. The only consistent measure of the price of housing to renters is the rent component of the consumer price

TABLE 3.2
Indexes for the price of housing to renters and all consumer prices (1961–85)

Year	All items	CPI rent component	Real rent index[a] (1981 = 100)	Average vacancy rate in metropolitan areas[b]
1961	100	100	162	n.a.
1966	111	104	152	3.2
1971	133	123	151	5.0
1971	100	100	151	5.0
1976	161	120	121	1.3
1981	237	157	100	1.2
1981	100	100	100	1.2
1986	132	133	101	1.6
1988	148	146	99	2.6

[a]Steele 1989; CPI rent component divided by Consumer Expenditure Deflater, to 1981; thereafter calculation by author
[b]Vacancy rates relate to privately initiated buildings of six units and over.
SOURCE: CMHC, various years

index (CPI). Rents rose slightly less than other prices in the 1960s, far less than other prices in the 1970s, and the same as other prices in the 1980s (table 3.2). There are many critics of the CPI rent component and most argue that the index understates the true rise in the price of housing to renters because it does not take enough account of depreciation (or it overstates quality improvement). Attempts to correct for this factor by researchers outside Statistics Canada are inevitably ad hoc, but their main conclusion is that the CPI rent index slightly understates the true rise in rents (Fallis 1985). Therefore, one can conclude that, on average, the relative price of rental housing declined significantly over the last twenty-five years and increased slightly in the last eight years.

Thus, the problem of homelessness has not emerged over a period when rental housing has become significantly less affordable. Some may find this conclusion surprising, and it is often forgotten in discussions of social housing policy. But it is an important part of the context. Of course, for certain individual households, and in certain specific neighbourhoods, the relative price of rental housing has risen significantly. But these are exceptions rather than the overall situation.

However, it may be that the relative price of the housing lived in by the poor has risen. And, therefore, the causes of this rise will have to be found in elements affecting the housing market of the poor but not other sub-markets. Gentrification, changes in urban structure, and many urban reform policies have hurt the poor. This is an important conclusion and one which sets the housing problem apart from many other social problems affecting the poor. For example, the poor were especially hard hit by relative price increases caused by the rise in oil prices. Everyone faced the same relative price increases. In such cases the poor can make common cause with others in seeking a government program to cushion the price increase. Or perhaps more realistically, when other more powerful groups seek to cushion themselves, they can invoke the plight of the poor. When the powerful are cushioned, it benefits the poor as well. But the poor have few allies in the urban housing market and, indeed, one can argue that many of the policies favoured by the middle- and upper-income groups indirectly hurt the poor.

Vacancy Rates
Although the data do not show that rental housing has become significantly less affordable on average, vacancy rates have declined significantly since the early 1970s (table 3.2) and are below 1 per cent in some large cities. When vacancy rates are very low in an unregulated rental market, a gap emerges between the rents charged on occupied units and the advertised rents on vacant units. Under universal and binding rent control this gap should not be large; although the most likely units to be vacated by tenants are those on which the controlled rent is nearest the absence of control rent. (The real 'bargains' are never vacated.) But control is never fully binding and the most likely time to evade rent control is between tenants. Also, new units or renovated units when placed on the market, even under rent controls, will be higher-rent units. There is anecdotal evidence that the gap can be as high as 40 per cent in Toronto. Thus, when vacancy rates are low, the data on average rents paid used in calculating the CPI do not represent the situation of new households or new arrivals struggling to find an apartment. It is likely that the rents for vacant apartments have risen faster than the rents for occupied apartments over the last eight years.

Furthermore, when vacancy rates are low, the matching of people and dwellings is more difficult, causing some problems for those who would like to move, but far greater problems for new arrivals or new households. All newcomers and all new households must bear extra search costs, and certain households fare worse than others. When vacancy rates are low, landlords can discriminate against certain types of tenants. When a single parent with a child or a visible-minority person applies for an apartment, the landlord can turn them away knowing full well another tenant can be found quickly. When vacancy rates are higher, the landlord is less likely to discriminate because the apartment might be vacant for some time before another tenant can be found. Thus, in tight rental markets possible 'problem' tenants – for example, families with children, especially single-parent families, those with psychological disabilities, or those without long job histories – will suffer. Also, tenants who are likely to move again soon, such as the young, will suffer, and landlords can more readily exercise their racial, religious, or other prejudices. The picture of those who will suffer begins to look like the description of the homeless in chapter 2.

In any housing market, there are two classes of private landlords: those who want trouble-free tenants; and those who are willing to rent to tenants who statistically are more likely to be troublesome, but charge a premium for doing so. To some extent rents reflect the costs of dealing with different types of tenants. For example, at one end of the spectrum, good tenants often receive long-tenure discounts. It is likely that when vacancy rates are low and most landlords are able to discriminate against possibly troublesome tenants, the premium charged by landlords who will rent to them will rise. The rents for possible problem tenants may have risen most rapidly of all. Some of these people will be forced to double up, to stay in emergency shelters, or to become homeless.

Real Household Incomes
There is still another way to view the problem of affordability. It might be that, although the relative price of rental housing has not risen, housing could be said to be less affordable if real income has fallen (just as all other commodities would be less affordable). The pattern over the last twenty-five years is clear (table 3.3). In the 1960s and 1970s real incomes rose significantly. The percentage of Canadians defined as living in poverty declined substantially from 1969 to 1979. Real per capita personal disposable income (PDI) rose almost 50 per cent in each decade. Thus, housing became more affordable, not less affordable, up until the late 1970s.

Household real PDI rose as well but less rapidly. Because household size is declining, household income does not keep pace with per capita income. This discrepancy creates more problems for obtaining housing

TABLE 3.3

Indexes of real personal disposable income (PDI), unemployment, and poverty (1961–88)

Year	Real PDI per capita[a]	Real PDI per household[b]	Unemployment rate[c]	Poverty rate[d]
1961	100	100	7.1	
1966	123	119	3.4	
1971	145	130	6.2	23.1 (1969)
1971	100	100	6.2	
1976	132	120	7.1	
1981	148	123	7.5	15.7 (1979)
1981	100	100	7.5	14.7
1982	99	98	11.0	
1983	97	92	11.9	
1984	101	94	11.3	17.3
1985	104	95	10.5	
1986	104	97	9.6	14.9
1987	105	98	8.8	
1988	107	99	7.8	

SOURCES
[a]Personal disposable income per capita from CMHC (1988), deflated by CPI to obtain real income
[b]Personal disposable income from CMHC (1988), number of households from Statistics Canada (1987 and 1988b), deflated by the CPI to obtain real income
[c]Bank of Canada (March 1989)
[d]Canada (1988)

than for acquiring any other necessity. Two people can get housing almost as cheaply as one person, although two cost almost twice as much as one to feed, clothe, and so on. Even when income is divided evenly, the splitting of a household means both parts are worse off because both must maintain a dwelling unit.

In the early 1980s, things changed dramatically because of the severest recession since the 1930s. Real incomes ceased growing and even fell. From 1981 to 1983, real per capita PDI fell 3 per cent and real household PDI fell 8 per cent. The poverty rate rose (although not as dramatically as one might have suspected). Housing became less affordable.

However, these are average data, which do not adequately represent the situation of the poorest households. The economy shrank in the early 1980s so that everyone, including the poor, found it harder to afford housing. But the burden of this recession was not equally shared. The unemployment rate rose from 7.1 in 1976 to 11.9 in 1983. Those who remained employed during the recession suffered a slight loss in real income; some even enjoyed a gain. Those who became unemployed bore the brunt of the adjustment cost as the economy contracted. Their incomes fell much more than the Canadian average; and for them housing became much less affordable.

Many of the poorest households derive their income from social assistance rather than from a job, and, therefore, data on per capita disposable income do not reveal how their situation has changed. Over the 1980s the real value of social assistance rates under General Welfare Assistance and Family Benefits Allowance increased significantly – as much as 45 per cent for some case types (Ottawa 1986). The problems of the early 1980s were definitely not caused by cut-backs in the real value of social assistance. The key point was that many people fell from being employed to being on social assistance and the level of social-assistance payments (despite real increases) makes it very hard to get by. Social-assistance payments are only about half of what Statistics Canada defines as the poverty line, making housing very difficult to afford. For example, in Ottawa, social-assistance recipients would have to spend about 60–70 per cent of their income to rent the average apartment appropriate for their family size (Ottawa 1986).

Since the recession, there has been a robust and prolonged recovery – the longest in the post-war period. Real personal incomes are rising again; poverty rates have dropped and the national unemployment rate is below 8 per cent (table 3.3). Many poor have participated in this recovery and their housing problems have diminished.

But the recovery is very uneven. Some regions have done better than others: the unemployment rate remains high outside central Canada. The 1986 poverty rate was 8.7 in Ontario and fell 27 per cent since 1983; the poverty rate in Newfoundland was 21.1 and fell only 5 per cent. Some sectors have done better than others: the real average industrial wage is just returning to its pre-recession level. And some households have done better than others. The most recent study of poverty in Canada (Canada 1988) has a chapter called 'The Changing Face of Poverty.' It begins: 'The 1971 report of the Senate Committee on Poverty chaired by Senator David Croll, *Poverty in Canada*, displayed a picture of an elderly man on its cover. Were that study to be done today, undoubtably its cover photo would show an elderly woman or a young single-parent mother and her children.'

The chapter goes on to characterize carefully the 'feminization of poverty,' which is widely recognized and of great concern. The pro-portion of low-income families led by women has increased dramatically from 17 per cent in 1969 to 37 per cent in 1986, an increase caused by the enormous growth of mother-led single-parent families, following mainly from marriage breakdown. Women continue to account for the majority of unattached individuals with low incomes (62 per cent in 1986), a circumstance that has changed little since 1969. The feminiza-tion of poverty took place in the 1970s but did not alter significantly during the recession and recovery of the 1980s. The dramatic change in poverty in the 1980s relates to age.

The percentage of elderly families in poverty dropped from 14 per cent in 1980 to 10 per cent in 1986; and the percentage of elderly singles in poverty dropped from 62 per cent to 43 per cent – still high, but a dramatic improvement. Optimism at these improvements is countered by pessimism at the rise of poverty among the young. In 1969, 21 per cent of poor families were headed by people under the age of 35; in 1986 it was 40 per cent. For poor individuals, the increase has gone from 25 per cent (1969) to 38 per cent (1986). Of the 3.7 million Canadians who remain poor, more than 1 million are children under 16 – one child in every six.

The recession and its uneven recovery have shaped the make-up of the poor and homeless, and so have the increases in marriage breakdown and the baby boom. All three forces have generated the single-parent families, the street kids, and the struggling young families and individuals portrayed in chapter 2.

These aggregate data on housing conditions are consistent with one another. Over the 1980s, the relative price of rental housing rose slightly and household real income fell significantly though it is now rising again. These relative price and real income changes have not produced any detectable decline in the physical adequacy of the housing of Canadians on average, nor has there been any general increase in crowding. There has been a significant increase in the percentage of renters spending more than 30 per cent of income on housing. But these are aggregate data and may not adequately reflect the situation of the poor. One should also consider how the incomes of the poor and the housing market they operate in are different from the general picture. Persistently high unemployment means some people have a low income despite general prosperity. Included in this group are increased num-bers of deinstitutionalized psychiatric patients and one-parent families.

GENTRIFICATION

Over the last fifteen years in many Canadian cities, middle-income households have moved into lower-income and sometimes deteriorating inner-city neighbourhoods. They have renovated much of the housing stock and transformed the area into a middle-class neighbourhood. The well-known examples come from all across the country: Kitsilano in Vancouver, Cabbagetown in Toronto, Centretown in Ottawa, the lower slopes of Mount Royal in Montreal, and the South End in Halifax. The process is most commonly called gentrification, although it has been variously called inner-city revitalization, an urban renaissance, and white painting. Gentrification has also been occurring in the United States, England, and Western Europe, suggesting that the forces behind the process are specific neither to individual cities nor to Canada, but are present through the Western world.

Gentrification is much praised for rejuvenating inner cities and for adding tax revenues to strapped city governments; it is also much celebrated for creating cosmopolitan and urbane communities. The process has been promoted and financially assisted by all levels of government, but it is not without costs because it removes low-rent dwellings from the housing market.

A range of explanations for gentrification have been made. (For recent surveys see Hamnett [1984] and Ley [1986].) Virtually all commentators have noted the surge in housing demand caused by the baby boom and by the decline in average household size. The total number of Canadian households increased by 29 per cent between 1976 and 1986; the number of households with heads aged 25–34 increased by 38 per cent and with heads aged 35–44 by 47 per cent. Total population increased only 11 per cent. In the last few decades, there has been a trend toward more persons remaining unmarried, later marriages, fewer children, postponed children, and more divorces (Miron 1988). These young, smaller, childless households tend to prefer inner-city locations. The rise in commuting costs made suburbia a less attractive location for them. There was also a social change in attitudes and values that favoured the more cosmopolitan atmosphere of the inner city, the conservation and restoration of older buildings, and the consumption and leisure activities traditionally found in the central city. Not only did the young urban professionals embrace this urban aesthetic, so did many with counter-culture life-styles including artists, gay people, and political activists. In Canada, unlike in the United States, this life-style was also embraced by many empty-nesters and families with children. Finally, gentrification has been associated with a shift in the urban economy from secondary (manufacturing) employment to tertiary (service) and quaternary (managerial, professional, administrative, and technical) employment. These jobs are concentrated in national and regional service centres of the urban hierarchy and within their downtowns.

The gentrification process removes many low-rent dwelling units from the rental market. Houses once rented to many households become single-family owner-occupied houses. Apartments are renovated and command much higher rents. Apartments and rented houses are demolished and replaced by more expensive housing. Rooming-houses, lodging-houses, and residential hotels seem especially vulnerable and are demolished or converted to more profitable uses.

The loss of low-rental housing stock is hardly surprising. By definition it is a part of gentrification, and the Canadian literature on the topic provides considerable documentation of its extent. The City of Ottawa lost 40 per cent of its rooming-house units from 1976 to 1979, with most of the loss occurring in the gentrifying neighbourhoods of Centretown and Sandy Hill. Another 600 units of lower-cost inner-city rental housing were lost in 1980–1 as a result of renovation and redevelopment (Ley 1985). The private rental stock in the City of Toronto declined by 11,000 units from 1975 to 1985, and much of the decline included low-rent units and rooming-houses (Toronto 1986). From 1973 to 1976, six inner-city neighbourhoods of Vancouver lost 2400 rental units, and from 1976 to 1981 another 1000 units per year were lost, mainly in the inner city. From 1976 to 1981 the number of residential hotels and lodging-houses on the edge of Vancouver's downtown declined from 1200 to 450 (Ley 1985).

Beyond the Gentrified Neighbourhood
The loss of affordable rental accommodation in certain inner-city neighbourhoods has been much decried. However, an analysis and evaluation of gentrification cannot focus exclusively on the gentrified community. All too often the analysis notes the loss of units and that existing tenants cannot afford the renovated or newly built units, and the analysis stops there. An analysis of gentrification in the context of the entire urban housing market is required. For example, what happens to the displaced tenants? What happens to rents, renovations, conversions, and new construction in the neighbourhoods they move into? Where would the gentrifiers have lived if gentrification did not

occur? What happens to rents, renovations, conversions, and new construction in the neighbourhoods where gentrifiers would have lived? Unfortunately, there exists almost none of this comprehensive analysis.

The lack of analysis[2] can be explained by several factors. It is very costly to track the people who leave the gentrifying neighbourhood and move to other parts of the city. And although social-science researchers might love to have complete longitudinal data sets, in an open democratic society the collection of the necessary data would be an unwarranted intrusion on individual privacy. We will always have to rely on case studies, many of which will not be strictly comparable to one another.

Analysis is also lacking because it is very difficult to develop a theoretical model to analyse sensibly the gentrification in an entire metropolitan housing market. The modelling of gentrification is an example of the more general problem of modelling housing-market dynamics. An essential feature of such a model is housing units of different qualities. With use and over time, housing declines in quality. Maintenance and renovation can slow or even reverse the decline in quality. In these models, the combination of demand-side forces, supply-side forces, and government actions determines the housing-market outcomes, which include the price of each quality level, the allocation of households of different tastes and incomes to the various qualities of housing, the rates of new construction at each quality level, the maintenance and renovation at each quality level, and the rate at which each dwelling declines in quality. Typically, in these models, new construction occurs at medium- and high-quality levels: the medium- and upper-income households live in newer housing and lower-income households live in older housing that has declined in quality.

Many models were originally developed to analyse housing filtering. In this process, higher-income households move into newly built housing. The housing they vacate falls in value and depreciates more rapidly, which, on balance, reduces the price of that quality housing. This reduction allows a household of lower income to move in, and so on through the quality levels. Higher-quality housing eventually filters down to low-income households. The process of filtering and the process of gentrification are very similar; indeed, gentrification is sometimes referred to as reverse filtering.

There are several approaches to modelling an urban housing market with dwellings that vary in quality. The computer simulation approach (for example, Ohls 1975), or the Urban Institute model, has not been developed for Canadian cities and cannot be used to study gentrification and its effects on the low-quality housing market. An alternative is a theoretical model (see Sweeney 1974; Braid 1984; and Arnott, Davidson, and Pines 1983). The Sweeney model cannot be formally applied here but its logic can be helpful.

A Commodity Hierarchy Model
In Sweeney's model, rental housing is partitioned into a number of discrete quality levels that form a commodity hierarchy, and each level has a market rental price that is different from other levels. Households all agree on the ranking of the quality levels, and each household rents one dwelling unit of a certain quality level depending upon its tastes, income, and the prices of all quality levels. In the short run, the total number of dwelling units of each quality level is fixed, but over time total supplies are modified by new construction, deterioration, and demolition. The number of dwelling units of a given quality level is increased as units deteriorate from a higher quality level or as new units are constructed at that level, and is decreased as units deteriorate from that level to lower levels. New units are built at various levels in the hierarchy depending on profits, which depend on rental prices at all quality levels through which the unit will pass. Similarly, landlords undertake maintenance, which sets the rate of deterioration, in order to maximize profit.

To see the logic of the model, consider a classic problem. If the government were to subsidize higher-quality rental housing, would the poor be better off because more housing would filter down to them? For some types of construction subsidy the answer can be no. Suppose that, before the subsidy, new construction occurred at quality level *C* and above, and then the government subsidized construction at levels *S* and above; and *S* is higher quality than *C*. In Sweeney's model, rents would fall at all levels above *S* but may actually rise at low quality levels. The result is the product of two factors. The subsidy reduces rental prices and increases quantities at higher quality levels so that some households move up and, therefore, reduce rental prices at levels below *S*. These reduced prices below *S* reduce new construction below *S* and so reduce supply at low quality levels because there are fewer units to filter down. At very low quality levels the downward pressure on rents caused by households moving up is more than offset by the upward pressure caused by reduced supply. A construction subsidy for higher quality levels can make the poor worse off! (Sweeney's analysis predicts that a construction subsidy for all quality levels at C and above would reduce rents for everyone.)[3]

Gentrification is too complex a phenomenon to be fully analysed using such a simple commodity hierarchy model, but these sorts of models are necessary to capture the repercussions of gentrification throughout the urban housing market. As the example above shows, the results of programs can be unexpected if one takes a comprehensive view of the housing market.

Let us consider a stylized conception of gentrification in a rental commodity hierarchy: households that otherwise would have rented high-quality housing decide to rent renovated low-quality housing. This removes a low-quality dwelling unit from the commodity hierarchy and adds a close substitute for traditional high-quality housing. In the medium run the rental prices on all lower-quality dwellings will be increased and some moderate-quality ones as well. There will also be pressure to use low-quality housing more intensively and to divide it up into smaller units, which suggests that those households displaced from a gentrifying neighbourhood are far from a complete list of those hurt by gentrification. The displaced face the costs of dislocation and higher rents. But everyone living in low-quality housing also faces higher rents. Thus, neighbourhoods outside the gentrifying areas are affected. And even if gentrification occurs in a solid working-class area, the neighbourhoods of the very poor will be affected as well. Furthermore, as some households move down in quality, a reverse filtering process occurs, and the least well-off households may be forced out of their housing and onto the street.

In contrast, rents on high-quality rental housing where the gentrifiers otherwise would have lived will tend to fall as the units are vacated. Moderate- and high-income tenants outside the gentrified neighbourhood can gain from gentrification. The gains and losses of existing landlords mirror those of tenants: owners of low-quality stock will gain and owners of high-quality stock will lose.

The analysis can be extended by adding an ownership commodity hierarchy as well. Suppose some gentrifiers would have bought housing outside the central area.[4] Instead, they buy low-quality central housing and renovate it. Sometimes they buy a house occupied only by the owner, sometimes by both an owner and tenants, and on other occasions only by tenants. The effect on displaced tenants and all other tenants remains as above. But original owners realize an increased price on their house. They may do especially well if they move to the suburbs where the gentrifiers otherwise would have lived. The relative price of suburban housing has declined. Many ethnic households have moved out of gentrifying areas into the suburbs and realized this double benefit. Like landlords, owners of central low-quality stock gain and owners of high-quality suburban stock lose. There will also be pressure on owners of low-quality stock to rent out a portion of their houses because the rents they could realize have risen.

The analysis of gentrification in a commodity hierarchy model draws out a number of ideas significant for the understanding of homelessness. Most important, it provides an argument to show why the relative price of housing for the poor can be rising when the relative price of housing on average is not rising. Thus, aggregate data on rent levels may mask what is happening to the poor.[5] Also, the deleterious effects of gentrification are felt not only within the gentrified neighbourhood but also outside it throughout the low-quality rental housing market. Inside the neighbourhood, many and probably a majority of original members gain from gentrification: landlords, home owners, merchants, and realtors. And the incoming residents like the change. This is a formidable coalition, indeed, whose strength is enhanced by a current public commitment to decentralized, local-area planning.

CITIES, HOUSING, AND THE POOR

The analysis also suggests homelessness is an outcome of a larger urban process in the 1980s. The Canadian economy continues to shift out of manufacturing and into tertiary and quaternary activities. These activities tend to be concentrated in the downtowns of certain command and control cities within the urban hierarchy: for example, Vancouver, Edmonton, Toronto, Ottawa, Montreal, and Halifax. There is pressure to expand and intensify the central business district (CBD). Many employees in such industries have come to prefer the cosmopolitan character and amenities of central living, which puts further pressure on the areas around the CBD. Many others share this change in preferences and prefer to renovate and enhance the existing built form rather than see it redeveloped at higher density with new structures. Conservation, liveability, environmental quality – these are the catchwords. The residential densities in the central neighbourhoods decline. The areas around the CBD contain most of the older housing stock; and many of the poor, young, elderly, and disabled live there. The process that is changing the internal structure of cities displaces these people and echoes through the low end of the housing market, leaving most of this group to pay higher rents and some without a place to live at all.

Some of the poor are pushed out of the central city and into the post-war suburbs, further complicating their problems. The jobs and social services for the poor are concentrated in the central city, although they are beginning to be found at dispersed locations in the suburbs. But the suburbs were built for people with cars. The poor often do not have cars and must face lengthy commuting by public transportation.

The Urban Process and the Internal Structure of Cities

'The housing problems of the poor are caused by the urban process itself.' The problem and the diagnosis begin to sound familiar. The same problem and same diagnosis were central to discussions of the urban problem in the late 1960s. Looking again at the major study of Canada's urban problems of the era – *Urban Canada: Problems and Prospects* (1970) by Harvey Lithwick – reveals a striking similarity. Lithwick wrote that 'the growth of large cities leads to competing demands for the one common feature of all cities, scarce urban space, driving core prices upward and households outward.' He noted how the poor were locked in the central areas 'with prices and rents continually squeezing them as urbanization proceeds.' He emphasized the urbanness of the housing problem of the poor, and that the problem did not simply occur in cities as it occurred in small towns and rural areas, but rather that it was the product of the urban process itself. 'We might call them problems *of* the city to distinguish them from the simpler *in* the city problems.'

Today, the social housing problem has similarities to the 1960s and the approach to analysis has similarities. But the parallel is not exact. The basic urban process is significantly different. In the 1960s, the driving force was urbanization and the growth of cities, especially the largest cities. Now, urbanization has stopped and urban growth rates are much lower, with some conspicuous exceptions. Both eras saw a shift out of manufacturing employment. In the 1960s, the process of internal restructuring was significantly different: the cities were growing rapidly and the CBD was expanding. But the areas of older housing stock were being demolished and replaced by high-rise apartment towers. The suburbs were growing as well. To accommodate the commuters, expressways were pushed from the periphery into the central city, further removing low-rent housing stock and wrecking neighbourhoods. In the 1980s, the loss of low-rent housing stock is associated with gentrification and the stopping of higher densities and expressways.

Urban Reform
The urban problems of the 1960s were 'the forgotten urban poor, the alienated young urbanites, the frustrated middle class seeking shelter, the accelerating pollution of the air and water in and around urban communities, the pointless transformation of most of our central cities into mammoth parking lots, and the general unsightliness of the urban landscape' (Lithwick 1970). And, of course, omnipresent was the spectre of the US city: inner-city decay and abandonment, middle-class flight to the suburbs, the ghettos of the poor in the centre, and race riots. Certainly no Canadian city looked like that, and perhaps none would have evolved into that, but there was always the fear.

Public-sector responses to the urban process and to attendant urban problems were varied. The federal government proved unable to respond at any systemic level. CMHC continued to finance public housing for the poor, later restraining it and expanding rent supplements and assistance for third-sector housing. CMHC also expanded assistance for new apartments and homes. The provinces did not respond systemically. Most expanded their housing assistance to poor and middle income alike, gave greater assistance to public transit and less to expressways, tried to streamline the subdivision approval process, and financially assisted local governments.

The urban housing problems of the poor had quite a high profile in the late 1960s but became less and less of a priority for senior levels of government in the later 1970s and early 1980s. The urban housing difficulties of the middle class became the priority.

The most dramatic response to the urban problem of the 1960s had occurred at the local level. (Chapter 8 provides a detailed analysis of the role of local government in housing policy.) The civic boosterism, which embraced growth, high-rise developments, and expressways, was replaced or at least severely constrained in city after Canadian city by a neighbourhood-based reform movement (Magnusson and Sancton 1983). 'The reform movement endorsed a land use policy of preservation and enhancement rather than substantial change; it was opposed to freeways and in favour of transit, opposed to high rise development and in favour of downzoning, opposed to urban renewal and in favour of neighbourhood enhancement, including protection of heritage, the environment and park land. The quality of life and urban liveability were slogans directing policies to social, cultural and environmental qualities' (Ley 1985). The reform movement also endorsed vigorous government intervention to shape urban structure, but wanted it rooted in participatory neighbourhood planning. The central areas threatened by CBD expansion, high-rises, and expressways were among the first to establish locally based plans.

The term 'reform movement' used here seems to imply a large cohesive force that dominated urban politics. This was not the case. In fact, the reform movement was a complex coalition of very divergent interests and many of its members felt the decisions of the era were a superficial response to fundamental problems (Caulfield 1974).

The reform movement was highly successful and many of its objectives were achieved. Major progress has been made on middle-class housing problems, pollution, and urban unsightliness – the list of urban problems of the 1960s. High-rise development was stopped, expressways were stopped, neighbourhoods were enhanced, and the spectre of the 1960s US city no longer troubles us. Although not espoused by all reformers, gentrification proceeded apace. The most conspicuous failure of the reform era was the provision of affordable housing for the poor. The process that, in the 1960s, was driving up inner-city land prices and gobbling up the old housing stock where the poor were living was constrained, but a different process was added with a similar effect on the poor. Again, the spectre of US-city decline has arisen, but now we hear of the 'Manhattanization' of the central city.

The reform movement, or at least the progressive component of it, was deeply committed to creating a central city where the poor could live. Many political activists first became involved while defending poor neighbourhoods against high-rise development and expressways. Many cities enthusiastically promoted the use of federal housing assistance programs, particularly the Residential Rehabilitation Assistance Program and the non-profit and co-op housing programs. Several cities established housing departments with a strong commitment to socially mixed neighbourhoods.

The progressive reformers were the advocates for the poor. They supported massive subsidies for third-sector housing, in conjunction with liveable city initiatives. Unfortunately, these subsidies did not materialize. It was naïve to believe that the massive subsidies would be forthcoming and it is obstinate to continue to believe they will be forthcoming.

The time has come to recognize the undesirable effects on the poor of some urban reform programs. Those who enjoy the fruits of gentrification must recognize that neighbourhood-based planning can just as easily thwart assistance to the poor as provide a way to hear the voice of the poor; that stopping expressways raises inner-city land prices; that a liveable inner city implies gentrification, which removes low-income housing from the market; and that downzonings reduce the expansion of the rental housing stock.

SUPPLYING MORE RENTAL UNITS

The processes that change the internal structure of cities have been removing low-rental housing. It is logical to ask next whether there have been additional units supplied anywhere. Additional rental units can come from two main sources: there can be more construction by the private sector, and there can be construction by the public sector and the publicly assisted third sector.[6] Unfortunately, there were fewer additional units from all these sources in the 1980s than were created in the past. Supply-side forces that were intended to redress the social housing problem have been weakened during the decade.

Private New Construction
Average incomes are rising, rents are rising slightly faster than other prices, vacancy rates are low, and real interest rates have fallen in the late 1980s. The horizon should be punctuated with cranes erecting apartments, but it is not. Certainly these same factors have produced much new ownership housing. (Chapter 6 offers more extensive discussion of the private-sector role in providing housing for the poor.)

Private rental construction is below what one would expect for several reasons: because of rent control, downzonings, changes in the income tax laws, and reduced government subsidies.

Rent control is a most contentious housing program, but it does have significant influence on the immediate problems of the poor and on how the entire urban housing market evolves, and so some of the advantages and disadvantages of control must be addressed. Rent control keeps rents below what they otherwise would be. It reduces some of the rent increases that follow with gentrification. There can be no doubt that rent control benefits some of the poor. Those who occupied a rental unit when controls were introduced or manage to obtain a controlled unit have their rents held down, and, thus, their housing is made more affordable. This lower price does not mean that the poor, on average, can rent better or more housing because, in aggregate, rent control reduces rental housing quality and reduces the total stock of housing below what it otherwise would have been. The lower rents do not mean that the poor have more housing; rather, lower rents mean they have more of other things like food and clothing. Rent control also increases security of tenure in some ways. Tenants are less likely to face an unexpected large rent increase, which would force them to move; and because housing expenditure is a lower fraction of income, an unexpected decline in their income is less likely to force them to move. But rent controls are a mixed blessing even for the poor. Rent control reduces vacancy rates and the total stock of rental units and encourages sitting tenants to stay in larger units. Poor tenants who wish to move find it more difficult. More important, new households – whether new arrivals from inside Canada, immigrants or refugees, the young setting out on their own, a released psychiatric patient, or one spouse of a marriage breakup – find it more difficult to find an apartment. Reduced rents also increase the likelihood that rental buildings will be demolished or converted to other uses, thus reducing the security of tenure.

In assessing the desirability of rent control, the immediate benefits of reduced rents must be weighed against reduced maintenance and reduced numbers of units because of demolitions, conversions, and less new rental construction. The trade-off against reduced new construction may at first seem easy to resolve. Perhaps by exempting new construction, such construction will not decline. The decline can be diminished somewhat but not eliminated, because investors always fear that control will be extended to their buildings. This fear is well founded, as the recent extension of rent control to include previously exempt new construction in Ontario shows. Or perhaps the trade-off seems easy because newly constructed apartments could not be afforded by the poor anyway. But we must consider the longer-run evolution of the urban housing market. Commodity hierarchy models suggest that more rental units, especially in the moderate-quality range, would reduce lower-quality rents as households move up and units filter down. The 1980s have been a critical period: we have reached a point in the fluctuations in the national economy when new rental construction ought to have surged. It did not, in part because of rent controls.[7] The housing market of the poor will be tightened in the future as a result.

Another factor restricting new rental supply has been downzoning in neighbourhoods around central cities. Again, there is a trade-off. The downzonings protected established neighbourhoods, permitted gentrification, facilitated the liveable city, and stopped much unsightly high-rise architecture. But in contrast to rent controls, there are few poor among the gainers. The high-rise apartments of the 1950s and 1960s may be unsightly, but they are where many poor now live.

Changes in personal and corporate income-tax laws have made investment in rental real estate less attractive. In the 1960s investors in rental real estate enjoyed several tax advantages. Losses generated by capital cost allowance (CCA) deductions were deductible against other income, making real estate an attractive tax shelter. Capital gains were tax free and much of the return to real-estate investment came as capital gains. Allowable CCA deductions were greater than the economic depreciation of the building. Soft costs during the construction phase could be deducted at the time they were incurred by the investor rather than capitalized (although at the time few individual investors used this provision).

Special tax advantages lead to an expansion of residential construction but also mean that the government loses revenues. Many people argue that this process is a poor strategy if the government truly wishes to increase rental construction. The process is inefficient because all investors enjoy tax reductions, and most of them would have built new buildings anyway. The government revenue loss is great compared to the relatively few *extra* buildings constructed as a result. Mainly high-income taxpayers use the special provisions; the process implies an income transfer to some wealthy taxpayers. Subsidies delivered through the tax system are hidden, often much more costly than forecast, and neither properly monitored nor evaluated by government (Auditor General 1986). As tax subsidies are used in more and more sectors, the income-tax system becomes more complex, is perceived to be full of loopholes, and falls into disrepute. The basic thrust of tax reform over the last thirty years has been to remove special tax advantages and treat all sectors equally. Working against this trend are initiatives by some taxpayers and those pursuing some public-policy goal to restore the advantages.

The 1971 tax reform removed the tax-shelter advantages for individual investors and included one-half of realized capital gains in taxable income. The Multiple Unit Residential Building (MURB) program restored the tax shelter in 1974, ostensibly for one year, but it kept being renewed until 1981. In 1978, allowable CCA deductions on wood-frame buildings were reduced. After 1981, only corporations whose principal business was real estate could deduct soft costs. In 1985, individuals were granted a $500,000 lifetime capital gains exemption that made real-estate investment much more attractive. But overall, real-estate investment now has fewer tax advantages, and the amount of private rental housing is lower as a result.

The 1987 tax-reform proposals continue the basic trend. They recommend that the allowable CCA deduction on new buildings be reduced from 5 to 4 per cent, that three-quarters of realized capital gains be included in income, that individuals retain only a $100,000 capital gains exemption, and that all taxpayers capitalize soft costs (DOF 1987a).[8]

Finally, private rental housing has not surged forward because federal subsidies to private rental construction have been reduced significantly. There has never been a constantly high level of subsidy, rather an on-again/off-again pattern. Things are currently off-again. The major private rental subsidies of the last fifteen years have been the Assisted Rental Program (ARP) and the Canada Rental Supply Plan (CRSP), neither of which is currently operating. ARP was regarded by many as an attempt to offset the effects of rent control and the income-tax changes, but only a permanent subsidy can provide a permanent offset. The effects of rent control and tax change on new construction are really just beginning to be felt now that compensating subsidies have been removed. CRSP was a program motivated by a desire to stimulate the economy rather than motivated by housing policy concerns. Subsidies to private rental construction will likely reappear sometime, especially when required by macro-economic policy.

Government and Third Sector

The supply of additional rental units for the poor has also been curtailed by changes in Canadian social housing policy. (Chapters 5, 7, and 8 also discuss the evolution of Canadian social housing policy.) The level of CMHC involvement in housing has been dramatically curtailed if it is measured as annual lending. In the late 1970s, CMHC was lending over $1 billion annually under all of its National Housing Act programs; the figure has fallen to about $265 million. These amounts are in current dollars; in real terms the decline has been even more dramatic. But these data are somewhat misleading in trying to understand the impact of government policy on housing for the poor. Most of the cut-backs have been of housing programs that assisted the construction of ownership and rental housing for moderate-income families. In 1978, CMHC

TABLE 3.4
Loans and subsidies under social housing programs ($ millions)

	1972	1974	1976	1978	1980	1982	1984	1986	1988
Loans									
Public housing	238	177	350	176	22	14	2	–	–
Federal/provincial housing	39	58	100	126	114	99	128	96	104
Non-profit corporations	42	124	288	121	5	1	–	1	–
Co-operatives	–	20	40	37	1	–	–	–	–
Total	319	379	778	460	142	114	130	97	104
Subsidies									
Differential interest and interest-reduction contributions	–	9	14	23	224	193	475	636	670
Public housing subsidies	30	63	117	179	267	399	453	497	548
Residential rehabilitation	–	1	29	88	107	135	202	103	146
Total	30	73	160	290	598	727	1130	1236	1364

SOURCE: CMHC, various years

changed its method of assisting new social housing projects from providing public loans and operating subsidies on rent-geared-to-income units to providing interest subsidies on loans raised privately. Thus, public lending for social housing programs declined but was replaced by interest contributions. Nominal subsidies under social housing programs have risen sharply during the 1980s (table 3.4). Using the CPI as a deflator they have increased in real terms as well. The annual level of new dwelling units supplied under social housing programs fell during the late 1970s, rose again in 1980 and 1981, declined for a few years, and has been up and down in the late 1980s (table 3.5). Thus, although total subsidies (to all existing social housing units) have increased in the 1980s, the annual new additions to the social housing stock have declined in the same period.

Furthermore, there has been significant change within the social housing component. Originally social housing had two major programs: public housing (including federal/provincial housing), with all tenants receiving a deep subsidy, and limited dividend (or entrepreneurial) housing, with all tenants receiving a shallow subsidy. Both programs were severely criticized. Public housing was provided in

TABLE 3.5
Dwelling units under social housing programs[a]

Year	Single detached	Multiple dwellings	Total	Limited-dividend entrepreneurial
1972	1,631	18,790	20,421	8,797
1973	1,174	17,509	18,683	4,526
1974	2,242	19,780	22,022	2,544
1975	3,547	18,680	22,227	10,895
1976	3,203	24,115	27,318	–
1977	3,331	12,619	15,950	–
1978	2,972	12,240	15,212	–
1979	2,574	7,392	9,966	–
1980	2,592	18,416	21,008	–
1981	1,718	20,254	21,972	–
1982	2,476	16,684	19,160	–
1983	1,941	16,331	18,272	–
1984	2,920	15,334	18,254	–
1985	1,864	17,785	19,649	–
1986	120	9,502	9,622	–
1987	328	15,895	16,223	–
1988	268	10,768	11,036	–

SOURCE: CMHC, various years
[a]Includes public housing, federal/provincial housing, non-profit housing, and co-op housing on new and existing properties

massive projects creating ghettos of the poor. The profit motive of limited-dividend owners was felt to be incompatible with the provision of housing assistance. New public housing development declined in the late 1970s and entrepreneurial projects were replaced by third-sector (non-profit and co-op) projects. Deep subsidies on a rent-geared-to-income basis also were made available to up to 25 per cent of tenants in private buildings and, much more frequently, to up to 25 per cent of the tenants in the non-profit and co-op buildings that were being built. The remaining tenants in the non-profit and co-op buildings received a shallow subsidy. It was felt that this mixing of deep and shallow subsidy to tenants would diminish the problems of the massive public housing projects. This commitment to social mix was made more complete in 1978 when new public housing projects with all tenants receiving deep subsidy were no longer supported. Instead, public housing, non-profit housing, and co-op housing became very similar. New projects would have about one-quarter to one-third of the tenants receiving a deep subsidy and the remainder a shallow subsidy. The mechanics of the program meant that the shallow subsidies were higher than before. The upshot of these changes was that the total number of units declined under social housing programs (table 3.5); more important for understanding the problems of the very poor, the proportion of rent-geared-to-income units declined significantly. The evolution of social housing policy meant that a smaller share of available funds was being spent to provide housing available to the poor. The annual number of new, deep-subsidy units declined.

A cruel irony is operating here. The commitment to social mix came out of a response to the public housing ghettos of the 1960s, and many progressive reformers pushed hard for change. But as the social mix was achieved, social housing policy evolved to give lower priority to the most disadvantaged.

REFLECTIONS ON SOLUTIONS

The analysis in this chapter has shown that homelessness is not the cruelest manifestation of a problem that hurts everyone but especially hurts certain vulnerable people. The average Canadian is well housed; average rents have risen only slightly faster than all prices in the 1980s; real incomes are now rising; unemployment is falling; and poverty levels are falling. Rather, homelessness is a problem affecting certain people in a certain part of the housing market. The causes are many and diverse, suggesting that the solution will have to be multi-faceted – tailored to the circumstances of each city, community, and household.

The many causes of social housing problems and homelessness identified in this chapter can be organized into three groups: those relating to income and employment; those relating to the changing internal structure of cities; and those preventing an increased supply of rental units. Recalling Lithwick's distinction, the causes in the first and third group mainly are causes *in* the city, whereas those in the second group are causes *of* the city. (The social and psychological dimensions of the problems concerning the poor and homeless are examined in chapter 2.) Proposed solutions roughly parallel these three groups.

Economic growth and a reduction in the rate of unemployment are vital to solving the social housing problem, and they make sound economic and social policy. A permanent job is surely the most comprehensive, dignified, and humane solution to the housing problems of many. Macro-economic policies, industrial and trade policies, and job-retraining and manpower policies must be part of a solution. And economic growth is critical to ensure that initiatives will be forthcoming to financially assist and support those people who cannot work.

Successful full-employment policies are not, however, a complete answer to the problem. Such policies could help the employable urban poor (sometimes referred to as the 'new urban poor'), whose numbers have risen recently. But a majority of people with severe housing problems could not take a job even if it were available because they are elderly, without job skills, physically or psychologically disabled, or single parents with young children. These people require financial assistance to secure decent housing. Canada has an extensive income-security system: the decline in poverty among the elderly as a result of enrichments to that system has already been noted, as have recent increases in the real value of welfare payments. However, the income-security system is not without its problems. Support levels are still so low for many that decent housing is often impossible. Many critics claim the system is cumbersome, contains overlapping programs, and is structured so that recipients have little incentive to work when they are able. Housing problems are often a manifestation of income problems, and some housing solutions can be found in higher levels of support under the income-security system and reform of that system to increase work incentives.

The income-security system provides financial assistance that recipients can use to rent housing in the private or non-profit housing market. There are no restrictions on how the money is spent[9] and it needn't go to housing, although, obviously, much of it will. We sometimes forget that income assistance is a major part of how governments help people to obtain better housing; indeed, that portion of income assistance spent on housing is much larger than all direct housing assistance put together.

A special sort of cash assistance – a housing allowance – could blend both income-security and housing objectives. A housing allowance is a cash payment to households that they use to obtain housing in the private or non-profit market; the amount of assistance usually depends on an individual's income and the amount of rent being paid. Economists have often recommended that many federal housing programs be stopped and replaced by a national housing allowance. The federal government has considered such a strategy but never implemented it; however, several provinces, including British Columbia, Manitoba,

Quebec, and New Brunswick, have established housing allowances. The need for more cash assistance to the poor could be met with either an income-security system or a housing allowance or both.[10]

Full-employment policies and an income-security system have been basic components of the welfare state and our social safety net over the last twenty-five years. (Chapter 4 contains a full discussion of how a consensus developed to support this welfare state and how the consensus has weakened in the 1980s.) Increasingly, social critics have argued that employment and income-support policies are not enough, an argument given more force when considering the plight of the homeless. The portraits in chapter 2 reveal the painfully personal and psychological aspects of the problems of homeless people. Full employment and income security must be complemented by programs to deal with these aspects. The range of needed programs – from those for battered women, to those for street kids, to those for released psychiatric patients – is very broad; and each city will likely have its special needs.

The approach of economic analysis and of much post-war social policy holds that if people don't have jobs or adequate income assistance, they will have poor housing. In order to improve their housing, they must first be helped to get jobs or their level of income assistance must be raised. Housing advocates, especially those who have been working with the homeless and with those of no fixed address, are now arguing that the first need is for permanent, secure, private shelter. Only then can people organize themselves and confront their problems sufficiently openly to consider looking for jobs, acquiring job skills, or even considering what income assistance is available and suited to them. The security of a home must come before the job, not after. The income-to-housing causality is probably appropriate for some households and the housing-to-income causality appropriate for others. For the latter, the solution must be assisted housing, regardless of which among the private, public, and third sectors provides the assistance and regardless of which manages the housing.

The programs in the first group of solutions – macro-economic policy, industrial and manpower programs, and income security – have been in recent years primarily the responsibility of the federal government, with some independent provincial initiatives. This locus of primary responsibility should remain. A greater role is being assumed by the private and third sectors in job creation and job training, but the fundamental responsibility for full employment and income security must rest with the public sector at the national level.

The second group of causes of homelessness and the parallel second group of solutions is much more local. (See also chapter 8 on local responses to homelessness.) Homelessness and social housing problems are caused by the changing internal structure of cities: the expansion of the central business district, the gentrification of low-income neighbourhoods, and the constrictions to new rental supply from downzoning and from reduced investment in the transportation system. In further contrast to the first group, the second group seems to become more acute as the economy booms. Our very prosperity and the urban form we want in our prosperity puts pressure on the affordable rental stock.

The solution cannot be to freeze the low-rental housing stock, forbidding its conversion to other uses. Some municipalities have tried this approach: although sometimes successful and even desirable in the short run, it cannot succeed in the long run. If the land or the building has a higher return in some other use, the landlord will continually struggle to convert to that use. His explicit allies will be the building, development, finance, and real-estate industries. More important, his implicit allies will be the companies that want to occupy a possible new office building, the higher-income households that want to move into the neighbourhood, and the shoppers who want a possible new boutique or sidewalk café. It is foolhardy to believe such an alliance can be stopped in the long run. A better long-run solution would have at least two components: measures to reduce the pressure on the central area, and measures to increase the supply of affordable rental units.

The means to reduce the pressure on residential areas surrounding the central business district are rather obvious: decentralization of jobs to suburban centres and transportation improvements to make these centres accessible within the suburbs. In most Canadian metropolitan areas there is at least nominal consensus that these measures are desirable. However, competitive civic boosterism often prevents their systematic application. There is less consensus about the desirability of improving transportation access to the central area. Such improvements diminish the relative advantage of central location. But these new or widened transportation corridors disrupt, even destroy, central neighbourhoods. And the central area now becomes accessible to an even larger surrounding population. On balance, such transit improvements may increase the total size of the metropolitan area and the total size of the central business district, but they reduce the relative attractiveness of central locations and reduce average rents across the city. Provided there are sufficient improvements to transportation within the suburbs and there is sufficient adaptability of suburban residential areas to allow affordable rental housing for the poor to emerge, the poor would gain from improved access to the central area, to which they might travel for work.

The most direct method for increasing the supply of affordable rental units is to increase the direct provision of rent-geared-to-income hostels and apartments. These would be built by the private sector; managed by the public, private, or third sector; and subsidized by the public sector. Creative initiatives in the private and third sectors can provide shallow subsidies, but the deep subsidy needed for the very needy must inevitably come from the public sector. Direct provision should be accompanied by measures to let the private sector increase the supply of affordable rental housing. The zoning in single-family neighbourhoods should be relaxed to allow basement apartments, duplexes, and granny flats. Zoning should be changed in many areas to allow redevelopment at higher densities, particularly along the major mass-transit corridors. The result need not mean massive high-rise buildings; considerable increases in density can be achieved with three-to-five-storey structures. Because the zoning change to allow increased density would confer a windfall gain on the landowner, consideration should be given to allowing increased density only when the redevelopment includes affordable units or assisted units.

A proposal to develop an assisted housing project, to relax single-family zoning, or to allow increased density is usually greeted with vociferous and organized local opposition. We seem to pay lip service to these proposals but refuse to accept them in our own backyards. The fears of local residents have to be dealt with because the political power of residents is undeniable. Required is a greater social understanding that urban prosperity and urban structural change impose costs on the poor. We need a social commitment and consensus to ameliorate some of these costs. Just as we built a social consensus nationally to develop the compassionate mixed economy, which we call the welfare state, so now we must build a social consensus to develop a compassionate city. Everyone – individuals, the private, public, and third sectors – must be involved in shaping the consensus and in shaping urban development. (Chapter 8 also discusses the need for a local response to neighbourhood opposition to social housing.)

The third group of solutions relates to additional reasons why new rental supply has not been forthcoming: rent control, income-tax changes, and reduced government subsidies. Rent control reduces the stock and quality of rental housing and increases the pressure to convert rental residential buildings to other uses. It also holds down rents for tenants, low and high income alike. Controls present a difficult dilemma: their benefits are immediate and obvious but tend to dissipate over time; their costs are less obvious and tend to increase over time. The longer that controls are in place, the more difficult politically it is to alter them. A gradual movement to decontrol is required, coupled with programs to protect and assist the very poor. There are numerous options for relaxing control and options for complementary programs. We need to recognize that control will increasingly become a cause of, rather than a solution to, the social housing problem.

Although tax changes over the last twenty years have reduced incentives to invest in rental housing, it would be wrong to call for a reversal of the changes. The income-tax system is not suited to pursuing housing objectives. It is much better to replace the income-tax incentives with explicit subsidies. The combination of tax and explicit subsidy has declined significantly and what remains is less directed toward the very poor. One of the sharp controversies in current housing policy is over the degree to which governments should assist moderate-income renters. Whatever the outcome of the controversy, we must ensure that the neediest are cared for. In recent years, our commitment to social mix, the third sector, and moderate-income renters, combined with a declining total commitment to housing, has meant that the poor are worse off. Whether the solution is a greater level of total assistance for housing or more targeting of the available dollars – and it is likely to be a bit of both – we must not forget the most needy in our society.

NOTES

1 I am indebted to referees and many discussants at the August 1987 symposium, especially Richard Arnott. I also benefited from comments provided by Jon Caulfield and John Sewell, colleagues at York (both disagreed with my characterization of the 1970s urban reform movement).
2 The major study of gentrification in Canada is Ley (1985).
3 Strictly, this result and the previous one hold if the subsidy is an increasing function of quality.
4 Most studies (Ley 1985 and 1986; Legates and Hartman 1986) show that the gentrifiers are not moving into the central areas from the suburbs but are moving from within the central area. The important issue is where the

gentrifiers would otherwise have lived had the gentrification process not occurred. Many likely would have lived in the suburbs.

5 It has been found that the price of the bundle of consumer goods bought by the poor is not accurately measured by the Consumer Price Index. The prices of goods bought by the poor have risen faster than the CPI.

6 There can also be conversion of ownership or non-residential buildings into rental units, and subdivision of one rental unit into several rental units. Relatively few units come from such sources because of zoning constraints and because the business of being a landlord has become less attractive.

7 The operating costs of landlords increased much faster than rents in the 1970s. Vacancy rates were very low. The surge in new rental construction in the 1980s would likely have been preceded by a significant rise in rents.

8 These changes, which broaden the tax base, are accompanied by reductions in corporate and personal income-tax rates.

9 Those receiving welfare and living in public housing must pay a fraction of their welfare payment for rent, which is set by regulation.

10 Steele (1985) is the most comprehensive analysis of Canadian shelter allowances.

REFERENCES

Arnott, Richard; Davidson, Russell; and Pines, David. 1983. 'Housing Maintenance, Quality and Renovation.' *Review of Economic Studies* 50: 467–94

Auditor General. 1986. *Report of the Auditor General of Canada*. Ottawa: Minister of Supply and Services Canada

Bank of Canada. 1989. *Review*. Ottawa: March

Braid, Ralph. 1984. 'The Effects of Government Housing Policies in a Vintage Filtering Model.' *Journal of Urban Economics* 16: 272–96.

Canada. 1985. *Consultation Paper on Housing*. Ottawa

– 1988. *Poverty Profile 1988*. Ottawa: National Council of Welfare and Minister of Supply and Services

Caulfield, Jon. 1974. *The Tiny Perfect Mayor*. Toronto: James Lorimer and Company

CMHC (Canada Mortgage and Housing Corporation). Various years. *Canadian Housing Statistics*. Ottawa

– 1988. *1985 Estimates of Canadians in Core Housing Need*. Ottawa. Mimeo

DOF (Department of Finance). Various years. *Economic Review*. Ottawa

– 1987a. *Income Tax Reform*. Ottawa

– 1987b. *Quarterly Economic Review*. Ottawa

Fallis, George. 1985. *Housing Economics*. Toronto: Butterworths

Hamnett, C. 1984. 'Gentrification and Residential Location Theory: A Review and Assessment.' *Geography and the Urban Environment* 6: 283–319

Legates, Richard T.; and Hartman, Chester. 1986. 'The Anatomy of Displacement in the United States.' In *Gentrification of the City*, ed. Neil Smith and Peter Williams. Boston: Allen and Unwin

Ley, David. 1985. *Gentrification in Canadian Inner Cities: Patterns, Analysis, Impacts and Policy*. Ottawa: Canada Mortgage and Housing Corporation

– 1986. 'Alternative Explanations for Inner-City Gentrification: A Canadian Assessment.' *Annals of the Association of American Geographers* 76: 521–35

Lithwick, Harvey. 1970. *Urban Canada: Problems and Prospects*. Ottawa: Central Mortgage and Housing Corporation

Magnusson, Warren; and Sancton, Andrew. 1983. *City Politics in Canada*. Toronto: University of Toronto Press

Miron, John. 1988. *Housing in Postwar Canada: Demographic Change, Household Formation and Housing Demand*. Kingston and Montreal: McGill-Queen's University Press

Ohls, James. 1975. 'Public Policy toward Low Income Housing and Filtering in Housing Markets.' *Journal of Urban Economics* 2: 144–71

Ottawa. 1986. *Manual for the Social and Health Policy Committee*. Ottawa: Regional Municipality of Ottawa Carleton. Mimeo

Statistics Canada. 1982, 1986, 1988a. *Household Facilities by Income and Other Characteristics*, 13-218. Ottawa

– 1987, 1988b. *Household Facilities and Equipment*, 64-102. Ottawa

Steele, Marion. 1985. *Canadian Housing Allowances: An Economic Analysis*. Toronto: Ontario Economic Council

– 1989. 'Income, Prices and Tenure Choice.' In *Housing Progress in Canada*, ed. J. Miron. Ottawa: Canada Mortgage and Housing Corporation

Sweeney, James. 1974. 'A Commodity Hierarchy Model of a Rental Housing Market.' *Journal of Urban Economics* 1: 288–323

Toronto. 1986. *Living Room II: A City Housing Policy Review*. Toronto: Department of the City Clerk

RAMESH MISHRA

4 The Collapse of the Welfare Consensus? The Welfare State in the 1980s

Social problems such as homelessness do not exist in a vacuum. The nature of the problem itself, the way it is perceived, and the kinds of solutions considered as feasible are shaped by economic, political, and social conditions, as well as by general beliefs prevalent in society at a particular time. This chapter puts the problem of shelter and homelessness into the wider context of the welfare state in Canada.

Broad post-war Western consensus about the welfare state developed around the idea that systematic government intervention in the market economy – including the provision of a range of public services to ensure prosperity, security, and equity – was both desirable and feasible. During the 1970s this consensus eroded in the West and three more-or-less distinct policy approaches have emerged instead: neo-conservatism, the mixed economy of welfare, and social-democratic corporatism. Although Canada has retained a far greater measure of consensus than have Britain and the United States, a mixed economy of welfare may be seen as the general perspective within which problems and policies are likely to take shape in the foreseeable future, including implications for the development of housing policy in general and housing of the poor and homeless in particular.

In this chapter, I examine trends in housing policy in the post-war years in the context of changes in Canadian political economy. Inter alia, this examination draws attention to the peculiarities of housing as a consumption good, which makes the universal form of social provision (along the lines of medical care or education) inapplicable to housing. The spatial and locational dimensions of housing make a selective approach equally inapplicable, creating yet more difficulties in helping the poor and the homeless. These constraints may be seen as challenging Canadian housing policy to make an adequate response.

THE BASIS OF THE POST-WAR CONSENSUS

It would be an exaggeration to say that, until the mid 1970s, the welfare state enjoyed something like universal consensus. Ideological and theoretical differences about the role of the state in the provision of goods and services have existed throughout the post-war period. Yet, in retrospect, what seems distinctive about Western countries in the 1950s and especially the 1960s was the widespread acceptance of the basic tenets of the welfare state. State commitment to maintaining full employment, providing a range of basic services for all citizens, and alleviating poverty seemed an integral part of a progressive capitalist society, so much so that such commitment became almost a bipartisan policy.

True, there was in this regard a major difference between Western Europe and North America (ignoring for the moment differences within each bloc). The idea of the welfare state found greater acceptance in Europe than in North America, especially in the United States. Canada stood somewhere between American and European patterns. Unlike most European countries but like its southern neighbour, Canada's commitment to full employment remained weak (Gonick 1978: 12–14; Therborn 1986: 112–13). In contrast, unlike the United States but in line with Europe, Canada had put together an impressive array of universal programs by the early 1970s that included medical care, family allowances, and old-age security.

The Curtis Report (Canada, Parliament 1944) had outlined the need for government intervention to ensure minimum standards in housing. The post-war years saw an active government role in assisting Canadians with home ownership. The Canada Pension Plan, the Canada Assistance Plan, and universal medicare were important developments in the 1960s towards establishing the Canadian welfare state. In the United States, too, the 1960s witnessed such bold measures as the War on Poverty, medical care for those over 65, and medical aid for those on public assistance. By the early 1970s, a more comprehensive approach, which included the provision of social housing, was beginning to emerge. The idea of collective responsibility for ensuring a basic minimum standard of living for all citizens had begun to find general acceptance in Canada. It appeared as though North America, with Canada in the lead, was ready to follow in the footsteps of Western Europe.

From the vantage point of the 1980s, the broad consensus within Western countries about the welfare state in the 1960s looks truly remarkable. What made for such a consensus and why did it weaken in the 1970s?

Keynes and Beveridge

The post-war welfare state rested on two pillars, one Keynesian and the other Beveridgian. Put simply, Keynesianism stood for the government's ability to manage the economy from the demand side in order to ensure a high level of economic activity and full employment. The Great Depression had shown that the economic and social costs of laissez-faire – a drastic fall in production, mass unemployment, political and social unrest – could be extremely high. Keynes believed that the waste and inefficiency of a market economy could be corrected through moderate forms of intervention. We might call this Keynesian aspect the 'economic' component in the idea of the post-war welfare state. The Beveridgian notion of social insurance (understood in the wider sense) against the hazards of the market economy, in contrast, formed the 'social' component. True, long before Beveridge, Western industrial countries had been developing forms of social protection underwritten by the state. But, in the context of the English-speaking world, the Beveridge Report (Beveridge 1942) formulated clear principles of state intervention and spelled out the institutional framework that would make a reality of state responsibility for maintaining minimum standards of life.

The hallmark of this approach, which saw a government policy of full employment as a basic prerequisite of national well-being, was a network of universal and comprehensive social programs. These provided adequate benefits to all without any stigma of charity and as a matter of the rights of citizenship in a modern democratic community. The Marsh Report (Canada, Parliament 1943), as well as being a response to the Beveridge Report, may justly be seen as the charter of the Canadian welfare state. It also showed the influence of Keynesian thinking (Guest 1985: 109–15; Kitchen 1986: 42–3).

Common to both Keynes and Beveridge was the assumption that the kind of state intervention and service provision they were advocating would complement a market economy. The welfare state was to be an integrative measure that would make liberal capitalism more productive economically and more just socially. The results far exceeded the expectations of these reformers. Post-war welfare capitalism was so successful economically and socially that the success redounded fully in favour of their integrative assumptions. It would take the stagflation of the 1970s to undermine these assumptions.

Social Science and Social Welfare: The Promise of Social Engineering
Among the intellectual developments that helped to legitimize the
post-war welfare state and the idea of social intervention and social
engineering more generally was the promise of a 'social science.' It was
more a promise than an accomplished fact, for, in stark contrast to
natural science and technology (highly advanced in their knowledge
base), the social field was characterized by the absence of reliable
knowledge. However, the success of post-war economic reconstruction
influenced by Keynesian thinking lent credence to the idea that
economics, at least, might be coming of age as a 'science.' By the early
1960s it appeared that economics had developed a range of reliable
techniques – backed by sophisticated theories and quantifiable models –
for managing the economy. Other social disciplines such as psychology
and sociology, it was believed, could travel the same road and in due
course emerge as sciences with well-tested theories that would enable
social phenomena to be understood and controlled with scientific
precision. The spectacular growth of the social sciences in the 1960s
attested both to the willingness of society to underwrite the development of social knowledge and to the hopes pinned on it. The
advancement of the social sciences promised better understanding of
social problems and their solution. This view encouraged the belief that
social engineering – whether under the auspices of the state or some
other agency – would succeed in the same way that industrial technology and economic management seemed to be succeeding in their
particular spheres.

An important source of support for the post-war welfare state was its
promise to create a more equal society through piecemeal, democratic
reform. To many social democrats the Western industrial society of the
1950s looked increasingly 'post-capitalist' and public ownership of
industry no longer seemed relevant to socialism (Crosland 1956). It was
believed that through a variety of policies – fiscal, industrial, and social –
the state could exercise control over the market economy in the public
interest. Above all, leaving *production* in the hands of private enterprise,
the government could none the less socialize *distribution*. The growth of
universal social programs and collective services enjoyed by all but
financed through progressive taxation could lead to substantial redistribution of resources from the rich to the poor – whether individuals,
social groups, or regions. For conservatives and liberals, state intervention seemed justified because it helped to make individual liberty and
the market economy more secure. In short, the main objectives were

security and stability. For social democrats, however, the welfare state held out the promise that, through peaceful and constitutional use of state power, society could be made more equal and moved further along the path towards socialism (Crosland 1956).

THE CRUMBLING OF THE WELFARE CONSENSUS

The factors that gave legitimacy to the post-war welfare state in the West included the Keynes-Beveridge rationale for state action in the context of a buoyant economy, the promise of a science of society, the efficacy of piecemeal social engineering, and the pursuit of equality through social welfare. In the course of the 1970s and the early 1980s, most of these supports weakened seriously.

First, from about the mid 1970s, the heady economic growth of the post-war decades gave way to lower rates of growth, if not stagnation, accompanied by inflation. From time to time this 'stagflation' threatened to turn into slumpflation. Unemployment rose to levels not only unprecedented since the 1930s but also totally unexpected in light of Keynesian teachings. The presence of inflation alongside economic recession and rising unemployment confounded Keynesian economics, which relied on the trade-off between unemployment and inflation (the celebrated Phillips Curve) to manage the economy. This unprecedented situation led to a collapse of confidence in the state's ability to manage the mixed economy.

Thanks to the high level of economic growth sustained through the three post-war decades, it had been possible to finance social and other government expenditure largely out of the growing national dividend. With economic growth slowing down or, worse still, turning negative and with unemployment rising, governments were faced with increasing expenditures and shrinking revenues, which meant continuing budget deficits and a growing national debt (Calvert 1984: 74–6). Faced with the prospect of weak economic activity or stagnation, governments were reluctant to raise additional revenues from taxation. Moreover, inflation, coupled with declining real incomes, precipitated tax revolts in a number of countries, reminding governments that in hard times citizens were not keen to see their shrinking income reduced further (Danziger 1980; Woodside 1982; Gough 1979: 145).

Ideationally, too, the situation was no less serious. At the heart of the Keynesian approach was the belief that governments could regulate demand, maintain employment, and control inflation through 'fine-tuning' the economy, i.e., through indirect forms of state intervention. But faced with continuing stagflation, governments found that Keynesian techniques were no longer working. The result was that the economic rationale of the welfare state weakened seriously, leaving only the social or the Beveridgian rationale in place. The Keynes-Beveridge package of welfare implied that state policies would sustain both economic well-being (full employment and economic growth) and social welfare. As the economic side of the equation lost its credibility, the social side of the equation became increasingly vulnerable. Indeed, neo-conservatives (and, from a different perspective, Marxists also) blamed inflation and recession squarely on the welfare state. Full employment and budget deficits, they argued, had fuelled inflation, while the increasing burden of taxation had weakened incentives for enterprise and wealth creation. Far from being a virtuous partner of the capitalist economy, the welfare state had turned out to be a parasite, whose insatiable appetite was sapping the strength and morale of its more worthy companion. The neo-conservative cure for the ills of the capitalist economy was, therefore, to free it from the embrace of the welfare state. Full employment had to go, social expenditures had to be cut back, taxation reduced, and the dynamism of the private sector restored. Rolling back the frontiers of the state was the key to economic recovery and a prosperous market economy. The dynamic and progressive union between the market economy and a comprehensive welfare state – the corner-stone of the Keynes-Beveridge approach – had proved to be a misalliance, harmful in the long run to both partners.

More generally, neo-conservatives challenged the very idea of the 'rationality' of government intervention. First, they argued, government action had various 'externalities' or unforeseen and unintended consequences. These were a major source of government failure. In trying to correct for market failure, government action could conceivably make matters worse. Second, much of government growth, including social programs and expenditures, resulted from pressures and exigencies of the 'political market.' This market involved a variety of sectional interests: politicians seeking votes, lobbies of various kinds, state bureaucracies, and professionals seeking to extend and consolidate their base. The public sector had become more a vehicle for advancing vested interests than for serving the common good. These very pertinent arguments challenged the naïve assumptions of earlier times about government action as ipso facto beneficial and in the public interest.

By the close of the 1970s, little was left of the promise of a 'science' of society. Economics, which was earlier believed to have come of age as a social science, was in deep trouble. Keynesianism was in disarray and neoclassical theories of the market economy were staging a come-back. But this new economics seemed more a matter of faith and common sense than science. The idea, so much in vogue in the 1960s, that economics was beginning to approximate the natural sciences seemed like pure nostalgia. In 1982, a leading economist wrote of the disarray of the profession, with 'no shared ideas about what was going on and why, and what could be done about our ailing economies.' The situation apparently paralleled the intellectual confusion and disarray 'during the early days of the Great Depression' (Thurow 1984: xiv, v).

But long before economics proved to be an emperor without clothes, sociology and social science (more broadly conceived) were also found wanting as reliable guides to action. By the close of the 1960s, many social commentators and analysts in the United States were finding the results of the War on Poverty and other Great Society programs disappointing. A great deal of effort and expenditure had gone into these with only meagre results.

Clearly, in the absence of a reliable science of society, social policy could not be a 'rational' undertaking, i.e., a form of intervention through which ends and means could be connected in a calculable way. It was largely a hit or miss affair. Piecemeal social engineering, i.e., ad hoc tinkering with social problems, now appeared to have unforeseen consequences that could create new problems (Mishra 1984: 33–4). The idea that a democratic state could manage social affairs effectively using piecemeal social action had proved unrealistic. Government failure now paralleled market failure. Friedman drew the necessary conclusion: 'Evidence that markets are imperfect does not create a case for government action which may be even more imperfect' (Friedman 1977: 7). Conceivably, state intervention could, therefore, do more harm than good.

Also beginning to concern many socialists and other grass-roots democrats was the feeling that unwittingly, the welfare state was becoming, or had the potential to become, an instrument of domination over the ordinary citizen. The growth of state bureaucracies and professionally managed services meant a top-down, hierarchical relationship between service providers and clients. There was little by way of democratic participation, not to say control, in the planning and provision of social-welfare services. It appeared as though monetary domination of the market-place had been replaced by an equally oppressive domination by state officials and professional services providers. Moreover, it was often the case that the prime beneficiaries of the welfare state were the middle and upper classes. Universality of service provision meant that the middle and upper classes received all of the basic services, yet the overall incidence of taxation was scarcely progressive. In the arena of housing, government stimulation of home ownership (as well as many other tax-related measures) benefited mainly middle- and high-income Canadians. In general, social programs were not designed to meet the needs of low-income and marginal groups. In sections of the left, scepticism about the big state was becoming more pronounced. By the late 1970s, when stagflation emerged as a serious problem and the future of the welfare state seemed in doubt, the welfare state had ceased to be an object of admiration for many, especially the young on the left. Increasingly, Marxists and sections of the non-Marxist left joined neo-conservatives in their critique of the welfare state.

Finally, the welfare state came under fire from the feminist movement, especially its more radical and socialist wing. Feminists argued that the post-war welfare state was sexist both in its policies and in their administration, and thereby perpetuated the oppression of women. Finding the Keynes-Beveridge welfare state to be based on patriarchal and sexist assumptions, many feminists looked towards developing self-managed, non-sexist social-welfare organizations outside the state sector (Wilson 1977; McIntosh 1981).

Thus, the broad consensus around the mixed economy and the welfare state so characteristic of Western societies since the Second World War weakened a good deal as the 1970s wore on. As Keynesianism and other social theories of the centre (which served either as a practical guide to state intervention or else as its intellectual underpinning) lost credibility, radical critiques of the welfare state from the right, the left, and feminists gained in prominence. In particular, the ideas, analyses, and prescriptions of neo-conservatives made a good deal of headway in virtually all Western countries.

THE 1980s AND BEYOND

The post-war consensus around the welfare state weakened seriously during the 1970s. What is the state of the consensus or rather dissensus as we move into the 1990s?

The breakdown of the Keynesian welfare consensus has resulted in the emergence of a variety of policy approaches. At least three different policy stances can be distinguished. They are (1) neo-conservatism, i.e., the type of approach associated with Thatcher and Reagan regimes abroad and with such provincial regimes in Canada as the Social Credit government in British Columbia; (2) the mixed economy of welfare, i.e., a moderate form of government retrenchment in social welfare, the approach prevalent at the national level in Canada generally; and (3) the post-Keynesian or corporatist welfare state, which exists in countries such as Sweden and Austria.

Neo-conservatism

Neo-conservatism is perhaps the best known and the most visible ideology of welfare that has tried to supplant Keynesian welfare ideology. Neo-conservatives would like to see the role of the government in social welfare reduced very substantially and would turn to voluntary and market-based approaches. As far as possible, they would devolve social-welfare tasks to lower levels of government, on the grounds that these levels are closer to the communities and the people. Decentralization is a part of neo-conservative thinking, but perhaps the word that captures the essence of this approach is 'privatization.' Prime Minister Thatcher's program of the sale of public housing in Britain is a dramatic example of privatization in welfare. Between 1979 and 1983, about one-half million public housing units were sold to existing occupants, sometimes at a discount of 50 per cent of their market price. Converting municipal housing into owner-occupied accommodation proved the most popular of the social policy initiatives of the Thatcher government (Riddell 1985: 154–9). In 1979, about 75 per cent of Labour voters approved of the proposal to sell council houses (Cowling and Smith 1984: 65). Indeed, the popularity of Conservative policy to privatize housing has led to a great deal of soul searching among Britain's socialists, so much so that universal home ownership has been proposed as socialist policy (ibid.).

Privatization means that the market and other non-government sectors are called upon to play an increasing role in the supply of services and programs hitherto provided by the state (e.g., private pension plans instead of government pensions, private health care in place of government programs). Services may be subsidized by the government but they are to be supplied by the private and third sectors. Ideally, the government's role in social welfare is reduced to providing a safety net for the population in need. For neo-conservatives, universal social programs, in particular, typify government involvement in unnecessary and wasteful expenditure. They would replace universality with selectivity, i.e., targeting programs on those in greatest need and leaving the majority of the population to fend for itself through voluntary arrangements.

As far as economic activity and employment are concerned, neo-conservatives are quite explicit in their belief that the market should have full play. Any governmental attempt to maintain high employment levels 'artificially' is not only doomed to failure in the long run, but is also likely to do more harm than good to the economy. Neo-conservatives, therefore, reject the Keynes-Beveridge notion of full employment as a sustainable, indeed desirable, goal towards which governments can work. Consequently, some unemployment is seen as inevitable and as the price to be paid for a dynamic capitalist economy.

Is there a general consensus around these beliefs in countries such as the United States, Great Britain, and Canada, where conservatives are in power? Scarcely. There is something of a paradox here. On the one hand, the electorate has put conservatives in power, and at least in the United States and Great Britain, these regimes have been closely associated with neo-conservative beliefs. On the other hand, public-opinion polls in all three countries have shown continuing support for social programs, as well as for government responsibility for collective well-being – two of the main ingredients of the post-war welfare state (Riddell 1985: 39–40, 162–3; Ladd and Lipset 1980; *Newsweek* 8 February 1982: 34; *Maclean's* 7 January 1985: 13–16; McKinnon 1983: 206). Continuing concern over unemployment rather than budget deficits suggests that the majority of the population has by no means accepted neo-conservative economic beliefs and priorities, or the government's apparent inability to maintain employment (*Maclean's* 1985: 13–14; McKinnon 1983: 190).

What, then, are we to make of the ambivalence of a situation in which a populace seems to be wedded to the goals and principles of the welfare state, while it puts a neo-conservative government in office? To understand this situation, we have to look at the nature of capitalist democracies. The capitalist element in these countries stands for a privately owned market economy, with its promise of dynamism and growth. The democratic element, in contrast, stands for values of justice and equity, community, individual liberty, security, and self-fulfilment. Because we live in social systems that are at the same time capitalist market economies and liberal democracies, it would seem as though two different sets of values and principles inform social practice. The singular achievement of the post-war welfare state until the mid 1970s was to harmonize these differing values quite effectively.

Let us take this analysis further. Continuing support for major social-welfare programs and for government responsibility for collective well-being suggests that the broad *aims* or *objectives* of the post-war welfare state continue to influence public opinion. The stagflation of the 1970s essentially demonstrated that Keynesian techniques for maintaining full employment, controlling inflation, and sustaining economic growth were no longer working. A weak and uncontrolled economy threatened both economic and social welfare. Thus, at the level of public opinion (as distinct from élite opinion), support for neo-conservative regimes betokens a readiness to consider *alternative means* to broadly *similar* social *goals*, i.e., economic growth tempered with security and equity. Indeed, this is what neo-conservative regimes generally promise the electorate: different means for reaching broadly similar goals. Thus, while denying the government's ability to maintain full employment, conservatives none the less win elections on the promise of 'jobs, jobs, and jobs' to be created, of course, by the private sector. In both the United States and the United Kingdom, what neo-conservative politicians promised were fiscally responsible governments. But fiscal balance was to be achieved largely through the miracle of a revitalized economy, which would create jobs and revive growth. To be sure, eliminating waste and inefficiency and cutting back on government bureaucracy have always been the stock-in-trade of neo-conservative politicians. But no government has ever been elected on a platform of substantially retrenching, not to say dismantling, the welfare state (Carroll 1984: 96; *Globe and Mail* 9, 10 November 1984). Clearly, then, there cannot be said to be a consensus anywhere on the ideology of neo-conservatism.

The Mixed Economy of Welfare
The mixed economy of welfare is somewhat difficult to pin down as an ideology (Beresford and Croft 1984; Hadley and Hatch 1981). It is largely pragmatic and accommodative in approach. It accepts the essential role of the government in ensuring the social welfare of the population through universal social programs, but finds government monopoly in service provision objectionable. By and large, it accepts the neo-conservative definition of economic problems: that budget deficits must

be reduced, and that taxation must not impede incentives to produce wealth. Continuing deficits, therefore, require containing, if not reducing, the scope of government.

However, issues of equity and justice are also acknowledged as important. The ideology of wholesale privatization is rejected. Rather, the aim is to contain and reduce the role of the government in social welfare and, thus, to encourage non-governmental organizations and agencies to play a larger role. Although the nature of the 'mix' of the various elements – government, for-profit as well as non-profit organizations, employers, families, and communities – remains imprecise, the basic idea is a reduced role for the government and a corresponding shift towards non-governmental organizations. This approach is considered desirable on both fiscal and administrative grounds: fiscal, in that it reduces the pressure on government financing; and administrative, in that it takes into account some of the general criticisms of the government – from both the right and the left. Less direct government involvement means less bureaucracy, more decentralization, more community involvement, and, in general, greater participation.

A basic ideological difference here is between those who see the situation primarily in terms of *decentralization*, with the government's role as that of ensuring adequacy of services through funding and the monitoring of standards; and those who see it essentially as a form of *privatization*, leading to a curtailment of the scope and responsibility of government. In any case, there seems to be a large measure of support for the idea that at least the *delivery* of social programs and services could be turned over more to non-governmental organizations. Again, the left would see these as, on the whole, being non-profit, community-based agencies. The right has a natural affinity for profit-making organizations. Overall, however, there is little doubt that, with all its ambiguity, a mixed economy of welfare seems to be emerging as the new orthodoxy in social-welfare ideology – at least in English-speaking countries.

The Post-Keynesian Welfare State

This model of welfare is based on the notion that the remedy for the various ills of the Keynesian welfare state is not a return to the marketplace or a discreet withdrawal of the state. Rather it is the development of a different institutional combination that will integrate the economic and social policy objectives of the welfare state more successfully than the Keynes-Beveridge approach was able to do (Mishra 1984: ch. 4). Like neo-conservatism, this model also can be seen as a different *means* to the broad *aims* of the welfare state, vis., economic growth tempered with stability, security, and equity. It seeks to sustain the basic value commitments of the welfare state embodied in the policy of full employment and adequate universal social programs for all. In dealing with the problems of economic and social policies of welfare capitalism, it moves beyond the 'hands-off' approach of the Keynes-Beveridge model towards a 'social-contract' approach. Basically, the model involves a framework of ideas and institutions in which the major economic (producer) interests – employers, employees, self-employed farmers, and others – recognize the legitimacy of *both* social and economic goals, and make a concerted effort to attain nationally agreed-upon goals such as controlling inflation, reducing deficits, improving productivity, maintaining competitiveness, maintaining employment, and sustaining social-welfare expenditures. Sweden and Austria are two countries generally recognized as having had a long and reasonably successful record of putting this model to work (Mishra 1984: ch. 4; OECD 1981; *The Economist* 1987: 21–6). Their success in balancing economic and social objectives over the last ten years, their search (especially in Sweden) for new institutional forms, and their attempt to strengthen and develop this model further suggest the continuing relevance of this 'third way' of organizing a post-Keynesian or advanced welfare state. In Canada, however, the mixed economy of welfare, privatization, and decentralization seems to be the basic idea around which social-welfare policy has tended to revolve so far.

CANADIAN SOCIAL WELFARE IN THE 1980S

Compared with the classical neo-conservative countries of this decade – the United States and the United Kingdom – Canada has followed a somewhat different course. Here we must acknowledge the political difference between the governments of the three countries. Apart from the brief interlude of the Conservative government of Joe Clark (1979–81), Canada has been ruled until recently by Liberals. Liberalism also seems to represent the prevailing consensus of values in Canada, which is more at the centre of the ideological spectrum than in Britain (to the left until the late 1970s), and the United States (to the right). Although Conservatives came to power in 1984 with a landslide victory and with solid support across the country, the government was nevertheless cautious in its moves, maintaining the continuing relevance of a centrist consensus. The prevailing national opinion on social welfare programs may be important here. Polls show quite clearly that the majority of Canadians are against slashing mainstream programs such as medicare, old-age pensions, and family allowances (*Maclean's* 1985: 14–16; McKinnon 1983: 199, 206). During the election campaign, Brian Mulroney had promised that the principle of universality of social programs would be fully respected. Despite this promise, the Mulroney government (1984–8) tried to open up for debate the question of universality (*Globe and Mail* 9, 10 November 1984; Prince 1985: 7; DOF 1984: 71). It also cut back on social expenditure (Prince 1986: 16, 40–1). At the same time, the retreat from the proposal to de-index old-age pensions, the affirmation of the principle of universality, and the decision to shelve the Forget commission's recommendations for the overhaul of the unemployment insurance program show the government's reluctance to make a radical departure from the status quo (Prince 1985: 7–8). Overall, then, it would seem that the Canadian consensus over social-welfare policy has remained relatively immune to neo-conservative influence at the national level. (Although it is too early to pronounce on its policies, the second Mulroney government has begun with a more determined assault on social expenditure.)

At the provincial level, governments have shown more pronounced ideological differentiation, although there is little evidence to suggest that public opinion regarding social welfare differs much across the country. None the less, variation in government ideology and policy at the provincial level (witness British Columbia [Carroll 1984]) remains an important counterpoint to the general continuity of restraint at the federal level.

From about the mid 1970s, federal governments have been following a policy of 'restraint' (i.e., holding down and even reducing social expenditure). This 'responsible' stance may have helped to sustain a centrist consensus around social welfare at the national level. As well, the general debate resulting from the crisis of the welfare state in the 1970s has exposed many weaknesses in the neo-conservative argument. For example, it is clear that the federal deficit in Canada is not a result of profligate social expenditure, but rather of a substantial reduction in revenues resulting from tax indexation and other measures (Economic Council of Canada 1984: 25–30). The growth of tax expenditures and allowances of various kinds since the early 1970s has meant a substantial loss of revenue for the government (ibid.). These measures have chiefly benefited businesses and high-income Canadians (DOF 1981; Ternowetsky 1984). On government subvention of business, the Tory government's own task force (Nielsen) speaks of government giving to business 'with both hands' (Study Team Report 1986a: 11). Indeed, it is in this area that government spending seems 'out of control' in that there is no clear accounting and evaluation of revenue measures. At the same time, reporting on the Canada Assistance Plan, the Nielsen task force found that government spending was far from excessive and there was little evidence of abuse of welfare (Study Team Report 1986b; Kirwin 1986: 39–40).

During the 1970s neo-conservatives were vociferous in their claim that the government's budget deficit was fuelling inflation. Ironically, under the Reagan administration, the budget deficit has sky-rocketed, yet inflation has dropped substantially (OECD 1986c: 37 and 1986d: 109). Further, evidence from Western Europe and elsewhere has shown that, contrary to neo-conservative belief, there is no evidence that a high level of government expenditure per se affects economic growth adversely (Canada 1985a: 576). Finally, the last decade or so has shown the resilience of the advanced welfare state (the model underlying Austrian and Swedish policies) in maintaining employment, reducing deficits, containing inflation, and generating growth through a co-operative and consensual approach (Mishra 1984: ch. 4; *The Economist* 1987: 21–6; OECD 1986a: 53, 56–7). These are among the developments that may be weakening the appeal of neo-conservatism among academics and intellectuals, and its influence on opinion leaders.

The Macdonald commission's (Royal Commission 1985) investigations confirm many of these points: 'no evidence of a major shift in the broad view of Canadians about the role of social security in modern society. The Canadian public does not support across-the-board cuts in our social services. Its support for the Canadian welfare state has survived the recent recession' (ibid.: 578). Indeed, the report states that 'the core of public support for our basic social programmes seems solid ... [We] see no convincing evidence of the emergence of new political consensus among Canadians that would mandate a dismantling of the welfare state' (ibid.: 577).

At the same time, the commissioners rightly note that 'the post-war consensus on social policy has weakened' and that, compared with the 1950s and 1960s, recent decades have witnessed a considerably stronger debate. The right has challenged the efficacy of government action in social welfare, while on the left 'a greater disillusion has diminished faith in social policy as an effective instrument of reform' (ibid.).

The Macdonald commission's own approach to unemployment suggests the way in which consensus has weakened, at least among opinion-forming élites. In company with the bulk of the economic community in Canada, the commissioners accept the inevitability of unemployment. They endorse the idea of a 'natural' or non-inflationary rate of unemployment in Canada of 6–8 per cent (Royal Commission 1985: 275–7, 362–3). This is a departure from the post-war notion of full employment seen by the architects of the welfare state (such as Beveridge and Marsh) as part and parcel of the welfare state, as well as its necessary underpinning. After seven years following the recession of 1982 the Canadian rate of unemployment has, at last, come down to pre-recession levels, but it still remains close to 8 per cent (7.8 per cent in April 1989) (Statistics Canada 1989: B-3). It is in abandoning the idea of full employment and in accommodating high rates of unemployment that departures from the tenets of the welfare state seem most pronounced in Canada.

As far as social-welfare services are concerned, the notion of a mixed economy of welfare is most likely to serve as a general guideline to policy changes in the near future. This means two things: first, a general recognition that there may be limits to what the state can do for its citizens by way of social welfare; and second, that although the government must remain responsible for maintaining core universal services of an adequate standard, objectives such as effectiveness, responsiveness, participation, and community involvement require pluralism and flexibility of approaches. There is therefore a case for devolving the *delivery* of services where possible to non-governmental organizations (for the nature of such organizations and their role in housing see chapter 7 in this volume). Generally, people on the left, as well as many feminists, look for decentralization and community-based services with popular participation (ibid.). Those on the right look to the market mechanism and profit-oriented organizations for enhanced efficiency, responsiveness, and consumer choice.

Policy choices are necessarily political. They also differ from one service area to another. In general, however, the mixed economy of welfare suggests developments along the following lines:

1 Unemployment is likely to remain high and to continue to present problems of adequate income protection for those out of work and their families. Many new jobs are also likely to be at low wages, which will increase the number of working poor. Political expediency might tempt governments to reduce expenditure on unemployment benefits, considering that the out-of-work group is a small, invisible minority without much popular support.

2 Within a broad framework of universality, selective and targeted programs will tend to increase. The problem of avoiding stigma and reaching target groups will be important. At the same time, governments may find it politically more expedient to cut back on programs affecting the poor and other minority groups rather than on mainstream universal programs. Seen in conjunction with no. 1 above, this could mean more poverty and inequality in Canada.

3 Non-government organizations – profit and non-profit – will be called upon to play a larger role in the delivery of social welfare. Problems of maintaining the quality of service and accountability will be important.

4 The 'social-engineering' approach of the late 1960s (the idea that with the help of the social sciences, the government could control and predict social behaviour and thus banish problems of poverty, dependence, and deviance) will be much less in evidence. Government policy is likely to be more 'contractual' and 'procedural' (e.g., employing a 'rights-and-responsibilities' framework). Voluntarism, including market forces, will play a larger part in problem solving. Government policy will aim at helping individuals, groups, and communities to help themselves.

HOUSING POLICY AND THE CANADIAN WELFARE CONSENSUS

The early part of this chapter divided the history of the post-war welfare state into two stages. The first, which lasted to the mid 1970s, was one of substantial consensus in Western countries around the principles and objectives of the welfare state. The second, which began around the mid 1970s, has seen a substantial weakening, if not the breakdown, of the consensus, with a number of policy paradigms emerging as alternatives. I have argued that consensus over social welfare has weakened rather less in Canada than, for example, in Britain or the United States. We may, therefore, expect a good deal of continuity of objectives and policies in the Canadian welfare state. To what extent is this assumption of continuity true of housing and what are the implications of the 'mixed economy of welfare' model for housing and homelessness?

The objectives of the welfare state may be expressed, in general terms, as a commitment to maintain a minimum standard of living with respect to a range of basic needs, such as education, medical care, shelter, and income security. But the nature of each sector of need, and the services and programs developed to meet them, differ in important ways.

Education and medical care tend to take the form of a standardized,

universally provided public service, aimed at an optimum rather than
a minimum standard. Equality of opportunity, with equal access to
valued educational and medical resources, is an important principle
underlying these two services. In contrast, income security and housing
aim at providing a basic minimum rather than an optimum standard.
Programs such as Old Age Security and the Guaranteed Income
Supplement for those over 65 reflect this idea of a national minimum
standard of living for all citizens. Accordingly, income-support services
aim at ensuring security rather than promoting equality. For example,
programs such as the Canada Pension Plan, Unemployment Insurance,
and sickness benefits are income-related and, as such, reflect the
inequalities of the market-place. In housing, too, policy objectives tend
toward a social minimum. State programs aim at ensuring a basic level
of adequacy – notably absence of overcrowding and access of basic
amenities – beyond which the housing standards of individuals and
families are supposed to reflect their market capacity. In virtually all
Western welfare states, the aim of housing policy has been to ensure a
national minimum standard of housing.

However, there are certain other peculiarities of housing or shelter
that need to be taken into account. Perhaps the most important of these
is that home ownership tends to be the predominant form in which
housing is consumed. Ownership of housing is attractive because it
makes shelter both a consumption good and also valuable private
property for the individual. Yet, given high urban housing costs, the
low incomes of many households, and the uncertainties of employment, universal home ownership cannot be a realistic goal for housing
policy. In Canada, for example, just over 60 per cent of all households
consist of owners and about 40 per cent of renters. This proportion has
scarcely changed since the late 1960s (Hulchanski and Drover 1986: 31),
although renters have increasingly become concentrated among low-
income households (ibid.: 32). This division of the population into
categories of owners and renters (a common-enough situation in most
countries) makes it difficult to provide housing as a universal program.
The strategy of universality, the hallmark of the welfare state, has been
applied reasonably successfully in the supply of medical care, education, and even income support (albeit universal programs per se cannot
meet all income needs). But the strategy of universality is not easily
applicable to housing because there is no readily available universal
means through which the welfare state could provide housing for all
citizens (short of a universal shelter allowance or public rental housing

for all). Yet 'selectivity,' i.e., targeting programs only for the poor and disadvantaged, also runs into difficulties because of the nature of the 'externalities' of housing. The NIMBY (not in my backyard) syndrome is particularly important because low-cost housing programs such as public housing projects and related measures impinge – environmentally, socially, and financially – on communities in a way that is perceived as negative. Hence, given its peculiar spatial and locational dimensions, housing is quite different in nature from medical care or income maintenance. As is well known, federal and provincial governments tried, during the 1970s, to overcome these externalities associated with public housing through compromises, such as third-sector and socially mixed housing, which introduced elements of universality. This, of course, meant that a good deal of housing subsidies went to non-poor households.

Among other relevant characteristics of housing as a field of public policy are the following. First, government economic policies such as interest rates affect housing starts and housing costs quite directly. Therefore, in some form or other, the government tends to acknowledge responsibility for the implications of its economic (including fiscal and monetary) policies for housing. Second, and this is a related point, the government becomes involved in housing from the vantage point of ensuring an adequate supply of capital for the house-building industry and as mortgage-insurance underwriters. Third, because the house-building and construction industry is a major sector of the economy (keeping in mind the multiplier effect of house building on the economy), governments tend to use housing policy as a tool of economic management, e.g., as an anti-cyclical device for job creation. Fourth, the housing market suffers from a number of 'imperfections.' An important one is that supply cannot adjust readily to changes in demand for housing (unlike most other commodities, housing cannot be moved quickly from a low-demand to a high-demand area). This factor can put the sellers of housing in an exceptionally strong position in relation to buyers, at least in the short run, and it is one reason why governments become involved in rent control in urban areas. These peculiarities of housing as a commodity help us to appreciate the nature and scope of government intervention in housing within the broad framework of the welfare state. They also point to the unwieldy nature of both the housing problem and forms of government intervention.

THE DEVELOPMENT OF HOUSING POLICY

An authority on housing and urban issues suggests that housing policy can be seen as developing through three fairly distinct stages. These are 'assisted-market,' 'social housing,' and 'comprehensive' stages (Donnison 1968: ch. 3). The reasoning underlying these stages may be stated as follows.

In the first stage, the emphasis of public policy is on strengthening mortgage and other financial markets in order to ensure a healthy flow of funds for residential building. Measures are also taken to ensure that there is an efficient and productive construction industry. In brief, the aim of government policy is to ensure the production of an adequate number of homes by helping the private industry and the market. The general belief underlying this policy is that economic growth produces rising incomes, while the production of an adequate number of homes ensures a rising standard of housing for the population as a whole through the so-called 'filter-down' process. The use of housing policy as a tool of economic management (i.e., through the stimulation or inhibition of house building) fits in quite well with the assisted-market approach. Overall, one might say that at this stage, housing policy is an extension of the policies of growth and management of a market economy to ensure prosperity.

The second stage sees the development of social housing for various disadvantaged groups such as low-income families. Although social housing can be provided through the market sector with government assistance (i.e., using producer subsidies), it usually involves other suppliers as well, notably the government itself and the third sector. The development of social housing policy is based on the recognition that the problem of housing is not simply one of production but also of distribution. Housing policy is also influenced by the perception that although the economy might be growing and average incomes rising, it cannot be assumed that all share equally in rising standards. Certain sections of the population may be falling behind others, in that their relative share of income is worsening. Besides, it also begins to be appreciated that certain sectors of the population may not only suffer economic but also social disadvantages in the housing market. In other words, the limitations of housing policy based largely on assumptions about the general benefits of economic growth and the allocation of housing through the free market become evident. The move towards social housing is prompted by yet another consideration, which is that economic development itself, e.g., urban renewal and inner-city business development, tends to create a housing problem by removing low-rent housing from city centres and by displacing individuals and communities through commercial development. Because growth creates 'diswelfares' with respect to shelter and other needs, compensatory policies of rehousing and redevelopment are seen as necessary to alleviate the problems generated by urbanization processes conditioned by market forces. Overall, however, the social housing approach remains a relatively minor corrective and a complement to an essentially market-based system of supply and distribution of housing. In short, social housing is seen as a necessary but delimited addition to the assisted-market approach. The role of the government in housing is still seen largely in 'residual' terms as dealing with that minority of the population who cannot fend for themselves in the market-place, and with that residue of problems generated by market processes that cannot be solved satisfactorily through the market.

In the third, 'comprehensive' stage of the development of housing policy, there is an appreciation of the fact that the 'housing problem' is not a neat 'one-off' problem, whether of production (e.g., clearing the backlog of needs unmet because of the Great Depression or the Second World War) or of distribution (e.g., solving the affordability problem of low-income groups through a once-and-for-all solution such as shelter allowances). Rather, it is recognized that if the government is to take its housing responsibility seriously, and if a national minimum standard of housing is to be assured for all citizens, then a wide range of instruments and forms of intervention – some short-term, others long-term – may be necessary. These interventions may include rent regulation, assistance with home ownership and rehabilitation, public housing, third-sector housing (e.g., housing co-ops), and shelter allowances. In short, a comprehensive housing policy recognizes that there are no 'quick fixes' to maintaining a social minimum. In a world characterized by change – economic, technological, and demographic – and by instability, government policy may have to run fast in order simply to stand still. The connection between housing and other aspects of social and economic policy (i.e., income security, employment, and taxation) is increasingly recognized as a factor in policy making, as is the relative nature of minimum standards in housing. Thus, 'comprehensiveness' implies that (a) the nature and scope of government housing policies and programs are wide ranging; (b) the objectives and principles of government policy in terms of commitment to equity and a national minimum are clearly spelled out; (c) the wide range of groups and classes served by government policy – whether directly through subsidies and loans or indirectly through tax expenditures – is recognized, and various policy interventions are considered in relation to one another; (d) a wide range of auspices – public, private, and third sector – is employed in the delivery of housing, in order to realize policy objectives more effectively; and (e) government role in housing is seen as 'institutional' rather than 'residual' that is, as a normal front-line function, rather than as a temporary or makeshift involvement in order to solve a specific problem (Guest 1985: ch. 1).

This three-stage classification provides a useful bench-mark for an understanding of housing policy in the post-war decades. It should be remembered, however, that it is an analytical framework or a heuristic device, i.e., an aid to understanding an untidy and complex social reality. These stages do not purport to describe reality, let alone to suggest a deterministic sequence through which welfare states go. With these caveats in place, it is useful to see post-war Canadian housing policy in terms of these stages.

HOUSING AND THE CANADIAN WELFARE STATE

It is a commonplace that despite the general blueprint for Canadian welfare drawn up by a series of reconstruction reports, notably the Marsh Report (Canada, Parliament 1943), there was very little government action following the war. It was not until the 1960s that the major building blocks of the welfare state were put in place. In housing, too, despite the recommendations of the Marsh and Curtis reports (Canada, Parliament 1944), the 1940s and the 1950s were dominated by a policy that answers to the description of the 'assisted-market' approach. The main concern of policy was to facilitate and stimulate the construction of houses and home ownership. A historian of Canadian housing policy writes that 'the best conclusion we can arrive at concerning national housing policy from 1945 through 1964 is that the Government of Canada was strongly in favour of the attainment of home ownership by every family' (Rose 1980: 35). The government, working through the National Housing Act (NHA) of 1944 and the Central Mortgage and Housing Corporation (CMHC) set up in 1945 to administer it, gave every encouragement to the house-building industry 'in its efforts to provide hundreds of thousands of homes for sale' during the next fifteen years (ibid.). Encouragements included providing mortgage funds, manipulating the rate of interest, and easing the terms of house buying. Mortgage funds were made available through the NHA at rates lower than those prevalent in the money market, while down payments were successively reduced as loan amounts were increased. The period of amortization was gradually extended from fifteen to thirty-five years to enable low-income families to acquire a home of their own. Indeed, until the late 1950s, the house-building industry was 'devoted ... to the production of one main product: the single-family detached house on vacant land, the only type eligible for National Housing Act financing' (ibid.: 36). Housing policy was dedicated to that one objective and almost totally neglected the provision of affordable rental accommodation for families unable to buy homes. One consequence of this policy was the stratification of housing tenure into owners and renters and the resulting problem of stigma: 'When a substantial degree of national resources and effort is devoted towards making every Canadian family a house owner, then there is a special kind of label, a special taint or blight to be placed upon those families who, despite all the favourable manipulations in the basic policy, cannot afford a house of their own' (ibid.).

The second phase of development in Donnison's classification, 'social housing,' was primarily an effort to address the housing needs of low-income Canadians who were not likely to become home owners. The 1960s brought a gradual recognition that an assisted-market approach centred on home ownership was not sufficient to meet the housing needs of many Canadians. The rediscovery of poverty and the explosive growth of inner-city problems in the United States created a much sharper awareness of the phenomenon of 'poverty in the midst of affluence.' Directly or indirectly, the uneven nature of the costs and benefits of economic growth also began to be recognized. Rapid urbanization during the 1950s and 1960s brought a greater awareness of the housing problems generated by urban development, especially inner-city business development in major centres such as Toronto, Vancouver, and Montreal. The NHA of 1964, which 'revolutionized the approach' to the public provision of accommodation for low-income people, symbolized Canada's move towards social housing. However, it was not until the close of the 1960s that real beginnings were made in the provision of public and other forms of non-market housing.

The formation of the Ontario Housing Corporation (OHC) in 1964 marked in the beginning of important initiatives at the provincial level in the provision of social housing. From the outset, the OHC took advantage of the liberal federal financing made available under the 1964 act for the building of public housing. Two important reports on housing (Canada 1969; Dennis and Fish 1972), one of which dealt exclusively with low-cost housing, gave voice to interest in moving policy beyond an assisted-market approach and provided the base for new policy initiatives at both federal and provincial levels. However, Canada's experiment with public housing was not to last long. In part, dissatisfaction with public housing projects helped to steer social housing towards the third sector, i.e., co-operative and other non-profit groups and organizations. The legislative consolidation of 1973 was important in this and in other respects, e.g., in providing for residential rehabilitation and assistance with home ownership for low-income families (Rose 1980: 54–64). In was not, however, until 1978 that the government announced a policy of moving away from public housing (Fallis 1980, 25). An important, if unintended, consequence of these developments was a shift away from housing directed at the poor. At any rate, the early 1970s did see the substantial development of policy initiatives and programs at both federal and provincial levels, edging Canadian housing policy in a comprehensive direction.

The early 1970s also witnessed an event that was to have profound consequences for the welfare state. The OPEC (Organization of Petroleum Exporting Countries) price shock of 1973 signalled the beginning of serious problems of inflation combined with economic recession throughout the Western world. Governments could no longer manage their economies through Keynesian fine-tuning measures. The long post-war boom had ended, bringing in its wake the unprecedented phenomenon of 'stagflation' and rising unemployment. As budget deficits began to rise, governments in many Western countries, including Canada, began to hold down – or worse, to cut back on – social expenditure. In Canada, the period of restraint had begun. Nevertheless, for a number of reasons, government expenditure on housing (especially if tax expenditure is included) seems to have risen rather than declined during 1973–83. First, compared to income-security transfers and expenditure on medical care and education, housing represented a much smaller outlay.[1] Second, as in the past, governments used the housing sector, to some extent, as a tool of economic management, in this case as an anti-recessionary device. True, the CMHC budget of 1978 saw a marked reduction in government allocation for social housing, but that reduction reflected government withdrawal from making direct loans for subsidized housing. Subsidies, in fact, continued to increase.[2] Third, the economic difficulties of the period exacerbated the housing problem via the issue of affordability, and strengthened the case for government intervention (Fallis 1985: 174–8).

Governments found themselves in a new and difficult economic climate and many housing initiatives tended to be ad hoc, piece-meal, and makeshift – a response to economic necessity and political pressures. Two new tax-related programs were introduced: the RHOSP (Registered Home Ownership Savings Plan), which made savings for buying a first home tax-deductible; and the MURB (Multiple Unit Residential Building) program, which made losses created by deprecia-tion of multiple-unit residential buildings deductible against other income. In addition, the AHOP (Assisted Home Ownership Program) scheme was expanded and an Assisted Rental Programme was initiated (Hulchanski and Drover 1986: sec. 3). The steep rise in interest rates in 1980–1 and the slump of 1982 saw further ad hoc responses, centred on the stimulation of house building, home ownership, and the provision of rental housing through various tax incentives and related measures. (The Canada Mortgage Renewal Plan, the Canada Rental Supply Program of 1981, and the Canada Home Ownership Stimulation Plan of 1982 were some of the principal measures.) As well, spending was increased on the Canada Home Renovation Plan and on the Canada Mortgage Renewal Plan. In 1982, for the first time since the introduction of social housing programs in 1973, the federal budget made a special additional allocation in this area. These programs were justified on economic grounds (e.g., job creation) as well as on others related to housing. Home-ownership initiatives were reintroduced in the 1983 and 1984 budgets, with the latter adding a mortgage-rate protection plan (ibid.).

It could be argued that the difficulties besetting Canada's welfare state in the 1970s halted the country's progress towards a comprehensive housing policy. Although it did not amount to a retreat from social housing in favour of an assisted-market approach, there is little doubt that the use of tax incentives and other tax-related measures encouraged the supply of owner-occupied and rental property through the market (Fallis 1985: 178). Government policy clearly benefited middle- and upper-income Canadians, both directly through these measures and indirectly through provision of lucrative tax shelters. In 1979, for example (the last year for which statistics on tax expenditures are available), tax expenditures on housing totalled 5.35 billion, compared with \$288 million provided in direct housing assistance for public, co-operative, and non-profit programs (ibid.: 180). In 1982, loans, grants, and subsidies to market housing totalled \$885.8 million compared with the \$747.7 million allocated to social housing (Hulchanski 1985: 5).

The 1970s saw the polarization of tenure by income, with renters increasingly concentrated among low-income persons (Hulchanski and Drover 1986: 30–3). Meanwhile, third-sector housing, which in 1973 seemed poised for a substantial development, made scant progress. Yet by the late 1970s, if not earlier, public housing projects, which at one time looked like a possible solution to low-income housing need, had been abandoned. Ostensibly, the major reasons were their institutionalized, ghetto-like character and their general unpopularity within the wider community. In short, public housing had largely been abandoned as a solution for low-income housing; yet, for a variety of reasons, third-sector housing made little progress. Not surprisingly, at the present time, public- and third-sector housing together constitute only about 4 per cent of all housing stock (ibid.: 13; Canada 1985a: 234).[3]

This period in Canadian government was characterized by unilateralism at both federal and provincial levels (discussed in chapter 5). Given the nature of Canadian federalism, a comprehensive housing policy was unlikely to develop, let alone succeed, in such conditions. There are other reasons, however, why third-sector housing has made limited progress. One of them is lukewarm government support, in turn related to the fact that this form of housing is not targeted on low-income groups, but rather uses an income mix to include modest-income Canadians as well. Some forms of third-sector housing are, of course, not meant to help low-income Canadians as such. Co-operative housing, for example, has a number of objectives, including that of providing moderate-income Canadians with an alternative form of ownership. In any case, if the stigma of creating a ghetto of the poor is to be avoided, then social mixing becomes a necessary strategy for both public- and third-sector housing (a form of universality through the back door). Yet, from the government's viewpoint, this strategy means subsidizing housing costs for households that do not (strictly speaking) need a subsidy, while depriving the poor of the assistance that they badly do need (CMHC 1983: 8). It has also become clear that if the low-income housing problem is essentially a problem of affordability, then subsidizing the income of the poor might be a better solution than subsidizing houses. Indeed, subsidized public housing cannot help low-income families who live in private accommodation and find shelter costs high relative to income. In recent years, the problem of low-income housing ('core housing need') is being defined increasingly as a problem of income and affordability, rather than of the availability of housing. Not surprisingly, proposals for a shelter allowance continue to come forward (Hulchanski and Drover 1986: 23–4; Steele 1985; Fallis 1985: 190), although their feasibility raises various questions, including the issue of divided jurisdiction in housing. These deliberations reflect broader trends and tendencies within the Canadian welfare state which I have termed earlier the mixed economy of welfare.

Although support for core social programs has remained high in Canada, the advent of a Progressive Conservative government in 1984 marked a shift (at least in ideological terms) towards restricting social expenditure, reducing the budget deficit, and giving market forces greater scope in the economy and in job creation (DOF 1984: 83–5). One of the new government's earliest acts related to housing was to cut back on social housing and housing rehabilitation programs (Hulchanski and Drover 1986: 33); but more important in policy terms may be the government's preference for 'targeting' social housing assistance more directly on lower-income Canadians. This was a major theme in the report of the study team on housing for the Nielsen Task Force on Programme Review (Study Team Report 1986c: 9): 'Housing programs have benefited Canadians at all income levels ... Even social housing programs have served moderate and middle-income households. It is time to redress this imbalance, to favour those with the greatest need for assistance.' The study team linked this point with the idea that it was not supply of housing but its affordability that was the problem (ibid.: 11).

While the Nielsen study team was still at work, the minister responsible for the CMHC issued a consultation paper on housing as a basis for developing more effective policies (Canada 1985b). An important part of the consultation process was, of course, the dialogue with the provincial governments. At the end of 1985, the minister announced new directions in Canadian housing policy (Canada 1985c). Social housing was to continue, but was to be more strictly targeted on the needy.[4] A new federal/provincial cost-sharing arrangement was to be put in place. Although the government did not propose a shelter allowance (it could not, of course, remove rent controls, which were provincial programs), its new package of social housing included rent-supplement programs and residential rehabilitation assistance for low-income households. The actual assortment of social housing programs was to be decided jointly by each of the provinces and territories with the federal government, in light of regional needs. In general, government policy was to move away from subsidizing producers towards subsidizing low-income consumers. In the arena of housing, Canadian government involvement was, up until that time, mainly through financial assistance to suppliers of housing and to home owners. Public- and third-sector housing have remained a minute fraction of the total housing stock in the country. Housing, therefore, remains to this day an eminently 'privatized' field. In any case, housing the poor and, in particular, the homeless requires a pragmatic and constructive approach, one that is prepared to employ a wide range of auspices stretching from public housing to private landlords. Fallis and Murray (appendix 2), for instance, remind us that '[Most] of the low-rental housing in Canada is supplied by private-sector landlords without government assistance. Much more attention must be paid to their financial plight. Being a small landlord must remain a profitable enterprise or our low-rental stock will gradually disappear. The income of tenants can be supplemented with a shelter allowance.'

An examination of Canadian federal/provincial housing policy suggests that Canada's entry into the 'social housing' stage coincided with the beginning of stagflation and other economic difficulties in Western countries in the early 1970s. In housing, the decade of 1974–84 can, with some simplification, be characterized as rich in programs but poor in policy. The volatile economic situation of the 1970s, culminating in Canada's deepest post-war recession in 1982 and the ensuing political pressures, elicited an ad hoc, makeshift, and short-term response on the part of the federal government. In part, housing policy was being used as a tool of macro-economic management; in part, it was shifting towards a mixed economy of welfare approach. Given the climate of fiscal restraint, the government stimulated the production of housing through tax expenditures, while easing off in the far more visible expenditures such as loans associated with social housing. Much of the housing assistance provided in this way was channelled through the private market. Meanwhile, social housing made limited progress – not, primarily, because of fiscal restraint. Public housing fell out of favour. And given the social mix involved in third-sector housing, it appeared to be a costly method of helping the poor. This meant lack of government (CMHC) support and encouragement of third-sector housing. Various organizational and financial weaknesses also hampered the progress of social housing. The upshot is that rental housing remains overwhelmingly in the market sector.

When the Progressive Conservatives came to power in 1984, the serious economic difficulties created by high interest rates, inflation, and the depression of 1981–2 had eased a good deal. Interest rates had come down from the record high of nearly 21 per cent in 1981 to around 10 per cent. Inflation had dropped from a high of over 12 per cent to nearly 4 per cent, and economic growth had resumed. Some of the ad hoc housing programs introduced in response to the stagflation of the 1970s and the depression of 1982 had already been phased out. The remaining tax-related programs, such as RHOSP, have since been gradually phased out by the Mulroney government, whose strategy of targeting assistance on those in greatest need, and relying generally on market forces for the supply of housing, seems to fit in with the idea of the mixed economy of welfare. At the same time, the continuity with pre-1974 policies should not be overlooked. It is as though after the interregnum of 1973–83, when housing policy was virtually put on hold, there has been a return to 'normal' conditions. Social housing has by no means been abandoned. Although the market remains the pre-eminent supplier of housing, a variety of auspices are to be employed. Above all, assistance dollars are to be made available to those unable to afford adequate housing.

This is a far cry from a comprehensive housing policy. Indeed, it seems to lack even a firm commitment to social and public housing. What are the implications of this approach for the problem of homelessness? The policy of targeting and selectivity implies that those unable to secure adequate accommodation or to pay for it are the ones earmarked for assistance. The flexible and plural approach suggested by the mixed economy of housing also bodes well for a practical solution to the problems of the homeless. That is the good news. At the same time, it is clear that the federal government's general economic and fiscal policy of greater reliance on market forces and private incentives is likely to worsen the problem of homelessness. (Accepting unemployment as inevitable, tightening up on unemployment benefits, and allowing tax-free capital gains with their predictable impact on housing market and house prices are only a few examples.) Tax expenditures related to housing, though less extravagant now than in the recent past, none the less involve a substantial transfer of income from the government to the well off. And there is little evidence that the government is willing to look at tax expenditures in the same way that it looks at subsidies and loans. Finally, the peculiar nature of housing, compared with services such as medical care or education, suggests that it may not receive the same level of support and endorsement from the public that mainstream, universal services enjoy. Yet, paradoxically, the very nature of housing – both as a basic need and as a commodity – calls for a 'comprehensive' housing policy if problems of equity are to be addressed. Only a stronger and more sustained commitment on the part of all concerned Canadians can ensure that the homeless and low-income householders are adequately housed. Otherwise the mixed economy of welfare, purporting to provide help to the disadvantaged through a flexible and varied approach, will, in fact, end up making the problems much worse even as it tries to 'solve' them.

NOTES

1 In 1982, for example, federal and provincial government expenditure on housing amounted to $2.4 billion compared with $21.7 billion on medical care and $23.2 billion on education (Canada, *Statistics Canada* 1986: 26, 30–1). Federal (CMHC) expenditure on housing has rarely exceeded 1 per cent of GNP (Hulchanski and Drover 1986: 8).
2 After 1978, social and market housing projects had to seek loans from the market (see Hulchanski and Drover 1986: 21–2; and chapter 3 in this volume).
3 Public housing production peaked at 20,000 units in 1970 (Chouinard 1986: 57). Between 1965 and 1981, public housing formed roughly 5 per cent of all dwellings completed in Canada, mostly between the late 1960s and the mid 1970s (Miron 1988: 252). See also chapter 3 of this volume.
4 In 1984–5, housing-related programs were estimated to cost $2 billion and tax expenditures $4.1 billion (Study Team Report 1986c: 1). According to another study, tax expenditures related to housing are 2–3 times direct government expenditure, a ratio that is almost the reverse of that in most other categories of social expenditure (Hulchanski and Drover 1986: 28). However, neither the government's *Consultation Paper* (1985b) nor the one on *National Directions* (1985c) pays any attention to tax expenditures on housing.

REFERENCES

Beresford, Peter; and Croft, Suzy. 1984. 'Welfare Pluralism: The New Face of Fabianism.' *Critical Social Policy* 9 (Spring): 19–39

Beveridge, W. 1942. *Social Insurance and Allied Services*. London: His Majesty's Stationery Office (HMSO)

Calvert, John. 1984. *Government, Limited*. Ottawa: Canadian Centre for Policy Alternatives

Canada. 1969. *Report of the Task Force on Housing and Urban Development* (Hellyer Report). Ottawa

– 1985a. *Canada Yearbook 1985*. Ottawa

– 1985b. *Consultation Paper on Housing*. Ottawa

– 1985c. *A National Direction for Housing Solutions*. Ottawa

– Parliament. House of Commons. 1943. *Report on Social Security for Canada*. Ottawa

– Parliament. House of Commons. Advisory Committee on Reconstruction. 1944. *Housing and Community Planning*. Ottawa

Carroll, W.K. 1984. 'The Solidarity Coalition.' In *The New Reality: The Politics of Restraint in British Columbia*, ed. W. Magnusson et al. Vancouver: New Star Books

Chouinard, V. 1986. 'State Formation and Housing Policies.' PhD diss., McMaster University

CMHC (Central Mortgage and Housing Corporation). 1983. *Section 56.1 Non-Profit and Cooperative Housing Program Evaluation*. Ottawa

Cowling, Mark; and Smith, Sue. 1984. 'Homeownership, Socialism and Realistic Socialist Policy.' *Critical Social Policy* 9 (Spring): 64–8

Crosland, C.A.R. 1956. *The Future of Socialism*. London: Jonathan Cape

Danziger, James N. 1980. 'California's Proposition 13 and the Fiscal Limitations Movement in the United States.' *Political Studies* 28, no. 4: 599–612

Dennis, M.; and Fish, S. 1972. *Programs in Search of a Policy: Low Income Housing in Canada*. Toronto: Hakkert

DOF (Department of Finance). 1981. *Analysis of Federal Tax Expenditures for Individuals*. Ottawa

– 1984. *A New Direction for Canada*. Ottawa

Donnison, D.V. 1968. *The Government of Housing*. Harmondsworth, Eng.: Penguin

Economic Council of Canada. 1984. *Steering the Course: Twenty-First Annual Review*. Ottawa: Minister of Supply and Services

The Economist. 1987. 'Sweden's Economy: The Nonconformist State.' 7 March

Fallis, G. 1980. *Housing Programs and Income Distribution in Ontario*. Toronto: Ontario Economic Council

– 1985. *Housing Economics*. Toronto: Butterworths

Friedman, Milton. 1977. *From Galbraith to Economic Freedom*. London: Institute of Economic Affairs

Gonick, Cy. 1978. *Out of Work*. Toronto: James Lorimer

Gough, Ian. 1979. *The Political Economy of the Welfare State*. London: Macmillan

Guest, Dennis. 1985. *The Emergence of Social Security in Canada*. Vancouver: University of British Columbia Press

Hadley, Roger; and Hatch, Stephen. 1981. *Social Welfare and the Failure of the State*. London: Allen and Unwin

Hulchanski, J.D. 1985. 'Tax Costs of Housing.' *Policy Options* 6, no. 5: 4–7

Hulchansi, J.D.; and Drover, G. 1986. *Housing Subsidies in a Period of Restraint: The Canadian Experience, 1973–1984*. Winnipeg: Institute of Urban Studies, University of Winnipeg

Kirwin, Bill. 1986. 'Nielsen Spending Review Defends CAP.' *Perception* 9, no. 5: 39–40

Kitchen, Brigitte. 1986. 'The Marsh Report Revisited.' *Journal of Canadian Studies* 21, no. 2: 38–48

Ladd, E.C., Jr; and Lipset, S.M. 1980. 'Public Opinion and Public Policy.' In *The United States in the 1980s*, ed. Peter Duignan and Albin Rabushka. Stanford: Hoover Institution

McIntosh, Mary. 1981. 'Feminism and Social Policy.' *Critical Social Policy* 1, no. 1: 32–42

McKinnon, Ian. 1983. 'What Does the Public Think about Deficits? What Does Bay Street Think about Deficits?' In *Deficits: How Big and How Bad?* ed. D.W. Conklin and T.J. Courchene. Toronto: Ontario Economic Council

Maclean's. 1985. 'A Confident Nation Speaks Up.' 7 January

Miron, J.R. 1988. *Housing in Postwar Canada*. Kingston and Montreal: McGill-Queen's University Press

Mishra, Ramesh. 1984. *The Welfare State in Crisis*. Brighton, Eng.: Wheatsheaf Books

OECD (Organization for Economic Cooperation and Development). 1981. *Integrated Social Policy: A Review of the Austrian Experience*. Paris

– 1986a. *Economic Outlook* 40. Paris

– 1986b. *Economic Surveys: Austria*. Paris

– 1986c. *Economic Surveys: Canada*. Paris

– 1986d. *Economic Surveys: United States*. Paris

Prince, Michael. 1985. 'Social Policy in PC Year One.' *Perception* 9, no. 1: 7–9

– 1986. 'The Mulroney Agenda: A Right Turn for Ottawa?' In *How Ottawa Spends: 1986–7*, ed. Prince. Toronto: Methuen

Riddell, P. 1985. *The Thatcher Government*. Oxford: Basil Blackwell

Rose, A. 1980. *Canadian Housing Policies: 1935–1980*, Scarborough: Butterworths

Royal Commission on the Economic Union and Development Prospects for Canada (Macdonald commission). Vol. II. 1985. Ottawa: Minister of Supply and Services

Statistics Canada. 1986. *Consolidated Government Finance*. Ottawa
– 1989. *the Labour Force, April 1989*. Ottawa
Steele, Marion. 1985. *Canadian Housing Allowances: An Economic Analysis*. Toronto: Ontario Economic Council
Study Team Report to the Task Force on Program Review (Nielsen). 1986a. *Economic Growth: Services and Subsidies to Business*. Ottawa: Minister of Supply and Services
– 1986b. *Canada Assistance Plan*. Ottawa: Minister of Supply and Services
– 1986c. *Housing*. Ottawa: Minister of Supply and Services
Ternowetsky, G. 1984. 'It's Time to Implement Tax Reform.' *Canadian Review of Social Policy* 12 (December): 23–4
Therborn, G. 1986. *Why Some People Are More Unemployed than Others*. London: Verso Books
Thurow, Lester C. 1984. *Dangerous Currents: The State of Economics*. New York: Vintage Books
Wilson, Elizabeth. 1977. *Women and the Welfare State*. London: Tavistock Institute
Woodside, Kenneth. 1982. 'The Tax Revolt in International Perspective: Britain, Canada and the United States.' In *Comparative Social Research*, vol. 5, ed. Richard F. Tomasson. Greenwich, CT: Jai Press

KEITH G. BANTING

5 Social Housing in a Divided State

Canada is governed in part through an endless succession of federal/ provincial meetings to which prime ministers, premiers, ministers, and officials troop with clockwork regularity. These meetings usually take place in tall, elegant buildings located in the heart of metropolitan centres, often only blocks away from the rooming-houses, residential hotels, hostels, and social housing projects that shelter many of Canada's poor and homeless. Mere physical proximity, however, cannot disguise the immense social distance between the world of federal/provincial diplomacy and the world of the poor, and the secret deliberations of federal and provincial governments must often seem irrelevant to the lives of those on the margins of the housing market.

In reality, however, the federal structure of our political system and the complex web of agreements between levels of government do have important implications for social housing programs. Rose (1980:16) has observed that 'the most important background fact in the Canadian housing experience is that Canada is a federal state.' The size of the stock of social housing, its internal configuration, its redistributive consequences, and its responsiveness to changing economic and political circumstances are all influenced by the division of power between federal and provincial authorities, and the annual ritual of secret negotiations between them.

This chapter investigates the nexus between federalism and social housing programs, and its consequences for the poor and homeless. Analysis of these relationships is complicated by the fact that the intergovernmental balance itself has changed repeatedly since the Second World War, and a historical perspective is, therefore, important to understanding the impact of different federal/provincial regimes on social housing. In examining the historical pattern, this chapter parallels the approach of chapter 4, which sets social housing within the context of the evolution of the welfare state as a whole. Federal/provincial relations in the field of social housing have been shaped and reshaped by the same linguistic, regional, and governmental conflicts that have pervaded social policy generally, and this chapter therefore begins with a discussion of the ways in which the federal/provincial balance has evolved in social programs generally. The second section then examines the specific case of social housing in greater detail, and the final sections explore the consequences of different federal/provincial regimes for the size, redistributive role, and responsiveness of social housing programs, as well as for the specific problems facing homeless Canadians.

SOCIAL POLICY AND CANADIAN FEDERALISM

As Alexis de Tocqueville observed about federations in general, it is 'as impossible to determine beforehand, with any degree of accuracy, the share of authority which each of two governments is to enjoy as to foresee all the incidents in the existence of a nation' (quoted in Birch 1955: 3). Nowhere is this problem clearer than in the impact of the emergence of the welfare state on the Canadian federation. The original British North America (BNA) Act was a nineteenth-century document reflecting the assumptions of the day about the appropriate role of the state. Welfare in the Canada of 1867 was largely a private matter, with the public sphere confined to rudimentary relief at the municipal level. Such a minor function of government did not command much attention in the BNA Act itself, and certainly such twentieth-century terms as income security, social services, and social housing do not appear in the list of jurisdictions parcelled out in sections 91 and 92. Hence the constitutional dilemma that has plagued Canadian politics throughout the last fifty years. Which level of government has the responsibility to respond to the social needs of an industrial society?

Given the local, private, and municipal nature of welfare in the 1860s, provincial responsibility seemed established in the constitution, and this assumption was seldom challenged until the inter-war years. As the scope of social problems inherent in a modern society and the constraints facing a purely local or provincial response to them became more obvious, advocates of social reform, including many provincial governments, focused their pressure on federal authorities. The federal response in the 1920s and 1930s was limited and often grudging; but after the dramatic centralization of power and politics during the Second World War, the federal government assumed the leadership in developing the Canadian version of the welfare state.

In part, federal leadership was grounded in formal constitutional change. Three amendments to the constitution expanded federal jurisdiction over unemployment insurance in 1941, pensions in 1951, and survivor and disability benefits in 1964. Elsewhere, the federal/provincial division in the social-policy sector was determined, not by constitutional amendment, but by the distribution of political power and financial resources between the two levels of government. In the post-war decades, the federal government was politically and financially dominant; that dominance found a constitutional outlet in the doctrine of the federal spending power.

The spending power lies at the heart of much of Canadian social policy, including the field of social housing. According to the traditional doctrine, the spending power allows the federal government to make payments to individuals, institutions, and other levels of government for purposes that Parliament does not necessarily have the power to regulate. That is, the federal government claims the right to give money away, and attach conditions if it wishes, even if the purposes fall entirely within provincial jurisdiction. This constitutional claim has never been settled authoritatively by the Supreme Court, and it was never fully accepted by provincial authorities, especially in Quebec. Nevertheless, the spending power proved to be a potent instrument, allowing the federal government to set the social-policy agenda and to shape the broad pattern of policy during the post-war decades in two ways. First, the spending power served as the basis of payments to individuals and private organizations, including direct assistance to non-profit groups and co-operatives in the field of social housing.[1] Second, it supported payments to provinces, including conditional grants for health insurance, post-secondary education, social assistance, and, most important for our purposes, social housing (Canada 1969a).[2]

Beginning in the mid 1960s, however, federal predominance was challenged by provincial governments; slowly the constraints on Ottawa's leadership grew. The dramatic resurgence of Quebec nationalism in the 1960s and 1970s generated strong opposition to federal 'intrusion' in provincial jurisdiction, and the province was soon leading the assault on federal dominance. Inspired by the Boucher and Castonguay-Nepveu reports (Quebec 1963, 1971), Quebec sought to establish a comprehensive *provincial* welfare state that would be fully controlled and integrated at the regional level and would reflect what nationalists saw as a distinctive cultural approach to the social needs of a modern society. Such a project required the province to liberate itself from the constraints inherent in federal conditional grants, to wrest control of unilateral federal programs from Ottawa, and to capture a larger share of public revenues.

Quebec's demands were increasingly echoed by other provinces. During the 1950s and 1960s, provincial governments had been growing steadily in size, bureaucratic expertise, and political self-confidence. In part, such expansion was the inevitable consequence of the fact that the primary policy concerns of the post-war era fell largely in provincial jurisdiction; but in part, it was also accelerated by the very conditional-grant programs that provincial administrations came to resent. From the late 1960s on, other provinces joined Quebec in complaining that federal shared-cost initiatives distorted their own policy priorities, and the conditions attached to the payments introduced distortions and inefficiencies in program design and delivery. Freedom from the constraints inherent in the federal spending power became a widespread provincial goal during the 1970s.

Provincial frustrations were exacerbated by the intense regional conflicts of the decade. Regionalism has been a constant feature of Canadian history since well before Confederation, but the conflicts engendered by the economic and energy issues of the 1970s were particularly acute. Provincial governments emerged as forceful advocates of distinctive regional interests, prepared to do battle with one another and the federal government in a wide range of policy fields. These tensions also flowed into the debate over constitutional reform, which had been stimulated originally by the possibility of Quebec's separation. Provincial governments, especially in the west, brought to the table their own list of constitutional demands, which were carefully crafted to strengthen provincial influence over public policy and tame a number of federal instruments, including the spending power. Social housing came to play an important role in this battle.

The federal response to the politics of language and regionalism oscillated between periods of grudging accommodation and periods of determined resistance. The cumulative effect, however, has been to constrain the role of the federal government in social policy generally, and to limit the flexibility inherent in the spending power in particular. This pattern became evident in a series of decisions in the mid 1960s. The Liberal government of Lester Pearson accepted that it could not prevent Quebec from establishing its own Quebec Pension Plan, and agreed that future amendments to the Canada Pension Plan would require the consent of the provinces. In addition, the federal government agreed that provinces could opt out of a number of shared-cost programs and receive full fiscal compensation. Quebec opted out immediately and, while the effect was largely symbolic because the province agreed to meet existing program standards, its action effectively served notice that the days of the traditional federal spending power were numbered.

During the late 1960s and the 1970s, federal authorities tacitly accepted a more constrained view of the spending power. The Trudeau government shied away from launching major new shared-cost programs, and in 1977 it accepted the decentralizing consequences of block funding for health and post-secondary education under the Established Programs Financing (EPF) Act. By abandoning the cost-sharing mechanism, the federal government hoped to gain more control over its own expenditure levels; but the provinces became freer to design their own programs and direct the resources as they saw fit. In addition, the federal government pronounced itself open to a constitutional limit on future uses of the spending power. During the first round of constitutional negotiations in 1969, Trudeau himself proposed a constitutional amendment that would have required that any new shared-cost programs be supported by a broad provincial consensus; and during another round of negotiations in 1979, the government proposed a variant on the same principle.

This pattern of incremental accommodation was temporarily reversed after the 1980 election. Under the banner of 'the new federalism,' the Liberals chose to challenge the twin forces of Quebec separatism and regionalism frontally by adopting unilateral action on a wide variety of fronts ranging from the National Energy Program to the threatened unilateral patriation of the constitution (Milne 1986). Their aim was to appeal over the heads of the premiers to the public and to sympathetic interest groups, in order to build a stronger political constituency and preserve as much room as possible for forceful federal action. In the social-policy sector, the high-water mark of federal assertiveness was the Canada Health Act, but the approach permeated other policies as well. A new EPF formula was imposed over provincial objections in 1982; and the federal government placed greater emphasis on the visibility of its role, stricter accountability to Parliament for the uses made of federal transfer dollars, criticism of provincial underfunding,

TABLE 5.1
Centralization of income-security expenditure

	1974	1976	1978	1980	1982	1984	1986
1 Income-security expenditure							
Federal	79.2	77.4	77.6	73.8	75.9	73.5	72.9
Provincial	20.7	22.5	22.4	26.2	24.1	26.5	27.1
2 Financing of income security							
Federal	85.5	84.6	85.6	82.8	84.7	83.1	83.2
Provincial	14.4	15.3	14.4	17.2	15.3	16.9	16.8

NOTE: Data on provincial expenditure includes municipal relief; federal and provincial tax credits are not included.
SOURCE: Calculated from data in Statistics Canada 1988

and stronger monitoring of provincial compliance with program conditions (Parliamentary Task Force 1981).

Not surprisingly, this period of unilateralism was marked by bitter conflict between the two levels of government. The 1984 election, however, ended this combativeness. The new Progressive Conservative government promised 'national reconciliation' and a return to a more collaborative style of federalism, with renewed emphasis on consensus and mutual accommodation. The most significant expression of the approach is the proposed Meech Lake Accord, which would – if ratified – establish new constitutional rules governing the exercise of the federal spending power. The consequences of the proposal are discussed in greater detail below.

The cumulative impact of twenty years of intergovernmental warfare in the social-policy sector has been to constrain the federal role and increase the responsibilities of provincial governments. The balance has certainly not returned to the situation prevailing in the inter-war period, because the federal government retains considerable weight in the sector. Nor has the decentralizing trend been uniform across all programs. Canada has increasingly edged towards a bifurcated welfare state, in which the income-security system remains relatively centralized while social services have become more decentralized.

The centralization of the income-security system can be seen in table 5.1, which presents two different measures of the extent of centralization for the period 1974–86. The first panel measures centralization in terms of which government actually pays the benefit directly to the recipient and demonstrates the continuing predominance of the federal government, which pays out approximately three-quarters of all income-security dollars. The second panel reveals the roles of the two jurisdictions in financing income security; in this case, intergovernmental transfers such as those through the Canada Assistance Plan are credited to the donor government rather than the recipient government. By this measure, income security is even more centralized, as over 80 per cent of the dollars flowing through the system are federal dollars, and this figure even ignores the portion of equalization grants that is devoted to social-assistance benefits. The pattern is thus clear: the income-security system remains highly centralized.

In contrast, social services such as health and post-secondary education have become more decentralized since the advent of block funding. These transfers are still subject to conditions. Although provinces may use the funds they receive for post-secondary education as they wish, the resources devoted to health care are still subject to the conditions laid down in the original legislation, which were specified in greater detail in the 1984 Canada Health Act. Nevertheless, provinces have gained greater flexibility under the EPF arrangements in two ways. First, they are freer to redesign their program delivery, especially in health care. Under the old approach, efforts to increase efficiency in various ways, such as relying more on convalescent homes than on hospitals, were undermined because the cost-sharing provisions did not cover such services. Second, provinces are free to transfer resources between health care and post-secondary education, or between the two programs and other provincial spending priorities; and the evidence is clear that they have done so in the case of post-secondary education (Johnson 1985).

FEDERALISM AND SOCIAL HOUSING

The evolution of federal/provincial relations in social housing has broadly paralleled that in the Canadian welfare state as a whole and has been driven by the same underlying political forces. None the less, social housing has also displayed distinctive features, and the record in this sector deserves closer inspection.

Two major threads run through the history of federal/provincial relations in social housing. The first is the classic tension between centralization and decentralization in the division of power between the two levels of government. It is here that the record most closely tracks that of social programs generally, with early federal dominance increasingly challenged as the post-war decades wore on. A second thread is also present, however. When two governments are active in the same sector, the mode of interaction between them is also important. In the case of social housing, there has been a continuing tension between unilateral and joint action. In some periods, the balance has tilted towards unilateral initiatives, with each government emphasizing its own programs and establishing direct relations with groups and individuals in the housing sector. In other periods, the balance has shifted toward joint federal/provincial programs that are financed through conditional grants and shaped by intergovernment bargaining. These two threads are closely interwoven in the history of this sector, and each has important consequences for the nature of the policy-making process and the shape of housing programs that emerge from it.

When peering back in time, it is useful to distinguish four broad periods: the post-war era of federal dominance in the 1940s and 1950s; the growth of the provincial role after the mid 1960s; the era of competitive unilateralism of the 1970s; and the era of accommodation from 1978 to the present.

The Federal Era

As chapter 4 emphasized, the early post-war years were animated by a tremendous faith in the capacity of the state to respond to the social problems of modern society. This faith was reflected most explicitly in the blueprints for post-war reconstruction, which envisaged the development of a comprehensive welfare state, providing a level of well-being and social protection previously unknown in Canadian life. Social housing was to be part of this vision. Both the Curtis and Marsh reports called for a major role for government in providing public housing for low-income Canadians (Canada 1944; Marsh 1943).

These expectations fell largely on the federal government. During the war, federal authorities had proved themselves effective in the housing sector.[3] A federal crown corporation, Wartime Housing Ltd, had provided inexpensive housing for workers swept into the cities by the demands of wartime production, and over 19,000 temporary units were constructed between 1941 and 1945. This momentum carried over into the post-war years, and by the end of the decade the newly created Central Mortgage and Housing Corporation (CMHC), which inherited this housing from the wartime agency, was 'the landlord of more than 40,000 families in 50 communities across Canada' (CMHC 1970: 12).

These housing drives were unilateral federal initiatives and, in the words of one internal CMHC memo, contributed to 'the belief in the public mind that the Dominion is indeed the only authority who can provide public housing' (Dennis and Fish 1972: 132). Federal authorities negotiated directly with municipalities, builders, and tenants, with little or no apparent objection from provincial governments, which were unprepared – politically, administratively, and financially – to assert themselves in the housing field. As a result, CMHC officials in branch offices across the country built up close relationships at the local level that continued into the following years.

This momentum did not survive the transition to peacetime, however. As the sense of crisis receded and returning veterans were assimilated into the housing market, federal enthusiasm waned and the government sought to limit its commitments. The pressure for partial withdrawal came not from outraged provinces but from federal authorities themselves. The Liberal government of Louis St Laurent was loath to launch a major public housing program, and expressed doubts about the constitutionality of such a course.[4] The government gradually sold off its existing stock of housing, and switched to a conditional-grant approach to social housing. Under the 1949 amendments to the National Housing Act, public housing projects were to be initiated by the provinces or by municipalities empowered to do so by the provinces. The federal government would contribute 75 per cent of the capital and operating subsidies, and provincial governments were free to pass on some share of their costs to municipalities.

The era of joint programs had arrived. The new arrangements transferred political responsibility for launching new public housing projects to the provinces. This system had political advantages for a federal government that remained lukewarm about public housing throughout the 1950s. The provinces were reluctant to become deeply involved, and their inactivity protected federal authorities from substantial expenditures. Thus, the federal government could always proclaim its willingness to fund any public housing projects with relative financial impunity. The president of CMHC explained to his minister in 1956 that 'this so-called "taps open" policy has the great tactical advantage of transferring the entire public housing debate to the provincial and municipal level. A restriction ... would "close the taps" and transfer public pressures back to the senior government, as was the case before 1949' (Dennis and Fish 1972: 176).

Within the rubric of conventional grants, however, the public housing program was a centralized affair. The new legislation officially cut the federal government off from direct negotiations with cities, but in practice informal dealings between CMHC officials and municipalities remained active; the provinces played a relatively passive role. As the predominant financial partner in these joint ventures, CMHC insisted on controlling each stage of a project, from the original request, through design and construction, to the ultimate appointment of a local manager of the completed dwellings. The process was often criticized as slow and cumbersome, and it was remarkable that any public housing was built at all. And, indeed, not much was. No matter how the count was made, fewer than 15,000 units of public housing were completed by 1960 (Rose 1980: 37). Administrative complexity was hardly the major reason for the scarcity of public housing projects, however. Slow progress was fundamentally a reflection of the limited nature of political support for such initiatives at all three levels of government.

The Provincial Challenge

The political landscape of housing policy was transformed in the 1960s. The decade witnessed the adoption of major components of the Canadian welfare state, such as the Canada Pension Plan, the Canada Assistance plan, and medicare, as well as a broad emphasis on redistributive policies in many sectors, including housing. The growth of interest in social housing reflected a belated response to fundamental changes in society. The steady process of urbanization since the war had created a decisively urban Canada and the needs of an urban society increasingly penetrated political debate (Rose 1980; Lithwick 1970). The re-emergence of poverty as a political issue in both the United States and Canada reinforced this trend, focusing attention on the plight of the inhabitants of inner-city areas. As a result, the social housing programs, which had existed on paper for twenty years, finally received substantial funding, and by the end of the decade federal and provincial leaders were appealing to their electorates in part with housing promises. 'Housing policy had arrived as a political weapon in the hands of the two senior levels of government' (Rose 1980: v).

Federal/provincial rivalry followed right behind. In 1964, the new Liberal government sought to stimulate public housing by amending the National Housing Act to provide a choice of methods for financing new projects. The prevailing assumption at the time was that strong municipal housing agencies would develop and take the lead at the local level.[5] In a critical decision, however, the Ontario government upset such calculations by announcing that Ontario municipalities would not be permitted to take advantage of the new legislation, asserting that 'if advantage is to be taken of the new provisions of the National Housing Act, this will be on a direct federal-provincial basis' (Dennis and Fish 1972: 146). To give effect to this decision, Ontario created the Ontario Housing Corporation, which rapidly expanded into a powerful agency that competed on an equal basis with the expertise and administrative capacity of CMHC. The Ontario corporation relied heavily on the new provision for financing public housing that allowed it to operate somewhat more independently of CMHC, and the province quickly developed an ambitious housing program.

Quebec soon followed, creating its own Quebec Housing Corporation, a decision that reflected the province's broader goal of recapturing jurisdiction over social affairs. When first introducing the proposal for a provincial housing corporation in 1965, Liberal minister Pierre Laporte lamented the negligence of earlier provincial leaders that had allowed Ottawa to pre-empt such a major role and looked forward to the day when the province would reclaim 'complete jurisdiction in the field of housing' (Dennis and Fish 1972: 153). The Quebec Housing Corporation was actually established two years later by the Union nationale government. Although the new government was not as enthusiastic about a large, *dirigiste* program of public housing as had been its Liberal predecessor, it was happy to advance the autonomist goal of greater independence from federal control.

Housing corporations or agencies quickly spread to other provinces. In one year, 1967, provincial bodies emerged not only in Quebec but also in British Columbia, Alberta, Manitoba, New Brunswick, and Newfoundland. Admittedly, there was considerable variation in the strength of these provincial agencies. Some, such as the Alberta Housing Corporation, moved towards the Ontario and Quebec model, building up considerable expertise and delivery capacity, and establishing themselves firmly between CMHC and the municipal level. Others simply oversaw federal/provincial exchanges, and continued to rely heavily on the administrative and technical facilities of CMHC. Most provincial corporations moved more slowly than Ontario in building a sizeable stock of public housing. Nevertheless, by the end of the decade, the federal agency was faced by a solid phalanx of provincial corporations with growing ambitions.

Intergovernmental frictions quickly emerged, and CMHC was forced into a defensive posture, responding incrementally to the specific pressures from individual provinces. The result was an increasingly asymmetrical pattern of intergovernmental relations. Relations between CMHC and the Quebec Housing Corporation, for example, were sensitive to the highly charged relations between Ottawa and Quebec City. Beginning in 1968, the province's insistence on greater autonomy in the field of social housing was translated into a series of annual master agreements, which reduced CMHC's role in project approval, design, construction, and management. When the first set of proposals from the Quebec Housing Corporation were ready, CMHC announced that $150 million a year would be available to the corporation without the necessity of formal approval of each specific project (Rose 1980).

This agreement upset relations between Ontario and the federal government. Ontario had developed by far the largest program of public housing of any province, and it had done so within the traditional constraints of the CMHC approval process. Now Ontario wanted the same treatment as Quebec, but the federal government responded only partially to the pressure. The approval process for public housing projects was streamlined, but the concession represented considerably less than the broad delegation to Quebec under its master agreement – and even this easing of the constraints was not offered to other provinces (Dennis and Fish 1972: 152).

By the early 1970s, the classic pattern of a provincial challenge to federal controls was playing out in the social housing sector. Since 1949, the federal government had repeatedly insisted that the primary responsibility lay with the provinces and municipalities. The provinces were now accepting that responsibility, in some cases aggressively, and were pressing for liberation from the detailed federal regulations that had built up over the years of provincial passivity. In effect, the policy of 1949 had succeeded far more than CMHC might have wished.

In all this, social housing was closely tracking experience in the social-policy sector generally. During the 1970s, however, housing developments moved in a somewhat distinctive pattern.

Competitive Unilateralism

The 1970s witnessed a shift away from joint programs, which had dominated social housing since 1949, towards unilateral action at both the federal and provincial levels of government.[6] This trend was facilitated by a proliferation of housing programs, which in part reflected a broadening of the goals of housing policy. With the inflationary pressures of the decade, the dream of home ownership was receding beyond the reach of a widening band of moderate-income families, and governments expanded their policy focus to incorporate this large and vociferous constituency through initiatives such as the Assisted Home Ownership Program and the Assisted Rental Program. In addition, however, program innovation was a response to growing resistance to conventional public housing, especially major projects that concentrated large numbers of poor families in what became, in effect, low-income ghettos.[7] Governments developed a wider set of policy mechanisms, ranging from support for non-profit and co-operative housing to shelter allowances, in the hope of integrating the occupants of low-income housing more fully into the wider community.

The proliferation of programs alone did not necessitate a shift to unilateralism. After all, new programs could have been delivered through federal/provincial agreements, as in the past. The primary reason for the renewed emphasis on independent action was the frustration generated by collaborative programs. From the federal point of view, the shared-cost mechanism had important drawbacks. First, not all provinces were equally capable of, or interested in, taking advantage of shared-cost grants for social housing; disadvantaged provinces had to make the greatest sacrifice to participate, and political enthusiasm varied enormously from one province to another. The result was a very uneven spread of federal social housing dollars, with a disproportionate concentration in Ontario. Second, the conditional-grant mechanism was obviously generating tensions with provincial governments. While Ottawa continued to resist provincial demands for block funding of existing programs, federal officials sought to avoid the shared-cost mechanism when planning new initiatives in social housing, a pattern consistent with the government's general approach to federal/provincial relations over much of the decade.

This trend became clear in the 1973 amendments to the National Housing Act. New initiatives, such as the Assisted Home Ownership Program and the Assisted Rental Program, were for the most part to be delivered directly by CMHC through its branch offices across the country. More important for the future, however, was that much greater stimulus was to be given to social housing delivered through non-profit and co-operative groups, and this support was also to come directly from CMHC.

Growing reliance on the third sector, which is discussed more fully in chapter 7, reflected several forces. Mixed-income projects in the non-profit sector were a means of avoiding the stigmatization associated with large tracts of public housing; and they also reflected the broader trend identified in chapter 4 toward a mixed economy of welfare, with non-state instruments of delivery playing a prominent role. In addition, the third sector offered rich opportunities to a federal government tired of working through provincial agencies. Unilateral programs would strengthen the federal government's links with non-profit and co-operative groups across the country, planting the government more fairly in another dimension of Canadian society. The visibility and public support generated by such programs were not lost on federal government facing constitutional challengers in many provincial capitals.

Federal unilateralism in the third sector did not eliminate intergovernmental conflict, however. Municipal non-profit corporations were eligible and soon emerged to take advantage of the legislation, operating separately from municipal public housing offices and sometimes maintaining separate waiting lists for accommodation, thus generating controversy at the local level. (On the role of municipal agencies, see chapter 8.) In addition, having received a promise of capital assistance from CMHC, non-profit corporations would then press the provincial government for rent subsidies for the units to be designated for low-income occupants, a pressure not always welcome in provincial offices. In the longer term, both the non-profit and co-operative housing sectors were to emerge as independent, active participants in the politics of housing policy, forming national organizations in part with direct assistance from CMHC, and lobbying both federal and provincial officials on policy directions.[8] In these ways, federal unilateralism was a source of friction within municipalities, between municipalities and provinces, and between the provincial and federal governments.

Unilateralism emerged at the provincial level as well, reflecting the growing self-confidence of provincial housing officials. A number of provinces established departments of housing headed by a full cabinet minister to provide a higher level of political direction to housing policy. Once again Ontario took the lead. The Ministry of Housing was established in 1973 to increase provincial policy co-ordination, to reduce municipal discretion, and to increase the province's leverage vis-à-vis Ottawa on funding issues (Rose 1980). British Columbia and Alberta followed quickly, with the Alberta department becoming a leading advocate of the transfer of housing responsibilities to the provinces. In this, it was supported vigorously by Quebec, especially after the election of the Parti québécois in 1976. Although the Lévesque government chose to expand the functions of the Quebec Housing Corporation rather than to create a new ministry, it began to plan for an expanded program of social housing and became a bitter critic of the federal role (Streich 1985: 58–62).

Unilateral programs quickly followed. According to one count, 'by 1976, there were fifty-three housing programs administered by the provinces independently of the National Housing Act, including direct construction and rental subsidies, housing rehabilitation, capital financing and rentals controls' (CMHC 1983: 49). As always in the housing field, there was dramatic variation in provincial activity during the 1970s, both as to the level of activity and the extent of unilateralism. As table 5.2 demonstrates, provincial spending did not reflect the severity of housing need; poor provinces, with the worst conditions, spent least. In addition, poor provinces emphasized shared-cost programs. Richer provinces, such as Ontario, Alberta, and British Columbia, in contrast, could afford the luxury of independence.

The 1970s thus produced a more complex social housing system: 'In the immediate postwar period and through much of the sixties, Canadian housing policy was largely defined and directed by the federal governments ... By the early 1980s, housing policy had come to be produced by eleven governments acting in varying degrees of unilateralism and collaboration'(Streich 1985: 31–2). Not surprisingly, the result was greater intergovernmental conflict. Led by Quebec, Alberta, British Columbia, and Ontario, the provinces pressed for a reduction in the federal role, making their case in federal/provincial negotiations in both the housing field and the wider struggle over the constitution. At the 1973 conference of ministers of housing, for example, Ontario and Alberta pressed the case for block funding of social housing. At that point, not all provinces were equally enthusiastic, and the minister from New Brunswick reminded the conference that his province was not 'jealous of its authority in the field of housing' (ibid.: 85). After the acceptance of the principle of block funding in the Established Programs Financing Act in 1977, however, the provinces developed a written consensus on such financing for social housing as well (ibid.: 86). By 1980, an interprovincial task force reported that three provinces had raised their jurisdictional sights even further: British Columbia, Alberta, and Quebec demanded a transfer of tax points along with a complete transfer of responsibility for housing to them.[9] Although other provinces still preferred block funding, they all agreed that provincial govern-

TABLE 5.2
Unilateral provincial expenditures and federal/provincial expenditures on housing, 1974–6

	Nfld	PEI	NS	NB	Que.	Ont.	Man.	Sask.	Alta	BC	Total
Expenditures											
($ per capita)											
Unilateral provincial	1	5	n/a	4	n/a	*21	5	10	107	31	21
Federal/provincial	21	19	11	13	13	14	35	10	16	10	14
Total	22	24	11	17	13	36	40	20	123	41	35
Housing need											
(% of households)											
Crowded conditions	23.6	12.8	12.4	15.2	12.4	6.8	9.2	9.8	8.3	6.8	9.4
No running water	16.3	13.9	7.8	7.8	1.1	2.0	9.8	16.2	7.4	2.0	3.9
No flush toilet	26.4	22.0	15.3	13.8	2.6	4.3	14.9	22.5	11.1	4.4	6.9

*Minus Ontario Purchase Grant Program
SOURCE: Canada 1979

ments should be 'totally responsible for the majority of policy, program development, program delivery and program administration' (Interprovincial Task Force 1980).

These tensions inevitably spilled over into the intense battle over the constitution in the late 1970s. Throughout the constitutional process, the federal government sought to focus attention on its own priorities – the patriation of the constitution, a charter of rights, and the amending formula – and to defer questions about the division of powers to a second round of negotiations. Provinces insisted that the first round must also respond to their concerns over the division of powers and financial resources, and repeatedly pointed to specific areas of tension and duplication of effort. Housing was a recurring example in this battle, especially for the premiers of the western provinces and Quebec.

The 1977 report of the Western Premiers' Task Force on Constitutional Trends, known as the 'Intrusions Report,' emphasized the areas of housing, urban development, and land use. 'In recent years, federal intervention has become more systematic and aggressive, and has begun to challenge provincial jurisdiction in a more direct way,' the report insisted; the result was to 'restrict provincial and municipal initiatives, distort provincial and municipal priorities, and strain both federal-provincial and provincial-municipal relations' (Western Premiers' Task Force 1977: 29, 3). A year later, Quebec published its own dossier noir, which criticized federal treatment of the Quebec Housing Corporation and attacked the federal role in housing and urban affairs as a contravention of the constitution. At the First Ministers' Conference on the Economy in 1978, a bitter confrontation broke out between René Lévesque and the federal housing minister, André Ouellet, and the battle became part of the Parti québécois campaign leading up to the referendum on sovereignty association.[10] Social housing had become a weapon in the struggle for hegemony among the governments of Canada.

Federal Accommodation
Over the next few years, the federal government slowly accommodated itself to these pressures in a series of steps that decentralized program delivery, tamed federal unilateralism, and launched the elaborate system of joint planning that exists today. The first stage came in the 1978 amendments to the National Housing Act. The changes reflected both the erosion of the federal government's fiscal position and its desire to keep the housing sector from adding more fuel to the constitutional

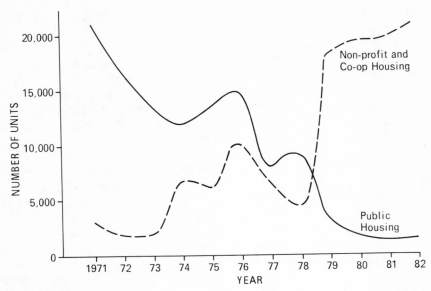

Figure 5.1
Public housing and non-profit/co-operative housing, annual unit commitments, 1971–82. SOURCE: after Streich 1985

fires. In order to reduce its annual cash requirements, the government shifted from a system based on the direct provision of capital to one based on the subsidization of the interest charges on private financing (Teron 1981). Under the new arrangements, known as the 56.1 program, public or private non-profit sponsors of social housing were expected to arrange a private mortgage. The federal government would then insure the mortgage and provide a subsidy to reduce the effective rate of interest to 2 per cent. As figure 5.1 indicates, this change radically reduced the construction of traditional public housing for which government provided the capital, and most new projects were soon proceeding under the new program.

In addition, the federal government moved to ease federal/provincial tensions. The Ministry of State for Urban Affairs was abolished, and a program of 'disentanglement' was announced to the 1978 conference of ministers of housing. The aim, the federal minister declared, was 'to extricate ourselves from the tangle of NHA programs and the duplication and overlapping of responsibilities' (Streich 1985: 198). Disentanglement took two forms. First, the new subsidy for social housing was not a shared-cost grant. In place of the mandatory sharing of subsidies for traditional public housing, the new subsidy was unilateral, and did not depend on financial participation by the provinces. The federal government hoped that the provinces would 'stack' additional subsidies on the federal base; in fact, the original Cabinet document on the scheme conceded that 'provincial subsidies will continue to be required if the program is to penetrate deeply enough to reach large numbers of those with very low income' (CMHC 1983: 48). None the less, federal support was not actually conditional on such stacking, and the federal government was soon to be disappointed by the provincial response. Second, the federal government agreed to withdraw from detailed project approval and inspection in the case of municipal and provincial projects. This decentralization would proceed within the framework of a global agreement negotiated with each province, but CMHC's role within the agreement was limited to budget allocations. All other aspects of project development became the responsibility of the province, which could target its allocations according to its own housing priorities.

These changes represented only partial decentralization, however. The federal government continued to deliver the *private* non-profit program that, as it turned out, provided two-thirds of new social housing in subsequent years. The federal government had offered to allow provinces to take over the private side as well, but only where they agreed to provide 25 per cent of the capital for the project; only two provinces were to make use of this provision.

The fate of the private non-profit sector revealed the growing polarization between the Liberal and Progressive Conservative parties towards federal/provincial relations in general and social housing in particular. The short-lived Clark government offered to withdraw the requirement of a 25 per cent contribution, and entered into negotiations with Ontario concerning provincial delivery of the private component, on the assumption that agreement would serve as a model for other provinces as well. Such negotiations might well have succeeded, because provinces regarded disentanglement as a success that should be extended (Interprovincial Task Force 1980). The negotiations were not complete, however, before the fall of the Conservative government. The re-elected Liberals, in the full flush of their 'new federalism' and resistance to provincial pressures, halted the negotiations. Because the projects were largely federally funded, provincial delivery would hardly appeal to a government intent on strengthening direct links between the federal government and individual Canadians. In the words of a CMHC

TABLE 5.3
Provincial variations in global agreement on social housing, 1983

	Nfld	PEI	NS	NB	Que.	Ont.	Man.	Sask.	Alta	BC
Provincial delivery	–	2	1,2	–	1,2	2	[a]	1,2,3	2	3
CMHC delivery	2,3,4	3,4	3,4,5	3,4	3,4,5	3,4,5,6	2,3,4,5,6	3,4,5,6	3,4,5	2,3,4,5,6
Provincial contributions					1,2	[b]		3,6		3

[a] Manitoba had a small allocation of 56.1 private non-profit global units for its use. However, these units were approved as if they were CMHC-led projects.

[b] Ontario Community Housing Assistance Program

CODE: 1, provincial non-profit; 2, municipal non-profit; 3, private non-profit; 4, co-operative; 5, DIAND non-profit; 6, urban native

SOURCE: CMHC 1983

(1983: 50) report, 'the principal rationale was the lack of federal visibility in projects that are provincially-led.'

As a result, decentralization remained stalled for the life of the Liberal government. CMHC retained direct delivery of the private non-profit program, and the federal government influenced the upper limit on the public side through its annual budget allocations. Some provinces preferred to continue to rely on CMHC delivery for large portions of the public non-profit program as well; table 5.3 illustrates these provincial variations. All in all, the 1978–9 adjustments had made only a modest dent in the federal role. They had, however, created the precedent for the future.

The second phase of federal/provincial accommodation began with the election of the Progressive Conservative government at the federal level in 1984. Provinces continued to press for the extension of the disentanglement provisions to all social housing, but this pressure ran into resistance at the bureaucratic level in Ottawa. This opposition, which was reflected in a major CMHC evaluation of the 56.1 program (CMHC 1983) and later the study team report on housing for the Nielsen Task Force (Study Team Report 1986), focused on both substantive and intergovernmental issues. Substantively, both reports insisted that resources were not being targeted on those most in need, and the program was having minimal impact on the housing problems of the poor.[11] The studies also attacked the growing imbalance between the two levels of government. The federal hope that provincial governments would stack their subsidies on top of the unilateral federal payment was disappointed. The CMHC evaluation of the 1978–81 experience concluded that provincial assistance had dropped to only 9.0 per cent of federal subsidies (CMHC 1983: 274); and three years later, the Nielsen study group concluded that provinces had reduced their spending on housing in general (Study Team Report 1986: 27–8, 46). The Nielsen group's analysis sounded hauntingly like many earlier Liberal speeches: 'Unless provinces significantly increase their financial contributions to social housing, there is a significant danger of the federal government paying the bills with the provinces having control over expenditures. Such a situation threatens federal accountability, visibility and control over program cost and effectiveness' (ibid.: 30).

The proposals advanced by the Nielsen group represented a reversal from previous Liberal inclinations, however. They advocated a major return to cost-sharing: provinces would be asked to share the costs of each program on a 50:50 basis. Failure to do so would jeopardize hard-won provincial delivery. Any province sharing costs equally would deliver the program; otherwise the government with the higher contribution would normally deliver the program; and 'under no circumstances should provinces not making financial contributions assume the delivery and administration functions' (Study Team Report 1986: 32). While the proposal held open the possibility of provincial control of both the public and the private non-profit sectors, it did so on much steeper terms. Not surprisingly, its authors anticipated 'some resistance to the proposed strategy' from the provinces (ibid.: 40).

This broad critique was accepted by the Progressive Conservatives, but its sharper edges were smoothed by the government's 'national reconciliation' and emphasis on federal/provincial consensus. An elaborate consultative process was launched, in 1985, with the issuance of the Consultation Paper on Housing (Canada 1985a); the minister travelled across the country for meetings with each province; and negotiations continued at a conference of ministers of housing in Calgary. The new policy, which was announced in December 1985, contained two broad thrusts.[12] First, federal social housing dollars would be much more tightly targeted on low-income households. Second, the federal government would accept the principle of provincial delivery of all social housing (except the co-operative program). Ottawa wished to retain a role in broad policy, however, and decentralization would therefore be subject to conditions set out in a global agreement between the two levels of government and in subsidiary operating agreements that would be renegotiated annually between Ottawa and each province.

The primary conditions, which are incorporated in the current agreements, fall into five categories:

1. *Distribution of federal resources:* Each province must agree to an allocation of federal resources among provinces based predominantly on housing needs. Federal expenditures do not depend, therefore, on the level of provincial activity as they did under traditional shared-cost programs.

2. *Cost sharing:* Given the consensual mode of the negotiations over the new system, the terms were predictably less stringent than those of the Nielsen group. Provinces must contribute 25 per cent of the costs to gain control over the delivery of a program, in effect, reverting to the traditional 75:25 formula established in 1949. Any province wishing to expand its housing effort further may inject additional money into the program; federal expenditures do not increase in this situation, however, and the effect is to shift the federal/provincial split closer to 50:50

for the enlarged program. Alternatively, provinces are free to mount independent housing programs.

3. *Allocational rules:* The agreements are much more detailed than the ones that established provincial delivery of the public non-profit program in 1977–8. The new system requires joint federal/provincial planning on all major allocational issues. First, the division of housing projects between public bodies on the one hand and the private non-profit sector on the other must be specified in the annual operating agreement, as are the basic principles governing the process by which individual groups are selected to deliver specific projects. Second, the allocation of assistance to different clientele groups is similarly identified. The federal rules require targeting on the poor for all new cost-shared units; and the balance between units constructed for senior citizens, families, and those with special needs is also subject to agreement. Third, the geographical distribution of new housing commitments within the province must also be set out in the annual operating agreement.

4. *Planning process:* To give effect to this allocational system, the agreements establish a joint planning and monitoring committee, known as the PMC, in each province that chooses to deliver social housing programs. This committee, which is chaired jointly, negotiates the annual operating agreements. The PMC is required to meet at least four times a year, establish a rolling three-year plan, evaluate existing programs, and recommend annual program levels for each region of the province to both levels of governments. If a province chooses to deliver native housing programs, a tripartite committee must be established, with representatives of the CMHC, the province, and native groups.

5. *Publicity:* The agreements call for joint publicity in the form of signs, plaques, ceremonies, and announcements. They call also for all publicity in both official languages, a matter of sensitivity in some western provinces.

The basic trade-off in the 1985 negotiations is clear. The federal government was prepared to surrender its unilateral role in social housing and to decentralize program delivery. In return, it wanted to retain considerable control over the basic parameters of housing policy. Indeed, in the case of the public non-profit program, which had been decentralized in the late 1970s, the new agreements represented a reassertion of federal influence. In effect, the new global agreements sought to control the distributional politics inherent in social housing. The federal bureaucracy was convinced that provincial and municipal

TABLE 5.4
Federal/provincial agreements on cost sharing and delivery of social housing, 1987

Province	Non-profit	Rent supplement	Urban native	Rural native housing (RNH)	Residential Rehabilitation Assistance Program (RRAP)			Emergency Repairs Program (ERP)
					Home owner	Rental	Disabled	
Newfoundland	Prov. 75:25	Prov. 75:25	Prov. 75:25	Prov. 75:25	CMHC + Prov. 75:25	CMHC	CMHC + Prov. 75:25 Urban Rural	Prov. 75:25
Prince Edward Island	CMHC	CMHC	CMHC	CMHC	CMHC	CMHC	CMHC	CMHC
Nova Scotia	Prov. 75:25	Prov. 45:55	CMHC	CMHC	CMHC	CMHC	CMHC	CMHC
New Brunswick	Prov. 75:25	Prov. 75:25	CMHC	Prov. 75:25	Prov. 75:25	CMHC	Prov. 75:25	CMHC
Quebec	Prov. 62:38 Public 75:25 Priv.	Prov. 62:38 Regular 75:25 Co-op	Prov. 75:25	Prov. 62:38 Non-Nat. 75:25 Native	Prov. 50:50 75:25	Prov. 50:50 Non-Nat. 75:25 Native	Prov. 50:50 75:25	Prov. 50:50 Non-Nat. 75:25 Native
Ontario	Prov. 60:40	Prov. 60:40	CMHC 75:25	CMHC	CMHC	CMHC	CMHC	CMHC
Manitoba	Prov. 75:25	Prov. 75:25	Prov. 75:25	CMHC 75:25 North + Prov. 75:25 South HAP	CMHC + Prov. 75:25 Urban Rural	CMHC	CMHC	CMHC
Saskatchewan	Prov. 75:25	Prov. 75:25	CMHC	CMHC	CMHC	CMHC	CMHC	CMHC
Alberta	Prov. 70:30	Prov. 70:30	CMHC 75:25	Prov.	CMHC	CMHC	CMHC	CMHC
Northwest Territories	CMHC	Terr. 75:25	CMHC	Terr. 50:50 HAP 75:25 RNH	CMHC	CMHC	CMHC	Terr. 75:25
British Columbia	Prov. 67:33	Prov. 67:33	CMHC	CMHC	CMHC	CMHC	CMHC	CMHC
Yukon	Terr. 75:25	Terr. 75:25	CMHC	CMHC	CMHC	CMHC	CMHC	CMHC

source: Data provided to author by CMHC.

decision-makers are more susceptible to local political pressures. In CMHC's view, the federal government must be involved to protect non-profit groups from losing out to provincial housing corporations in the competition for new units, to prevent disproportionate attention to senior citizens at the expense of families, to target assistance on the poor, and to forestall the possibility of new housing commitments all appearing in the constituency of the provincial minister of housing. Not surprisingly, provincial officials reject this view as federal paternalism, and insist on their commitment to responsible delivery of social housing.

None the less, provincial governments proved willing to accept this broad approach at least in part. In the first round of agreements under the new system, all but one province chose to deliver the basic housing and rent-supplement programs. Admittedly, provinces proved less anxious to take over other programs. Only four provinces chose to deliver the rehabilitation and native housing programs, with Quebec alone assuming responsibility for the entire package (see table 5.4 for details). This response reflected in part the wider decline of interest in social policy identified in chapter 4, and in part an easing of provincial expansionism, especially in the western provinces, which became less interested in major new responsibilities than they had been in the affluent climate of the 1970s. Financial commitments by the provinces also differed. Most chose the basic formula of 75:25, but Ontario, Quebec, and Alberta initially opted for larger programs with larger provincial commitments, resulting in financial splits ranging from 60:40 to 70:30. When the dust had settled, however, the provincial role in the delivery of social housing had expanded considerably.

Provincial governments can also expand their role further by launching unilateral initiatives outside the framework of the global agreements. Such independent programs are free of federal conditions and can be used to dilute federal priorities. For example, in the face of intense housing pressures in Ontario and especially Toronto, the province announced a succession of unilateral commitments. In 1986, 'Project 3000' was mounted to provide 3000 non-profit units for hard-to-house groups such as low-income singles, ex-psychiatric patients, and elderly or battered women; in 1987, 'Project 3600' promised another 3600 units over two to four years; and the 1988 budget added another 30,000 units over three to five years (Ontario 1988). Because Ontario rejects Ottawa's insistence that social housing be targeted exclusively on low-income people, it simply adds unilateral provincial units to each new project to ensure a more socially integrated approach to social housing in the province.[13] Federal officials claim that the overall balance within new projects even in Ontario is still more targeted, but the federal impact is clearly less than in provinces without such room for independent action.

The Contemporary Pattern

The history of the federal/provincial balance in social housing parallels the broader trends in the federation and has been shaped by the same underlying political forces that shifted the equilibrium in social policy more generally. As elsewhere, the broad pattern is one of decentralization, from the centralized activities of the 1940s to the global agreements of today. The trend has not been as consistent; unilateralism in the 1970s represented the reassertion of an independent federal role in housing. In principle, however, the new global agreements tame federal unilateralism and devolve the delivery of social housing to the provinces.

Comparison with the other major components of the social-policy sector discussed earlier qualifies this picture somewhat. The social housing system remains relatively centralized by the standards of health and education. Despite all the talk of block funding in social housing, the new global agreements do not introduce block funding on the model of the Established Programs Financing (EPF) Act. Rather, they consolidate social housing in the traditional condition-grant mode, and they therefore resemble the Canada Assistance Plan (CAP) more than EPF. Even by the standards of CAP, social housing remains centralized in several critical ways. First, CAP remains an open-ended program; the CAP 'tap' is open for all eligible activity, and total federal expenditures are still driven by provincial decisions. In contrast, the social housing 'tap' is under federal control, at least in terms of the level of new spending. Second, social housing transfers are subject to much stricter conditions. Federal housing dollars are now subject to specific rules concerning the incomes of those housed, for example; in comparison, CAP is silent on provincial welfare rates; and the income limits set for recipients of other services funded under CAP are now so high as to exercise little constraint on provincial programs (Health and Welfare Canada 1985). Third, planning and monitoring of social housing through joint committees is much more formal and stringent. During the drafting of CAP, officials in Health and Welfare Canada pressed hard for an annual review of the administration of the program, province by province; but this suggestion was eliminated from the draft legislation at the last moment in response to pressure from provinces and senior officials in the central agencies of the federal government (Splane 1985). As a result, federal officials have difficulty enforcing the few conditions that do exist, especially in provinces that rely in part on municipal delivery of benefits.

Thus, the brave new world in social housing has an old face. Indeed, its reliance on the conditional-grant mechanism evokes a certain nostalgia for the days before EPF. The reasons why the pressures of the last generation appear to have had less impact on social housing are reasonably obvious. In practice, public housing began as a predominantly federal service, delivered by a federal agency with branch offices across the country – and provinces have had to struggle to capture it. Other social services began as provincial programs – and the federal government has had to struggle to influence them. Different starting points produced different end points. Several other factors also muted decentralist impulses in housing. Historically, provincial administrative capacities have varied more than in health or post-secondary education, and therefore a provincial consensus on proposals for real block funding or a transfer of tax points proved elusive. And important interest groups in the third sector that grew up around the strong federal presence in housing during earlier years, such as the non-profit and co-operative movements and native organizations, have resisted unconditional decentralization.

Do the new arrangements represent an end point, a stable equilibrium in social housing? Such a prediction would defy the entire, restless history of federal/provincial relations in Canada. Admittedly, a reassertion of federal unilateralism seems unlikely, even though the Liberal opposition in the House of Commons attacked the agreements as the abandonment of a national housing policy.[14] Revoking the principle of provincial delivery would undoubtedly provoke serious conflict with some provinces and would require an act of considerable political will by a new government. In the current political climate, the conditional-grant mechanism seems safe from federal hawks.

Canadian history confirms, however, that conditional grants are not necessarily immune from provincial hawks. Close collaboration and co-operation can easily turn to mutual frustration and recrimination, and battles over federal conditions are inevitable. This dynamic emerged almost before the ink was dry on the new agreements, as provincial and municipal officials protested the stringent income limits for households in new social housing.[15] These early complaints have been echoed by senior officials, especially in those provinces that have maintained large, active housing corporations. In early 1988, for example, a senior Ontario official strongly criticized CMHC's 'incredibly detailed guidelines [that are] intended to ensure rigid conformity across the country' (Wilson 1988). The competitive process required for the selection of delivery groups, federal controls over the transfer of allocations among projects, and the rigid caps on project costs all frustrated provincial officials. 'This absolute lack of flexibility stifles ... the ability to make decisions based on a clear understanding of the local provincial housing environment' (ibid.). Not all provinces are equally assertive about expanding their jurisdiction, and it is possible, in the current financial climate, that poorer provinces might simply walk away from the process, forcing CMHC to resume direct delivery of some programs.[16] Nevertheless, if the past is any guide to the future, strong provinces will press against the outer limits of conditional-grant programs, and over time they may wear down federal resolve.

The more that social housing becomes defined as a provincial program that the federal government is simply cost-sharing, as opposed to a federal program that the provinces are simply administering, the more the basic political legitimacy of federal conditions will erode. The federal conditions are not entrenched in legislation, as in the case of the Canada Health Act. They must be sustained politically in the annual ritual of intergovernmental negotiation over the operating agreements. As one federal official admitted privately: 'Our ability to enforce these conditions does not depend fundamentally on all those bits of paper. It depends on the political will of the day. If the minister decides to go easy on the provinces, there are few real sanctions that the bureaucracy can bring to bear.' In the first rounds of bargaining, the federal government prevailed, with only minor concessions, on its controversial objective of targeting new social housing commitments exclusively on the poor. The impact of joint planning on other issues on which federal government was less committed is not clear, however. Non-profit groups, for example, have complained that they have been shut out in some provinces.[17]

Constitutional changes, such as those proposed in the Meech Lake Accord or perhaps some successor agreement, might accentuate this trend. At the present time, the prospects of the accord's ratification are highly uncertain. If the agreement were to be ratified, it would establish a firm constitutional foundation for the federal spending power, but would also subject its exercise to limitations. The accord proposes to add the following section to the Constitution Act:

106a. (1) The Government of Canada shall provide reasonable compensation to the government of a province that chooses not to participate in a national shared-cost program that is established by the Government of Canada after the coming into force of this section in an area of exclusive provincial jurisdiction, if the province carries on a program or initiative that is compatible with the national objectives.

(2) Nothing in this section extends the legislative powers of the Parliament of Canada or of the legislatures of the provinces.

Although there is considerable debate about the implications of Section 106a, it would probably increase regional variation in future social programs in two ways. First, federal authorities would most likely build considerable flexibility into new shared-cost programs so as to accommodate diverse provincial preferences from the outset and thereby minimize the incentives for provinces to opt out. Second, some provinces, especially Quebec, would probably opt out as a matter of principle and be bound only by the 'national objectives' of the program (Banting 1988).

The centralized nature of the current federal/provincial agreements in social housing runs counter to the ethos animating the Meech Lake Accord. Admittedly, social housing may not fall within the strict legal reach of Section 106a because the federal government might contend that social housing is not 'an area of exclusive provincial jurisdiction,' citing both the recent history of direct federal delivery and existing case law, especially CMHC *v. Coop. College Residence Inc.* Nevertheless, while social housing might escape the legal claws of Meech Lake, it would be unlikely to escape its political claws completely. The accord is premised on an accommodative approach to federal/provincial relations and an acceptance by the federal government that it should not dictate the specifics of social programs to provinces. If the accord is ratified, its ethos might well spill over into the housing sector and erode the willingness of future federal ministers to insist on detailed controls over provincially delivered social housing projects.

There are dangers in such a world, even for provincial ministries of housing. If federal control over social housing is worn down, federal commitment to the sector may also wither. Deprived of the political benefits and visibility inherent in control, ambitious federal politicians might naturally look to policy instruments in federal jurisdiction when responding to the social concerns of their electorate. Certainly the tax-transfer system, with its direct link between the federal government and citizens in every region, would be an inviting alternative. It is possible that such dynamics would make shelter allowances a more active issue in federal policy debates. It is also possible, however, that political excitement at the federal level would move beyond social housing altogether.

FEDERAL MODELS AND SOCIAL CONSEQUENCES

Social housing has witnessed a struggle for hegemony among governments that has been accompanied often by strong rhetoric and sharp conflict. Underlying these battles, and contributing to their intensity, have been competing visions or models of Canadian federation and its future. Centralized and decentralized models of federalism have lain at the heart of constitutional controversy in this country since its birth. The centralized model is premised fundamentally on the primacy of a single pan-Canadian political community, and insists on the need for a strong central government that speaks for individual Canadians across the country and nurtures a common political loyalty that transcends our more local attachments. The decentralized model, by contrast, celebrates our regional and linguistic communities, and emphasizes the importance of strong provincial governments that can respond effectively to regional diversities and speak forcefully for them on issues of national debate.

In a less dramatic way, the tension between unilateral and joint programs also captures the essence of different models of federalism. Unilateralism reflects a classical conception of a federal state, in which each level of government acts independently within its own jurisdiction and is accountable directly to its own electorate, with few formal mechanisms integrating the policies of the two in a comprehensive way. Joint action, in contrast, reflects an alternative model, often called collaborative or co-operative federalism, in which governments mount common programs that are financed through conditional grants and managed through continuous intergovernmental negotiation.

Individual Canadians, however, might wonder whether all this really matters. Are federal/provincial battles simply a game beloved by bureaucrats and politicians, driven by a territorial imperative, but devoid of real consequences – 'full of sound and fury, signifying nothing'? Or do subtle shifts in the models that structure the distribution of power have major impacts that are visible at the grass roots, where real people need better housing? The complexities of federal/ provincial relations do, in fact, have important implications for the broad patterns of public policy. In exploring these social consequences of federalism, it is useful to distinguish between the degree of centralization on the one hand, and the extent to which governments rely on unilateral as opposed to joint programs on the other. Although these two threads are interwoven and confounded in day-to-day practice, their implications are distinctive and warrant separate examination.

Centralization and Social Housing
The extent to which power over social policy is centralized in the hands of the central government or decentralized to provincial governments has important consequences for both the scope of social action and the redistribution that flows from it.

The Scope of Social Action
Political theorists have long argued that decentralized government means limited government.[18] This view can be traced back to early American theorists, for whom federalism was part of a larger system of divided jurisdiction designed to restrain the powers and growth of the state. Modern studies of the welfare state tend to confirm this view by demonstrating a clear relationship between levels of welfare spending and political centralization; other things being equal, countries with decentralized governments devote a smaller proportion of their national resources to social security than do those with more centralized governments (see Cameron 1978; Wilensky 1975; Castles and McKinlay 1979).

In Canadian history, certainly the growing power of the federal government and the expansion of welfare proceeded in tandem, and most observers conclude that the two processes have been intimately related. Indeed, the inadequacy of social policy during the 1930s' depression convinced an entire generation of constitutional scholars and social reformers, in English Canada at least, that decentralized authority was a formidable barrier to social progress. Provincial responsiveness during the inter-war period was undermined in part by the problems of fiscal imbalance, with spending responsibility lodged firmly at the local level but the broadest taxing powers reserved for central government. In addition, provincial authorities were well aware of the constraints inherent in the mobility of capital and labour in a federation. The premier of Manitoba wrote to the prime minister in 1927 that 'if any City or Province singly adopted plans to solve unemployment, that City or Province would become the mecca to which the unemployed in other cities or provinces would drift' (Schofield 1983: 92). The reports of a long stream of government commissions in the 1930s and early 1940s are replete with similar arguments.

Federalism was not the only – or even the most important – factor limiting social policy in those decades. Canada was still undergoing the transition from an agricultural to an industrial economy; the unionization of the urban work-force was only in its early stages; left-wing protest was still consolidating itself in the form of the Co-operative Commonwealth Federation; Keynesianism had yet to reshape the orthodoxies of policy makers. As these forces came into play during and after the Second World War, constitutional road blocks that had seemed insurmountable in the 1930s proved much more manageable. As a result, it is difficult to sort out the independent influence of the division of powers.

Nevertheless, there can be little doubt that decentralization did complicate inter-war efforts to respond to the social needs of the time. The centralization in this sector after the Second World War circumvented barriers confronting provincial action, facilitating the development of a modern social-security system. Undoubtedly some expansion would have come in the post-war era even without major changes in the federal/provincial balance. But centralization aided a larger expansion than Canadians could have legitimately expected from the institutional framework of the inter-war years.

This dynamic was at work in the specific case of social housing as well, although the impact was more modest, because federal enthusiasm for public housing was restrained throughout the 1950s. Nevertheless, CMHC kept public housing on the national agenda. As the government most distant from local resistance to public housing projects, the federal government could remain a somewhat detached supporter. Rose (1980: 30) describes the politics at work in the early years in the following terms:

The federal role was fostered by the outright and fairly strong hostility to public housing programs, a hostility far more evident within the councils of local government and the legislatures of provincial governments than elsewhere in Canada. At the federal level, there was, by the late 1940s, at least a decade of major housing [experience] ... The Marsh Report and the Curtis Report were further influences at the federal level that helped to weaken whatever antagonism existed ... There was never in Ottawa the strong anti-public housing lobbies which were evident in Washington from 1933 onwards.

As a result, according to Rose, federal policy was 'primarily an instrumentality to encourage the assumption by the provinces of their rightful constitutional responsibility.' (ibid.: 182) Without that pressure, even fewer units would have been built, except perhaps in Ontario.

In more recent decades, when provinces developed greater interest in social housing, the federal impact became more subtle. In effect, the federal government became the guardian of a wider mix of policy instruments. This conclusion challenges the argument often advanced by public-choice theorists that it is decentralization that encourages experimentation and diversity, as provincial governments develop their own approaches to problems and then learn from each other's successes and failures. Whatever the merits of this argument when viewed from a nationwide perspective, it pales when attention shifts to the range of policy options maintained in any single province. The national political constituency is more complex than that of any province. The nature of housing problems varies enormously across the country, as does the relative political strength of builders, tenants, non-profit organizations, the co-operative movement, and native groups. In responding to regionally diverse constellations of needs and pressures, the federal government developed a larger menu of nation-wide programs than any single province would likely have chosen to support, and citizens therefore enjoy a more diverse set of choices.

The federal government has tried to entrench this diversity through the new global agreements. Fear that individual provinces might sharply narrow the range of delivery groups or beneficiaries lay behind the requirement for joint planning on major allocational decisions. Even these provisions failed to reassure important interest groups, such as the co-operative movement and native organizations. The co-operative movement was convinced that at least half the provinces had no commitment to co-operative housing, and that some provinces were actively hostile.[19] As a result, the movement mounted an intense lobby of MPs and Cabinet ministers to ensure that support for co-operative housing remained a unilateral federally delivered program; and in this, it succeeded. In addition, the federal government responded to the concerns of native organizations by insisting that any province assuming responsibility for native housing had to adopt the tripartite planning committees mentioned earlier.

Redistribution
Historically, centralization also transformed the redistributive impact of social-security programs. The expansion of the federal role did not

necessarily make social programs more redistributive between high- and low-income classes, but it did transform social security into a powerful instrument of redistribution among different regions of Canada (Banting 1987). As Gunnar Myrdal (1957: 46) argued almost thirty years ago, the development of social security and greater progressivity in taxation were 'two mighty policy trends which have forcefully contributed to equalization between regions' in Western nations. Such policies have little to do with regional policy per se; but, in Stuart Holland's words (1976: 56), the welfare state 'is the submerged but massive part of the iceberg of state interventions' that favour poorer regions.

In Canada, centralization was a prerequisite for this process of nation-wide redistribution. As long as welfare was a municipal or provincial responsibility, redistribution took place within the confines of the local economy; the poorest regions always had the greatest needs but the fewest resources with which to respond. The growth of federal social programs, however, generated substantial interregional redistribution because the populations of poorer regions have larger proportions of elderly, unemployed, and needy people than do others, while the revenues to finance federal programs that help these people are raised in disproportionately greater amounts in more affluent regions.[20]

Defenders of a strong national role in social housing make the same argument.[21] Only the federal government has the capacity to equalize access to housing because, in the words of the Matthews Report (CMHC 1979a: 24), 'provinces which can least afford a redistributive housing policy are the same provinces which have a disproportionate share of households requiring assistance.' This pattern was highlighted most graphically by the experience of unilateral provincial programs during the 1970s. As table 5.2 demonstrated earlier, purely provincial spending accentuated, rather than compensated for, regional inequalities in housing: poor provinces with the poorest housing spent least, while rich provinces pumped substantial resources into the sector. Traditional open-ended shared-cost programs, in which the overall level of activity depends on provincial decisions, do not escape this dynamic. During the 1950s and 1960s, the federal government's reliance on the conditionalgrant mechanism meant that the regional distribution of federal housing dollars was distorted by provincial fiscal capacity and interest in public housing. The result was a very uneven distribution of federal assistance, with well over half of all units being built in the richest province, Ontario, a considerable embarrassment in a federation increasingly sensitive to such issues.

TABLE 5.5
Allocation of federal social housing units by province, 1986

Province	Distribution of households in core housing need (per cent)	Allocation of federal housing units (per cent)
Newfoundland	2.1	2.5
Prince Edward Island	0.5	0.7
Nova Scotia	3.9	3.5
New Brunswick	3.4	3.5
Quebec	22.0	27.4
Ontario	32.0	31.4
Manitoba	6.2	5.1
Saskatchewan	5.2	5.3
Alberta	8.4	7.9
British Columbia	16.3	12.7
Canada	100.0	100.0

NOTE: Data on federal housing units represent 95 per cent of the units made available for the Non-profit Housing Program, Rent Supplement, and Rural and Native Housing Ownership and Rental Programs. The remaining 5 per cent of the units were to be allocated through negotiation with the provinces. Data on housing need are for 1982.
SOURCE: Data on core housing need are from the Study Team Report 1982, table 2. Data on the allocation of federal units are from the 1986 Global Agreement on Social Housing.

Direct federal delivery in the 1970s, in contrast, facilitated a more equitable regional distribution. CMHC devoted considerable effort to measuring housing needs across the country and moved towards a needs-based allocation of federal expenditures among the provinces. The transition was not complete when the global arrangements were renegotiated in 1986; but a provisional formula was adopted and the governments committed themselves to develop a mutually agreed needs-based model. This quest for an apolitical allocational system is probably chimerical. Federal/provincial bargaining over the distribution of federal resources is a quintessentially political process; and despite improved data, consensus on a revision to the 1986 formula continued to elude governments as the decade drew to a close. Nevertheless, as the partial evidence in table 5.5 suggests, the distribution of federal social housing expenditures among the regions of the country is more equitable than in the 1960s, and the remaining deficiencies appear to favour poorer provinces, especially Quebec.

Modes of Interaction
With two governments active in the same sector, the relations between them shape the policy-making process and the nature of the programs that are developed within it. The tension between unilateral and joint action in social housing has important implications for the responsiveness of the system to new problems, the level of co-ordination among programs, and the openness of the process to groups and the public.

The Responsiveness of Policy
The extent of centralization is not the only dimension of a federal state that conditions its responsiveness to new social problems. The nature of relations between levels of government is at least as important in facilitating or inhibiting change.

Unilateralism enhances the flexibility enjoyed by governments to respond to their own political constituencies and facilitates experimentation in policies and delivery mechanisms. In so doing, it opens up more avenues for new concerns to enter the system, establish a toe-hold in public policy, and then spread from one jurisdiction to another. It was not an accident that the period of greatest unilateralism in social housing – the 1970s – also saw a proliferation of new approaches to meeting housing needs. Joint programs, in contrast, set alternative dynamics in motion. New initiatives require the agreement of governments espousing different political ideologies, pursuing different policy agendas, and answering to different constituencies. At the extreme, programs controlled by various governments are subject to multiple veto points that slow the process of innovation.[22] At minimum, collaborative action produces a more tortuous policy process and raises the level of consensus required for new initiatives. As we shall see more fully below, provinces wishing to respond to homelessness have sometimes found it faster to act unilaterally, outside the framework of global agreements.

Federalism and Co-ordination
The modern state is a sprawling apparatus that delivers thousands of programs through hundreds of departments, commissions, and agencies. Policy makers face a constant struggle to co-ordinate increasingly complex policy systems, and success in this effort is never more than partial. In such circumstances a citizen faces a bewildering organizational maze when seeking help from government; and citizens with

especially complex or multi-faceted problems, such as the poor and the homeless, must co-ordinate their relationships with a diverse set of bureaucracies – a degree of co-ordination that governments themselves are unable to achieve.

Co-ordination problems are inevitably accentuated in a federal system, especially when both orders of government occupy common policy sectors and relation between the two levels are conflictual, as has often been the case in Canada. Much depends, however, on the nature of program links. The unilateral approach of the 1970s preserved flexibility but at the cost of a lack of integration in social housing as a whole. Streich observed (1985: 108) that 'housing became a field of policy duality or interpenetration to an increasing extent; federal and provincial policies operated within the same housing markets often in pursuit of different objectives without any coherent policy framework. Under these conditions, the potential for complementarity was not great.' In contrast, the onset of joint planning and the consolidation of the delivery of major programs in provincial hands in the 1980s hold out the possibility of higher levels of integration. The conflicting objectives of governments should increasingly be resolved in federal/provincial meetings rather than be played out as independent initiatives in the housing market; and the commitment of the federal government in the 1986 agreements to consult with the provinces before introducing any new programs extends such joint planning into the future.

Provincial delivery also increases the scope for co-ordination between social housing and other programs relevant to the needs of the poor. As noted earlier, the Canadian welfare state has increasingly settled into a bifurcated pattern, with the federal government being the predominant force in income security and provincial governments predominant in social services. Given this broader context, centralized control over social housing was always somewhat anomalous, and the decentralist impulses of the last generation have increased the possibility of linkage between social housing and related social programs. While income security as a whole is primarily federal, social assistance itself is firmly under provincial, and in some cases, municipal direction. The wider range of personal and family services, health care, and employment programs for those on social assistance is also largely in provincial hands. Because the problems faced by the poor are seldom restricted to the housing market, decentralization of social housing creates opportunities for more integrated responses to their needs.

Federalism, Groups, and the Public

In a democratic system of government, the openness of the policy process to the public and groups in the community is an important test of the health of the political order. Given the contemporary context of the social housing debate, the openness of the process is especially relevant. In an era of protracted fiscal restraint in government, innovative proposals increasingly depend on new forms of collaboration among government, the private sector, and the non-profit sector. It is important, therefore, to ask whether the evolving system of federal/ provincial relations has implications here as well.

According to defenders of the classical model of federalism, unilateral action prevents the lines of political accountability between governments and their electorates becoming obscured or attenuated by multiple layers of responsibility and control. In the political vernacular of the 1970s, governments have 'visibility.' Political debate, as a result, focuses on substantive issues rather than intergovernmental complications, and there is less danger that concerns of interest groups will be shut out by an overriding imperative to reach a federal/provincial compromise.

The collaborative model, in contrast, is often criticized for accentuating the closed and secretive nature of policy making in Canada. Decision making retreats into closed federal/provincial meetings that issue bland communiqués which are indecipherable to all but the *cognoscenti*; public debate is muffled, as governments avoid comments that might jeopardize negotiations; interest groups have difficulty in getting their concerns onto the negotiation table; and voters are uncertain about which set of politicians to hold responsible for policy failures. This critique of federal/provincial negotiations as a mode of government was given fresh currency by the controversy over the Meech Lake Accord, but it is a long-standing complaint about Canadian federalism.

The new world of federal/provincial collaboration in social housing betrays many of these attributes. Policy is increasingly hammered out in annual negotiations between Ottawa and each province in the Policy and Monitoring Committee (PMC). Debates within this committee are closed to the public and to other participants in social housing such as municipalities, the private sector, non-profit groups, and the beneficiaries themselves. Only in the case of provincial delivery of native housing programs is the clientele represented directly on the PMC. Indeed, it may even be difficult for other interested groups to determine which level of government has ultimate responsibility for particular housing problems.

This new federal/provincial order has mixed implications for collaborative projects involving government, non-profit groups, and the private sector. In one sense, decentralization should help. A defining characteristic of such partnerships, especially in a regional country like Canada, is their local nature, and provincial delivery of a wider range of housing programs should increase the scope for innovation. In some regions there does seem to be active consultation with the third sector and municipalities in the development of new provincial initiatives. Nevertheless, the emphasis on federal/provincial planning constrains the opportunities here. For example, chapter 6 describes the initiative of Governor Dukakis of Massachusetts in creating a tripartite advisory body called the Massachusetts Housing Partnership, representing the three sectors: public, private, and non-profit. The board meets on a quarterly basis to review housing problems in the state, advise on policy issues, and nurture collaborative projects developed at the local level. Although such a model is available to any provincial premier in Canada, it would inevitably operate in tension with the realities of federalism, especially in provinces that do not have large unilateral programs. Important parameters of social housing in the province would continue to be determined in federal/provincial meetings, which would be closed to the other participants in social housing. Provincial officials might carry the message forward from a tripartite advisory forum, but they would sit across the table from federal officials constrained by the objectives of their own political masters who must respond to nation-wide concerns. Whether the credibility of a partnership forum would survive the marginalization inherent in divided jurisdiction is doubtful.

THE HOMELESS IN A WORLD OF GLOBAL AGREEMENTS

The social housing agreements examined in this chapter deal with the full range of housing needs and are not focused particularly on those at the very margins of the housing market – the homeless and those at risk of becoming homeless. Indeed, the word 'homelessness' does not even appear in the global agreements between the two levels of governments. Nevertheless, the evolving federal/provincial balance in social housing is relevant to the needs of people with no fixed address.

The global agreements structure general social housing programs,

TABLE 5.6
Special-purpose housing under the non-profit housing program, 1984–5

Special-purpose type	Nfld	NB	PEI	NS	Que.	Ont.	Man.	Sask.	Alta	BC	Canada	%
Children's Aid Society							9	19			28	1.1
Ex-prisoners					1	53			9		63	2.4
Transients	5				32	56	8			87	188	7.1
Unwed mothers						10					10	0.4
Victims of family violence	6			15	35	149		11	21	19	256	9.7
Alcohol and drug abusers				8	15	39	70	30	24	20	206	7.8
Physically disabled adults	5			8	151	79		100	10	37	390	14.8
Physically disabled children									16		16	0.6
Disturbed children					15	7		2		8	32	1.2
Mentally disabled adults	16	45		36	78	91	14	44	61	358	743	28.2
Mentally disabled children	5				8	9	8		12		42	1.6
Nursing homes	87						82	446		50	665	25.1
Total	124	45	0	67	335	493	191	652	153	579	2639	100

SOURCE: Data supplied by CHMC

which do assist many who might otherwise be homeless. Moreover, with the return to a strong emphasis on targeting federal assistance, future social housing commitments should produce more units for the poor. The size, distribution, and diversity of the social housing program are therefore important to the homeless in Canada. This point, although undoubtedly true, should not be overstated. The social housing sector remains small, and the great majority of those on the margins of the housing market are unlikely to gain access to it. In addition, regular social housing projects have traditionally been less responsive to certain categories of the homeless; single persons often receive a lower priority than the elderly and families with children, and many people in need of special support services cannot be accommodated in regular projects.

The interests of the homeless have been more directly addressed by the separate provision in the global agreements for 'special-purpose' housing. Until now, the special-needs program has provided a variety of types of accommodation, ranging from emergency shelters and transition homes to permanent housing that incorporates special support services. As table 5.6 indicates, the beneficiaries have been diverse: the elderly in nursing homes, battered women and their children in transition houses, the mentally and physically handicapped in community-based housing, substance abusers in special centres, parolees in half-way houses, and the transient in emergency shelters. Between 1979 and 1984, approximately 15,000 units of special-purpose housing were built, although, as table 5.7 reveals, there was considerable provincial variation in the commitment to such accommodation.

Under the global agreements established in 1986, up to 10 per cent of new commitments could be allocated to special-needs housing, and this program has been used to tackle the problems of the truly homeless. During the International Year of Shelter for the Homeless, for example, the province of Quebec mounted a special program 'aimed specifically at the homeless clientele' under the umbrella of the Canada-Quebec global agreement (Société d'habitation du Québec 1987). There have been important limits to this vehicle, however. Given the 10 per cent cap, a major response to the particular needs of the homeless has had to come from the allocation to other groups with special needs, including nursing homes for the elderly and transition houses for victims of family violence, both of which are supported by powerful political constituencies. A radical shift in the allocation towards shelter for those actually on the street has not been easy.

Provinces seeking prompt action have found the complexities of

TABLE 5.7
Special-purpose housing by province, 1979–84

Province	Number of units	Percentage of all social housing
Newfoundland	562	19
Prince Edward Island	283	38
Nova Scotia	696	16
New Brunswick	1,091	40
Quebec	2,239	6
Ontario	2,079	6
Manitoba	764	19
Saskatchewan	833	11
Alberta	760	7
British Columbia	5,161	29
Canada	14,468	12

SOURCE: Study Team Report 1986: 65

federal/provincial diplomacy a significant constraint. The response of the Ontario government to homelessness during the winter of 1987 is a case in point. Rapid economic growth and the inflow of people from other provinces had generated acute pressure on the housing market, especially in Toronto and Ottawa. The number of homeless people was rising dramatically and beginning to exceed the capacity of existing emergency hostels. Not surprisingly, the plight of the homeless in a wealthy province during the International Year for Shelter of the Homeless became a major issue in the media and political debate, and the government knew that the pressure would intensify with the onset of winter. The provincial government decided to develop a major initiative on homelessness as quickly as possible. The package that was unveiled in mid December was a purely provincial initiative, however, with no federal funding under the global agreement (Ontario, Ministry of Housing 1987). Working through the federal/provincial mechanism would have been much slower and would have involved a painful reallocation within an already stretched program. Also, a unilateral provincial initiative escaped federal conditions that focus effort on new housing stock, allowing Ontario's crash program to concentrate on the rapid acquisition and repair of existing buildings.

Provincial responsibility for the homeless is now being further entrenched by refinements in the global agreements. As the Nielsen

Task Force pointed out, special-purpose housing often involves a transfer from health and social-service budgets to the housing budget. For example, the move to community-based facilities rather than institutional care for the physically and mentally handicapped eased health and welfare costs but increased the demand for social housing. The federal government was not slow to point out that social-service budgets are cost-shared under the Canada Assistance Plan on a 50:50 basis, while housing budgets are most often shared on a 75:25 basis. Moreover, the federal contribution to heath care is locked in under the EPF formula and does not decline if health costs shift to the housing budget. Not surprisingly, the Nielsen Task Force recommended federal/provincial negotiations 'to shift responsibility for subsidising special purpose housing to health and social service budgets' (Study Team Report 1986: 67).[23]

Such negotiations are now under way, and the federal government is in the process of phasing out elements of the special-needs program. Emergency and transitional housing, including shelters for the homeless, are to be transferred to the Canada Assistance Plan over a five-year period. The consequences of this shift are more than financial. It also represents a decentralization in policy control since, as discussed earlier, the Canada Assistance Plan is a more flexible instrument than the global agreements, placing far fewer conditions on the exercise of provincial discretion. Current changes are firmly consolidating provincial and municipal responsibility for policies relating to homelessness, bringing with them all of the strengths and weaknesses of decentralization.

The framework of political institutions constitutes a hidden influence on the policies of contemporary government. The imprint of a particular set of institutions is seldom sufficiently visible to generate intense public interest, and constitutional patterns can be as important as many of the more dramatic clashes of personalities, ideologies, and interests that dominate the public stage. Institutions do not by themselves determine policy outcomes but they do constitute a filter that shapes the play of contending economic and political forces.

Throughout the post-war era, the social housing sector has been shaped and reshaped by repeated shifts in federal/provincial relations. The post-war dominance of the federal level was challenged by increasingly active provincial governments, and two decades of occasionally intense conflict produced an accommodation in the form of the new global agreements, which retain a federal role in policy but decentralize the delivery of major social housing programs. Intergovernmental relations have also alternated between unilateral and joint programming. Unilateral federal action in the 1940s gave way to joint action through conditional grants in the 1950s and 1960s, which was supplemented by competitive unilateralism in the 1970s, which in turn gave way to joint planning in the 1980s.

This evolving regime of federal/provincial relations has been important to social housing. The historically strong role of the federal government has shaped the amount of social housing; the diversity of programs, delivery mechanisms, and beneficiary groups; and the distribution of social housing subsidies across the regions. At the same time, however, centralization of social housing undoubtedly made co-ordination with other relevant social service programs, which were under provincial control, more difficult.

Changes between unilateral and joint programs, in contrast, have important implications for flexibility, co-ordination, and openness. On the one hand, unilateralism preserves maximum flexibility for experimentation and greater openness to outside groups, but cannot ensure the integration of social housing programs operated at two levels. On the other hand, the consequences of joint action represent the obverse of unilateralism. Conflicting objectives are co-ordinated in meetings rather than played out in independent policies, but the policy process is inevitably slower and more cumbersome.

The new global agreements establish a new blend among these enduring cost and benefits. Whether co-ordinated policy and decentralized delivery is a stable combination remains to be seen. The history of Canadian federalism suggests that stability is an illusive goal, and that the balance between governments will continue to evolve. It is certain, however, that social housing policy will be hammered out in federal/provincial meetings held behind closed doors in elegant buildings located only blocks away from the tenements, hostels, and projects sheltering Canada's poor and homeless.

NOTES

1 See *CMHC v. Coop. College Residence Inc.* (1975) 13 ER (2d) 394 (Ont. CA); also Scott and Lederman (1972).
2 Until the constitutional reforms of 1982, the spending power also provided

the basis for the unconditional equalization payments to provincial governments.

3 Many of the early activities of the federal government as a mortgage lender of last resort and provider of mortgage insurance arose out of the federal responsibility for banking.

4 The dual nature of St Laurent's opposition to public housing is reflected in the observation attributed to him that subsidized housing was 'unconstitutional and a threat to democracy' (House of Commons, Debates, 1948, vol. II [15 March 1949], 1492).

5 The expectation that the amendments would stimulate municipal activity is clear in the speech of the minister responsible for housing during second reading of the bill in Parliament (House of Commons, Debates, 1964, vol. IV [28 May 1964], 3717; see also Dennis and Fish 1972: 14; CMHC 1970: 22, 26; and Feldman 1963).

6 By far the best source on this period is Streich 1985.

7 The first major expression of this growing opposition to large-scale public housing projects came in the report of the Hellyer Task Force (Task Force on Housing and Urban Development 1969). The critique was to be reinforced a few years later by the Dennis Report (Dennis and Fish 1972).

8 The key organizations are the Cooperative Housing Foundation of Canada and the Canadian Association of Housing and Renewal Officials (CAHRO), which publishes the magazine Canadian Housing and incorporates many officials in the non-profit sector, especially public non-profit corporations.

9 Such a transfer of tax points involves the federal government lowering its tax rates and the provinces raising their tax rates by the same amount at the same time, thereby diverting revenue from federal to provincial coffers.

10 See Streich 1985. Ouellet replied vigorously that the Quebec Housing Corporation was responsible for the slow progress on social housing, pointing to its long-standing failure to complete all of the housing authorized by CMHC. The Quebec Housing Corporation, he insisted, was 'an elephant that moves at a turtle's pace' (ibid.: 121).

11 The 1983 CMHC evaluation, which calculated that only 21 per cent of the occupants of non-profit housing were poor, sparked widespread media coverage and contributed to a growing polarization of debate over the appropriate role of social housing. (For a critique, see Manchee 1984.) The Nielsen study was even more critical, concluding that 'the record of current programs in meeting social housing needs is dismal' (Study Team Report 1986: 39).

12 See the statement by the federal minister, Bill McKnight, and the responses of opposition critics in House of Commons, Debates, first session, vol. VI (12 December 1985), 9432–8; see also Canada 1985b.

13 Ontario's preference for socially integrated projects is deeply rooted in the local political objections to large public housing projects established in the province during the early post-war era. The federal decision in 1985 to target federal social housing dollars exclusively on core housing needs therefore posed a bigger problem for Ontario than for other provinces.

14 After the announcement of the new approach in the House of Commons, the Liberal housing critic Sheila Copps observed that 'we have just found out today that a minister is quite prepared, like Pontius Pilate, to wash his hands of the issue of social housing for Canadians' (House of Commons, *Debates*, vol. VI [12 December 1985], 9434; see also her comments in *Canadian Housing* 3, no. 5 [1986–7]: 18).

15 See, for example, the comments sprinkled through the proceedings of the symposium on the new programs held by the Canadian Association of Housing and Renewal Officials (as reprinted in *Canadian Housing* 3, no. 5 [1986–7]).

16 Shortly after signing the global agreements, Saskatchewan decided to reduce its housing commitments as part of an austerity drive. As a result, it withdrew from the delivery of several smaller programs, retaining only the basic housing and rent-supplement programs.

17 See, for example, 'Social Housing 1987' in Canadian Association of Housing and Renewal Officials (1987).

18 The next few paragraphs are drawn from Banting 1985a.

19 Goldblatt 1987. The fears of the co-operative movement were exacerbated in the midst of negotiations over the new global agreements by the leak of a BC cabinet document that suggested that the province would channel all the federal dollars into shelter allowances. The active BC co-operative movement was particularly distressed (*Globe and Mail* 15 July 1988).

20 For estimates of the size of the interregional redistribution that results, see Banting 1987, ch. 6.

21 It is possible to argue that the federal government is likely to develop social housing programs that are more vertically redistributive as well. As the government most distant from local resistance to traditional public housing, Ottawa may be politically freer to insist on targeting social housing expenditures on low-income individuals. The historical record is mixed, however. Public housing in the early period of federal dominance was certainly a low-income program; and in recent years federal authorities have been leading the drive for targeting on 'core housing need.' In other periods, however, the federal government has shared – and in some cases led – the reaction against this approach. In 1969, for example, the Hellyer task force vigorously articulated the objections to the traditional concept of public housing (CMHC 1969).

22 The classic instance of this pattern is pensions policy. See Banting 1985b.
23 A similar issue concerns housing subsidies to social assistance recipients in social housing. If the cost was borne through CAP rather than through the social housing legislation, the cost to the federal government would be reduced (Study Team Report 1986: 60).

REFERENCES

Banting, Keith. 1985a. 'Federalism and Income Security: Themes and Variations.' In *Ottawa and the Provinces: The Distribution of Money and Power*, vol. 1, ed. T. Courchene, D.W. Conklin, and G.C. Cook. Toronto: Ontario Economic Council
– 1985b. 'Institutional Conservatism: Federalism and Pension Reform.' In *Canadian Social Welfare Policy: Federal and Provincial Dimensions*, ed. J. Ismael. Kingston and Montreal: McGill-Queen's University Press
– 1987. *The Welfare State and Canadian Federalism.* 2nd ed. Kingston and Montreal: McGill-Queen's University Press
– 1988. 'Federalism, Social Reform and the Spending Power.' *Canadian Public Policy* 14, supplement: 81–92
Birch, Anthony. 1955. *Federalism, Finance and Social Legislation in Canada, Australia and the United States.* Oxford: Clarendon Press
Cameron, David. 1978. 'The Expansion of the Public Economy: A Comparative Analysis.' *American Political Science Review* 72: 1243–61
Canada. 1944. *Report of the Advisory Committee on Reconstruction.* Vol. IV (Curtis Report). Ottawa
– 1969a. *Federal-Provincial Grants and the Spending Power of Parliament: Working Paper on the Constitution.* Ottawa: Queen's Printer
– 1969b. *Report of the Task Force on Housing and Urban Development* (Hellyer Report). Ottawa
– 1979. *The Relationship between Social Policy and Housing Policy: A Federal Perspective.* Ottawa
– 1985a *Consultation Paper on Housing.* Ottawa
– 1985b. *A National Direction for Housing Solutions.* Ottawa
Castles, F.; and McKinlay, R.D. 1979. *Democratic Politics and Policy Outcomes.* Milton Keynes: Open University Press
CMHC (Canada Mortgage and Housing Corporation). 1970. *Housing in Canada, 1946–1970.* A Supplement in the 25th Annual Report of Central Mortgage and Housing Corporation. Ottawa
– 1979a. *Report of the Task Force on Canada Mortgage and Housing Corporation* (Matthews Report). Ottawa
– 1979b. *Evaluation of the Neighbourhood Improvement Program, National*

Housing Act. Ottawa: Neighbourhood and Residential Improvement Division

– 1983. *Section 56.1 Non-Profit and Cooperative Housing Program Evaluation*. Ottawa

Dennis, Michael; and Fish, Susan. 1972. *Programs in Search of a Policy: Low Income Housing in Canada*. Toronto: Hakkert

Federal-Provincial-Territorial Conference of Ministers of Housing. 1985. Communiqué. Calgary, 4 July 1985

Feldman, Lionel. 1963. 'A Housing Project Wends Its Weary Way.' *Canadian Public Administration* 6: 221–32

Goldblatt, Mark. 1987. 'Some Observations on the 1986 Federal Cooperative Housing Program.' Paper presented to the 1987 Annual Meeting of the Canadian Association of Housing and Renewal Officials. Ottawa

Health and Welfare Canada. 1985. *Notes on Welfare Services under the Canada Assistance Plan*. Ottawa

Holland, Stuart. 1976. *Capital versus the Regions*. New York: St Martin's Press

Hum, Derek. 1983. *Federalism and the Poor*. Toronto: Ontario Economic Council

Interprovincial Task Force on Future Fiscal Arrangements for Housing. 1980. *Report*. Edmonton: Housing and Public Works Department, Government of Alberta

Johnson, A.W. 1985. *Giving Greater Point and Purpose to the Federal Financing of Post-Secondary Education and Research in Canada*. Ottawa: Secretary of State

Lithwick, Harvey. 1970. *Urban Canada: Problems and Prospects*. Ottawa: Central Mortgage and Housing Corporation

Manchee, Rod. 1984. 'Evaluating Federal Non-Profit Housing Programs.' *Perception* 8, no. 1 (September–October): 26–8

Marsh, Leonard. 1943. *Report on Social Security*. Ottawa: King's Printer

Milne, David. 1986. *Tug of War: Ottawa and the Provinces under Trudeau and Mulroney*. Toronto: James Lorimer

Myrdal, Gunnar. 1957. *Rich Lands and Poor*. New York: Harper and Row

Ontario. 1988. *Ontario Budget 1988*. Toronto: Queen's Printer

– Ministry of Housing. 1987. 'Hosek and Sweeney Launch Initiatives to Address Homelessness.' News Release, 17 December 1987

Parliamentary Task Force on Federal-Provincial Fiscal Arrangements. 1981. *Fiscal Federalism in Canada*. Ottawa: Minister of Supply and Services

Quebec. 1963. *Report of the Study Committee on Public Assistance*. Quebec: Editeur officiel

– 1971. *Report of the Commission of Inquiry on Health and Social Welfare*. Quebec: Editeur officiel

Rose, Albert. 1980. *Canadian Housing Policies: 1935–1980*. Toronto: Butterworths

Schofield, Josephine. 1983. 'The Politics of Welfare: Canada's Road to Social Security, 1914–1939.' PhD diss., University of British Columbia

Scott, Frank; and Lederman, William. 1972. 'A Memorandum Concerning Housing, Urban Development and the Constitution of Canada.' *Plan Canada* 12: 33–44

Société d'habitation du Québec. 1987. 'Housing for the Homeless and for Special Needs: Call for Proposals.' Montreal and Quebec City

Splane, Richard. 1985. 'Social Welfare Development in Alberta: The Federal-Provincial Interplay.' In *Canadian Social Welfare Policy: Federal and Provincial Dimensions*, ed. J. Ismael. Kingston and Montreal: McGill-Queen's University Press

Statistics Canada. 1988. *National Income and Expenditure Accounts: Annual Estimates 1976–1987*. Ottawa. Minister of Supply and Services

Streich, Patricia. 1985. 'Canadian Housing Affordability Policies in the 1970s.' Kingston: PhD diss., Queen's University

Study Team Report to the Task Force on Program Review (Nielsen). 1986. *Housing*. Ottawa: Minister of Supply and Services

Teron, William. 1981. 'The Management View of Restraint.' In *The Politics and Management of Restraint in Government*, ed. P. Aucoin. Montreal: Institute for Research and Public Policy

Western Premiers' Task Force Report on Consititutional Trends. 1977. *Report*. Tabled at the 18th Annual Premiers' Conference, St Andrew's, NB

Wilensky, Harold. 1975. *The Welfare State and Inequality*. Berkeley: University of California Press

Wilson, D.A.M. 1988. 'Address to the Symposium of the Institute of Urban Studies and Housing.' Winnipeg

LANGLEY KEYES

6 The Private-Sector Role in Low-Income Housing

This chapter analyses the role of the private sector in providing housing for low-income households in the context of the housing markets and institutional constructs of the United States. In examining the potential of private developers, landlords, and financial institutions to provide shelter for people of low income in existing and newly developed housing, it explores four major categories of inquiry.

First: What is the nature of the present low-income housing problem? To what extent do homelessness and the threat of homelessness represent new phenomena in the annals of low-income housing crises? Who are the homeless and to what degree is their problem solely one of access to permanent shelter?

Second: What has been the experience of the private-sector/low-income nexus since the start of the New Deal in 1932 in the United States when the federal government first became involved in housing issues? In what way is past experience useful in framing the present private-sector role?

Third: How is the housing market perceived by the private sector, i.e., what are the constraint and opportunity areas that motivate and discourage the involvement of the private sector, particularly with regard to the low-income issue? In other words, what is the lens through which the private sector views its activity?

Fourth: How can the private-housing sector interact with the two other sectors relevant to the housing world – third sector and government – to provide affordable housing for low-income people? What are the possibilities for a 'synergistic relationship' among the three sectors?

Analysing these four issue areas and their interrelationship is a productive way of focusing on the potential and limitations of the private-sector role in shelter provision for low-income households. Given that the analysis addresses these questions as they apply to the United States and that the book for which it is written is concerned with Canada, a central task is to structure a general framework of analysis that can provide a useful heuristic device for consideration of the Canadian experience. The focus, then, is less on facts and figures as they apply to the United States and more on the mode of analysis and policy formulation which that experience evokes.

The four issue areas could be used equally well to organize inquiry into the housing situation in Canada or the United States. The questions posed in each are addressed with respect to Canada in several other chapters in this book, especially chapter 3 on the urban housing market. Although it is true there are many differences between Canada and the United States – for example, there are different attitudes to the role of government, and the cut-backs in federal housing assistance have been more severe in the United States – there are fundamental similarities as well. A basic cause of housing problems for people in both countries is lack of income, exacerbated by gentrification, deinstitutionalization, and the feminization of poverty (see chapters 2 and 3). These similarities are sufficient that the framework of this chapter could be applied to Canada, and that the examples of private/public partnerships could be applied in Canada.

Before exploring the four categories of inquiry, it is important to set out operating definitions of the actors in the housing development and management process. This book has framed the discussion around the roles of three critical sets of actors: the private, public, and third sectors.

THE THREE ACTORS IN THE HOUSING DEVELOPMENT PROCESS

The Private Sector

The private sector is made up of the developers, owners, and financiers in the housing field who operate from the profit motive. Although there are often other reasons for their being involved in housing – the desire to build a physical product, the love of 'deal making,' an inherited business – these actors are in the trade because generally it is financially a better choice than an alternative one for using their energy and money. From one perspective, the sole factor that unites these diverse parties is the profit motive, for their roles vary greatly as a function of the segment of the housing market in which they have chosen to stake their claim.

Given the range, size, and mission of organizations involved on the private side of the housing agenda, it is almost a misnomer to place them all under one heading. Central-city resident landlords of small buildings have more in common with their tenants than they do with the huge private developers who deal in high finance and negotiations with public actors. Organizations involved in financing housing can quickly shift their interest from residential construction to other commodities where the returns are higher. The housing construction business is characterized by easy entry and exit. A hammer, a strong back, and the necessary zoning put a person in the business. Although housing is unique among consumer goods in its utilization of capital, it doesn't take much to capitalize a small producer or owner.

The Public Sector

The public sector consists of governmental units at three levels: federal, state, and local. At each of these levels, government has three potential roles by which to affect the development and management of housing: (1) regulation, (2) support, and (3) subsidy. In its *regulatory* role government establishes what Lawrence Friedman has called 'negative legislation'[1] establishing laws and regulations governing the physical quality of residential structures. In its *support* role government helps to bulwark the elements of the private housing production system. In its *subsidy* role government provides financial resources to make housing available to people who would not otherwise be able to afford it. How that subsidy is channelled and to whom – the government itself, the non-profit sector, or the private sector – is a continuing issue of debate. Historically, there have been significant shifts among the levels of government in utilizing each of these devices, a point explored in some detail later on.

The Third Sector

There is only a limited tradition in the United States of non-profit sponsorship of housing. Tax-exempt organizations involved in the production and maintenance of housing have emerged since 1960 as a significant force in the housing field, although the third sector comes nowhere near its European counterpart.

The third sector for housing production is made up of community-development corporations, other non-profit housing service and production organizations, and the support entities that provide technical assistance and financing to them. Its advocates argue that the non-profit movement represents the wave of the future in terms of low-income units – the only way to 'decommodify' housing for poor people. Other observers are less euphoric. They recognize the significant role that non-profit organizations can play, but they see that role as limited and consistently dependent on a close working relationship with both the public and the private sector.

THE LOW-INCOME HOUSING MARKET AND THE HOMELESS

The Nature of the Current Low-Income Housing Market

The current phenomenon of homelessness in the United States is a dramatic indication that the housing market is not working for people at the low end of the income scale. The private housing market has always been problematic for this group. Effective market demand – the ability of the household to pay for shelter – has historically intersected the housing supply curve at a point below the threshold of a socially acceptable standard of housing. The gap between what the private housing market has been able to provide for effective market demand and the level of housing need based on acceptable physical standards and affordable cost has always constituted the arena for public or non-profit intervention.

From the perspective of a housing market analyst taking a long view of housing policy, the critical question to ask about the current housing plight of the poor as symbolized by homelessness is: In what way is the situation quantitatively and qualitatively different from the perennial housing problem of low-income people? Is the homeless issue simply the most recent formulation, the idea in good currency, of a long-standing problem – that of providing adequate housing for people who can't make it in the private market? Or is there something unique about the current situation that differentiates it from past crises? At the risk of truncating a complex set of issues, one can summarize the arguments from 'business as usual' and 'singular crisis' as follows.

The business-as-usual position argues that although there are some interesting and perhaps unique factors behind the current crisis of homelessness – the failure of deinstitutionalization, the feminization of poverty, and the decline in the stock of 'bad housing' – the central issue confronting low-income households remains one of income, the inability to pay for private shelter. If the households on the street are simply the tip of the homeless iceberg, then the theme becomes the familiar one of how to provide standard housing for people who cannot compete in the private market. 'Homelessness' as a proxy for all low-income households with shelter problems is simply the current formulation of the central issue of housing policy in the United States: how to bridge the gap between housing need as measured by some normative standard and effective market demand, the ability to command housing resources in the market-place.

The singular-crisis position focuses on the differences between the housing issues facing today's homeless and potentially homeless and the traditional challenge of providing housing for low-income people. Several of these differences are a consequence of the particular characteristic of today's housing market. Others are related to the changes in public policy that impinge on the housing needs of the poor.

The housing problem of low-income people has shifted from one of shelter adequacy to one of affordability. No matter how one slices the statistics it is clear that the poor are paying more for shelter in 1989 as a percentage of their income than at any time in recent memory. 'Since 1975, rental cost increases have outpaced increases in income by 11 percent. Real incomes actually have declined an average of 4 percent for the poorest fifth of households. As a result, the "rent burden" ... rose from a median of 48 percent in 1978 to 58 percent in 1983 among renters with incomes below $10,000 (in 1983 dollars) ... Of renters with less than $7000 income in 1983, more than half paid at least 60 percent of income for rent' (National Governors' Association 1986: 5).

At the same time that affordability, rather than physical adequacy, has become the central issue, the amount of physically inadequate housing, i.e., low-rent housing, has declined during the past two decades. Urban renewal and highway building levelled a good deal of substandard stock during the sixties. The phenomenon of housing abandonment that raced through major cities in the early 1970s resulted in more structures at the low end of the quality scale falling to the wrecker's ball. Gentrification in the late 1970s and 1980s upgraded areas that had been bypassed by urban renewal and code enforcement. Single-room occupancy units (SRO) were reconverted to single-family condominiums. Thus, low-rent stock filtered up or out of the market. Either way, the units were no longer available to low-income people.

In comparing the business-as-usual and singular-crisis positions, I conclude that rents escalating well above the rate of inflation, the demise of old substandard stock, the disappearance of rooming-houses, and the gentrification of urban neighbourhoods represent qualitative shifts in the urban housing market. The perennial issue of housing need outstripping effective market demand has been ratchetted up to a singular level of urgency by the restructuring of many of the nation's housing markets.

That market structure has been exacerbated by three significant social and policy trends: (1) the rising poverty gap and the feminization of poverty; (2) the unmet promise of deinstitutionalization; and (3) cut-backs in federal housing programs.

The Poverty Gap and the Feminization of Poverty
Although inflation has abated and the economy has been on a five-year roll, a percentage of the population has significantly less housing buying power than it did a decade ago. Several aspects of national and state policy intersect to make this the case. Five and one-half million people work at or below the minimum wage, which is set by statute and has been the same since January 1981. A person working full time at the $3.35 hourly wage earns $6968 a year – substantially less than the poverty level for a family of four, which was roughly $11,000 in 1985.[2] Minimum wage buys one very little in the housing market. Operating on the traditional 25 per cent of income, a family dependent on one minimum-wage earner should pay about $150 a month for rent, a figure approximately half the national median rent in 1983.

Demographic shifts, marriage patterns, and eased divorce laws have combined to plunge a group of families – single women with children – into the ranks of the very poor. The feminization of poverty is a stark reality of the late 1980s.

Deinstitutionalization
The chronically mentally ill (CMI) who once resided behind institutional walls must now fend for themselves in the private housing markets of the nation's cities. Often lacking the support system to cope with the most fundamental aspects of independent living, let alone the complex challenges of a tightening housing market, many of the deinstitutional-ized or never-institutionalized are adrift on the streets.

Cut-backs in Federal Housing Programs
During the Reagan administration, the role of the federal government in the housing field underwent a major transformation. The Department of Housing and Urban Development (HUD) was no longer the leading public actor in the effort to make decent housing available to those who could not afford it in the market-place. Rather than struggling with the complexities of the low-income housing issue, the administration

moved to the sidelines. The diffusion of the national housing coalition, a sophisticated set of arguments limiting the federal role in the housing process, a temporarily soft rental market at the lower end of the spectrum in the late 1970s, and a costly federal supply-side subsidy program converged to give the Reagan administration an 'open season' on federal housing programs when it took over the White House in 1981.

The Reagan revolution has had a profound impact on housing and community development. Armed with the arguments of thoughtful critics of the federal housing system as it existed in 1980, a political mandate, a weakened housing coalition, and a compliant HUD secretary, the Reagan administration worked hard to remove the federal government from a central role in housing policy and expenditures. It was extremely successful in so doing.

For example, commitments of federal subsidized housing units of all kinds were down to less than 100,000 by fiscal 1987 compared to 363,000 in 1977. Budget authority for HUD, which accounted for 7.4 per cent of the total federal budget authority in fiscal 1978, was proposed by the administration for less than 1 per cent for 1988 (National Association of Home Builders/Realtors/Bankers Assn 1987: 4).

The reordering of national priorities from social programs to national defence, the devolution of housing responsibility to state and local governments, privatization, deregulation, and tax reform and reduction have produced a situation in which 'housing policy has suffered in the debate over the proper size and functions of the federal government, and on how the federal government should relate to state and local governments and to the private sector in meeting the needs of society' (ibid.).

This quotation is taken not from the literature of low-income housing advocacy groups but rather from the recently published 'Towards a National Housing Policy,' developed by the National Association of Home Builders, the National Association of Realtors, and the Mortgage Bankers Association of America, all mainstream private-sector housing interest groups.

Homelessness and the threat of homelessness, and the declining real incomes of low-income households, represent more than business as usual for the nation's poor. Chapter 3 reaches the same conclusion that it is not business as usual in Canada, and for basically all the same reasons.

Who Are the Homeless?
To analyse the role that the private sector can play in dealing with the

homeless and those at risk of being homeless, it is important to understand not only why there is pressure on the low end of the nation's housing markets but also the characteristics of those households who occupy the ranks of the homeless and near homeless. The changing nature of the market helps explain why there is a problem at present. The characteristics of the homeless indicate the degree to which permanent shelter per se can solve the problem. The distinctions among homeless individuals and households critical for the private market can be captured in the following terms: the economic homeless, the situational homeless, the chronic homeless, and the hidden homeless.

The *economic homeless* are those households that are out in the street simply because they cannot find an affordable place to live. They lack the economic resources, nothing more. They are victims of a tightening housing market. Their lives may be in turmoil and that turmoil is a function of being without a home. This category – generally, but by no means always – consists of female-headed households and has been dubbed the 'new homeless.'

The *situational homeless* is a category made up of households that are without permanent shelter because they are fleeing from some dangerous or traumatic situation: a battering husband, abusing parents, or personal disorganization renders them incapable of managing the demands of finding and maintaining housing. Short on skills, long on hard times and disordered lives, such households require a supportive environment in which to gather their resources and sort out their lives so as to become sufficiently independent to 'make it' in the housing market.

The distinction between the situational and the economic homeless is not always clear-cut and is often the basis for debate.[3]

The *chronic homeless* category is made up, for the most part, of individuals (rather than families) who because of substance abuse, drug or alcohol addiction, or chronic mental illness are unable to organize themselves in the housing market without support. The category also includes bag-ladies and vagrants – often disoriented individuals – who always have been described as 'street people.' These are people for whom housing is not enough, even in the long run.

There is much debate about the distribution of the homeless population among the three categories described above. Several years ago the 'news' was that 'many of the homeless people wandering the streets of American cities and crowding into emergency shelters are mentally ill' (Bassuk 1984: 40). Shortly thereafter the 'new homeless' were discovered: intact families who found themselves on the street for the first time priced out of even the worst rental units (Karlen et al. 1986: 20). Recently, Ellen Bassuk's study of households living in shelters in Massachusetts has highlighted 'the breakdown of the family,' the homeless children with battered mothers that I have called the situational homeless (Bassuk 1985).

Although the distribution varies from city to city, there is increasing recognition that any homeless population is likely to have elements of all three categories. From a housing perspective, the critical issue in any given market area is knowing the distribution of the local homeless among the categories and, therefore, the degree to which housing is the entire or only partial solution to the problem at hand.

The *hidden homeless* are households 'at risk' of becoming homeless. Including this group broadens the definition of homeless to encompass the households whose accommodations may be upgraded to a condominium, whose rent may soar, or who may become unable to continue the strain of doubling up with family or friends. The magnitude of households on the edge of homelessness varies from city to city. Perhaps the best indicator of the potential scale is the housing vacancy rate. In 'hot' real-estate markets in the country – New York City, most of Massachusetts, and San Francisco – the submerged part of the homeless iceberg runs deep and wide. The 1983 Annual Housing Survey estimates that there are 6.3 million households in the nation paying more than 50 per cent of their income for rent. Thousands of those families must be on the edge of disaster. Stemming the tide of the homeless requires that those 'at risk' of being on the street be kept in their place in the market, however difficult the circumstances of their current situation. This characterization of the homeless is consistent with the continuum of housing problems set out in chapter 2, but further refines the classification of the homeless at the extreme end of the continuum. This refinement is applicable to Canada as well.

THE HISTORIC ROLE OF THE PRIVATE SECTOR IN THE PROVISION OF LOW-INCOME HOUSING

Before examining how the private sector currently regards the low-income housing issue, it is important to frame a longer view of how 'the privates' have dealt with the issue in the past and how public policy has influenced that involvement.

Although I have argued for the singular nature of the current crisis, it must be emphasized that from a policy perspective the challenge remains the same: how to bridge the gap between effective market demand and housing need, the financial distance between what the private market produces and what low-income people can pay for. In exploring the current role of the private sector in dealing with low-income housing, I will deal first with the historical interaction of the private- and public-sector's response to the low-income housing issue in the United States. (Where we go from here is certainly not inexorably determined by where we have been, but one ignores history at one's peril.)

It must be emphasized that most low-income people in the United States do not live in public or subsidized private housing. Unlike in European countries, the public and non-profit housing sectors in the United States are a minor part of the overall housing equation. Although subsidized units in private developments have been expanded significantly during the past decade (and in fact constitute the Reagan administration's primary means of housing low-income families), most poor people do not benefit from these subsidies and must rely on the extent to which their wages or welfare cheque can compete successfully for shelter in the private market. Thus, in Massachusetts, roughly 33 per cent of the households on Aid to Families with Dependent Children (AFDC) that are low income by definition live in subsidized units of any kind. The private sector, without public subsidy, remains the largest provider of housing for people of low income.

The relationship between the private sector and the public on housing issues was very much a local affair until the coming of the New Deal in the 1930s. That local interaction focused on the regulatory model: i.e., an emerging public construct that limited what private housing developers could build and how they could manage. The presumption of reformers at the turn of the century was that enlightened housing codes and zoning regulations would bend the private market to accommodate low-income people in physically adequate housing. Many who laboured on the great code battle of the progressive era came to an alternative conclusion: that regulation was not enough because the private sector would never of its own volition build decent housing for low-income people. The needs/demand gap was simply too great.

Early in the twentieth century, housing's equivalent of Cartesian dualism emerged; it was the view that 'the publics' had to handle the poor and 'the privates' could deal only with the market. Housing reformers looked to European models of state-built housing or third-sector developers as the mode by which low-income people would be provided with affordable and physically adequate shelter. When public housing finally passed the US Congress in 1937, it was only after great struggles with the private sector, which saw in its emergence the Red tide of socialism.

With the arrival of public housing, the reformers who had fought for decades finally felt that public policy with regard to housing the poor had entered the age of enlightenment. However, the euphoria was not to last.

For the thirty-year period from the start of the New Deal in 1932 to the coming of the Great Society in 1960, a sharp division existed in the housing world between the public and the private sectors. The public sector led by the federal government was responsible for providing publicly owned units through local housing authorities. Under attack by an increasingly conservative Congress during the 1950s, the once idealistic and energetic public housing program became beleaguered and involved in a 'dreary deadlock' with the private sector.[4]

The public/private polarization was overcome during the 1960s in two significant ways. First, Washington hit upon the idea of getting private developers to build and manage private housing that would be publicly subsidized so as to bring rents down to a level affordable for low-income people. For the next twenty years, each successive federal administration worked to find ways of maximizing the cost effectiveness of supply-side subsidies to the private sector and thereby harnessing them to the needs of the low-income population. Second, public housing was transformed by legislative changes from a public production program to one that relied upon the private sector to build and manage developments and that used public subsidies to lease units from private developers. Public housing became, then, a financing formula for both supply- and demand-side subsidies channelled to the private as well as the public sector.

The 1960s was also the decade in which the third sector emerged as a major actor on the housing scene. Its relationship with the other two sectors is complex, often encouraging, never more so than at present.

Throughout the twenty-year period from 1960 to 1980, the relationship between the private and public sectors took on many permutations as efforts were made to find the most cost-effective way of utilizing public subsidies and the support and regulation needed to involve the private sector in housing low-income people.

From 1932 to 1980, while debates abounded on how the federal government should engage in the housing business and how it should work with the private sector, bipartisan political support existed for the federal government as the key public actor in the housing field. The high-water mark of federal commitment to the goals of the 1949 Housing Act – of a decent home and suitable living environment for every American – was the landmark housing legislation of 1968, the Magna Carta of federal housing involvement. That bill created two new major subsidy programs, one for rental and the other for home ownership; it expanded the public housing program that Washington promised would solve the low-income housing problem through a series of 'top-down' federal initiatives.

The evangelical enthusiasm of 1968 was dampened by the Nixon administration's housing production moratorium in 1973. Responding to criticism, scandals surrounding several of the programs, and warnings about future program costs, President Nixon declared time out for reappraisal.

However, the flow of federal housing funds did not stop in 1973. A deep subsidy, private supply-side initiative called Section 8 emerged from this period of re-evaluation. The program provided federal subsidy for both capital and operating costs of new and rehabilitated housing for low-income households. But enthusiasm had diminished for 'solving' the low-income housing problem by the production of units subsidized by the federal government. Increasingly, researchers argued that the 'housing problem' was an affordability issue and as such could be better handled by demand-side efforts than by supply-side subsidies to private housing developers. A housing allowance experiment surfaced in the wake of the 1973 moratorium as the first federal demand-side subsidy to low-income tenants in private housing.

While there was a sustained federal effort to produce subsidized units during the Carter administration, the intellectual and political climate was being set for the Reagan administration's assault on the federal role in housing. John Weicher (1980: 159) is among the critics of the housing policy of the 1960s and 1970s who argued that the housing problem essentially had been solved, with the exception of some tough pockets, and that those spots that remained would be remedied 'from rising incomes rather than from governmental programs.'

The national housing coalition, with membership ranging from public housing and non-profit advocates to developers and bankers, never regrouped after the 1973 moratorium. Two other factors paved the way for the Reagan administration's retreat from long-standing national housing policies. The Section 8 program turned out to be very expensive and far too easy a mark for profit-making developers. In addition, high vacancy rates in low-rent private housing stock in many of the nation's housing markets meant that a demand-side strategy (i.e., subsidizing private rental units) made sense.

Federal policies during the past seven years have focused on removing the federal government from the housing business. Leasing units from private producers has taken on a variety of forms – vouchers, certificates, allowances – but the approach is essentially similar: housing should be viewed as an income problem and private rents subsidized to raise the purchasing power of the low-income household. The result has been token funding for some of the poor for a limited time only.

Throughout the period from the New Deal to the present, a central concern of housing policy-makers has been to find ways of ensuring a steady supply of 'reasonably priced' financing for housing production and ownership. The Federal Housing Administration and the Veterans' Administration made it possible for moderate-income people to buy into the ownership market. The secondary mortgage market made possible by a variety of federally inspired initiatives ensured that mortgages could be bought and sold like any other form of financial paper, thus ensuring – with the exception of some rural areas – a uniform flow of capital across the country for housing. But the engine of private finance has never been a vehicle that has helped the poor directly. Without subsidy – direct or indirect – the world of private finance has focused on housing demand as defined by the market, not housing need as defined by policy-makers. However, when layered on top of private financing vehicles, public subsidies make it possible for low-income households to benefit from housing financed by private institutions. Certainly, public financing undertaken by state housing finance agencies for private rental and ownership has benefited from the sophisticated financial infrastructure that is currently in place.

With the federal withdrawal of subsidies, the states have come to the fore. The public/private partnerships that have emerged at the state and local levels provide much optimism for the capacity of the three sectors to work productively on the low-income issue, particularly if the federal government were to re-emerge in a leadership role.

The National Association of Home Builders (1986: 1) makes this point clear in its recent report:

[The National Association of Home Builders] ... approached this [study of low-income housing issues] believing that economic growth and the unfettered market can go far towards meeting most housing needs. Thus we have emphasized the importance of freeing housing markets from unnecessary regulatory burdens that boost housing costs. And we have urged the expansion of public/private partnerships that combine the creativity and resources of entrepreneurs, private foundations, and state and local government. We find, however, that the federal government still has an important role to play in housing many lower income people ... [federal] attention to housing problems is dictated both by established national housing goals and by the need to avoid social frictions stemming from housing difficulties.

Taking the long view of the interaction between the private and public sectors on the low-income housing issue, it is interesting that what began as polarization in the 1930s and became a synthesis in the 1960s has emerged in the late 1980s as a situation in which the 'privates' are pleading with the 'publics' and the federal government to get back into the business of worrying about low-income people, a reversal of historic roles.

Having passed national housing legislation for the first time in seven years in 1987, the US Congress, both the House and the Senate, is now looking at fundamental aspects of national housing policy: an evaluation of where the nation is and where national housing policy ought to be going in the post-Reagan era. At present, 'virtually no knowledgeable observer believes that the housing needs of the nation's poor are being met ... the arithmetic of the incipient crisis is plain to see. The nation's demand for low-cost housing is rising steadily ... but the supply of low-cost housing, both private and public, is going down at an ever-increasing rate' (*Newsweek*, 4 January 1988: 18).

What have we learned about the private-sector's role in the provision of housing to serve the nation's poor? What can be expected of that sector in helping to meet the 'arithmetic of the incipient crisis'? The debate has moved well beyond the polarization of the 1950s in which the public sector built for those with lowest incomes and the private sector built for everyone else. Today, the private sector is more than prepared to build for low-income households. But it wants deep subsidies to do so. The challenge is how to produce sufficient federal subsidy to pull the private sector in and provide low-income rents without 'breaking the bank' as the Section 8 program is seen to have done. Cost effectiveness and deep subsidy may be a contradiction in terms when applied to new production. The past seems to suggest the federal government should move into a private, subsidized production program with caution. Where it exists, such a program must pry loose local and state resources, both public and private. Moreover, housing should be built only in those areas where housing availability rather than affordability is the central issue. Where there are weak markets and numerous vacancies, long-term demand-side subsidies of the private stock are a legitimate means of sheltering low-income households.

The housing problem of low-income people has moved from being defined as one of standards to one of affordability. Federal policy in the past eight years has championed demand-side utilization of the private market to close the affordability gap. Yet there are problems. Demand-side subsidies carry restrictions that units remain available to the low-income tenants for a certain time period. When these restrictions lapse, there is a danger that the housing will fall out of the subsidized, i.e., low-income, sector and be recaptured by the market where rents will rise to meet the highest bidder. How to hang on to units in private subsidized developments becomes a challenge posed by the current state of the privately subsidized stock.

Critics of the private role in low-income housing production maintain that the conflict will always be there as long as subsidized housing is produced by the private sector, i.e., the desire on the part of the 'privates' to take the units and run. Spokespersons for the private sector maintain, however, that the issue is one of contract terms at the front end of the deal. If private owners understand that they have to maintain the subsidized housing as subsidized housing in perpetuity, they will discount their terms accordingly.

An increasing number of states and localities have come to focus on public/private partnerships for the production of low-income housing; it is clear, therefore, that if the federal government is once again to take a lead role in working with private sponsors of housing for low-income people, it will of necessity work in a governmental structure more locally based than was the case in the pre-Reagan days. Although national policy may set the parameters for the expenditure of federal dollars, much flexibility will be given to localities and states to work out their own programmatic initiatives.

There are creative efforts afoot. The challenge for the immediate future is to structure a role for the federal government that energizes the local public/private partnerships with financial incentives that stimulate an equitable, economic, and efficient response.

THE PRIVATE-SECTOR LENS OF ANALYSIS

How private-sector housing people view the low-income issue (i.e., the extent to which it is of concern to them) is a function of: (1) the segment of the market towards which they have geared their business; (2) their personal attitude and experience; (3) and the pressures and cues they receive from the public (and sometimes the third) sector with which they must interact as they go about the process of building or managing their product.

Market segment: Developers of luxury homes in an exclusive southern California suburb are not confronted on a daily basis with the issue of low-income families and how their product can be utilized by such families. Inner-city landlords who own several small rental properties in a racially and economically changing neighbourhood must, by definition, engage with the issue posed by renters of limited means.

Attitude and experience: Where in the system the private housing people operate is not the only consideration in determining involvement with poor people. Attitudes and experience are also relevant. Many of those in the development or the management end of the business view the low-income issue with fear and trembling: Low income is code for racial and social problems; low income means unpaid rent and damaged property, outraged neighbours, and problems with the local officials. Dealing with 'those people' means trouble, and it is best to avoid them. Conversely, there are private housing people who embrace low-rent housing as an issue with which they feel not only comfortable but also morally engaged. These individuals take pride in their ability to work with poor tenants and to integrate them into their developments. 'How to do well by doing good' is an adage with meaning to some people in the private sector.

In the real world, a spectrum of attitudes exists between these extremes. Most private housing people fall somewhere between confident affirmation of the low-income issue and persistent and dogmatic avoidance – with the balance tipped towards the avoidance end. Owners of low-rent, private rental property in the central city can be as negative about dealing with income-limited households as the luxury suburban builder can be.

For those in the private market confronting the homeless issue, low-income tenants become increasingly less desirable as they move from the 'economic' to the 'chronic' end of the homeless spectrum.

Private sponsors see themselves in the business of providing shelter for which they receive rent. To the extent that people need more than shelter (for example, services for abused women and the chronic mentally ill), the private sector sees the operation shifting away from their interests. There are, of course, private landlords who are comfortable dealing with people who have mental handicaps or are among the disorganized 'situational' homeless.[5] But other actors and social-service providers have to be involved, and the simplicity of a 'market solution' becomes complicated by the need for support systems sponsored by the public and third sectors.

Public pressure: Attitude alone is not the determining factor of whether or not a private housing person is involved with any of the homeless categories. The choice to deal with people of limited means may not be left entirely to the 'free will' of the developer or manager. The institutional and political world in which those who provide private housing must operate has a good deal to say about the extent to which the private housing world must confront the low-income challenge and the four categories of homelessness described earlier. The key to private involvement is very much determined by the interaction among the three sectors – particularly the private and public – on the low-income issue.

The private sector operates in a complex world that influences how and if it must confront the low-income segment of the housing market. Government, in all three of its roles – regulatory, support, and subsidy – shapes and challenges the 'privates' as they go about the business of building and managing housing in the market-place.

Developers or managers discover that embracing low-income tenants may be a necessary part of dealing with a state financing agency or municipal boards. For example, the Massachusetts Housing Finance Agency (MHFA) requires that 25 per cent of the units built with its resources must be dedicated to low-income households. If developers want access to the below-market interest rate offered by MHFA, they have to accept the low-income requirement. At times, when MHFA has been seen as the 'only financing game in town,' private developers have found themselves dealing with low-income rental units as a necessary part of getting access to capital.

A study of MHFA done in the early 1970s explored how the concept of MHFA's 'mixed-income' housing worked in practice. The conclusions confound the conventional wisdom that diverse social classes cannot share the same buildings. Life-styles across income were found to be remarkably similar. Moreover, developments with the highest level of tenant satisfaction at all income levels were those built by sponsors who had never dealt with low-income or subsidized development before becoming involved with MHFA. These so-called market-oriented developers geared their projects to the unsubsidized market and consequently were seen as running more desirable projects than were those developers who were described as 'subsidized' and who had normally focused their attention on a low-income clientele.

Municipalities have increasingly come to utilize zoning and permit granting as means of extracting low-income units from developers who would otherwise build solely for the market. Chapter 8 discusses the extent of such activities in Canada. Inclusionary zoning, linkage, and comprehensive permit-granting are examples of public imposition of low-income housing requirements on the private sector. From the developer's point of view, such requirements are costs of doing business and must be discounted like any other. Depending on how desirable the deal is from other perspectives, a developer may be willing to allocate units to poor households or to pay a fee for someone else to build low-income units.

Clearly such public pressure on the private sector is possible only in markets in which the developer sees significant financial returns despite public agencies 'hiving off' resources for low-income people. Thus, in Boston and San Francisco, two of the hottest real-estate markets in the United States at present, discussions of linkage and inclusionary zoning have a saliency that would not be generated (at least at the moment) in Houston or Detroit, where the residential real-estate market is flat on its back.

An important distinction exists between public requirements that private developers include low-income units within their developments for which they provide the subsidy through the internal manipulation of their *own* financing, and inclusionary policies that presume the subsidy for the low-income units will come from elsewhere (i.e., the public sector). When the subsidy comes from government, it has less financial impact on private developers (and thus presumably is more acceptable to them). As the federal government has pulled further back from the subsidized housing business, the availability of such funding has become more problematic in areas where the state government has not picked up the slack. Internal subsidies clearly cost the private sector more than subsidies provided by 'the publics' and therefore are viewed by for-profit developers with a suspicious eye in other than the most profitable markets.

Some actors in the private-development community see the imposition of low-income requirements on the part of localities as yet another of the hurdles erected by the public sector to make it difficult for the private sector to proceed. Other developers recognize the fact that, given the absence of deep federal subsidies, 'the internal subsidy' extracted by the local public sector is perhaps the only way newly constructed units can be made available to people with limited financial resources.

The public extraction of low-income units from private developers is a variation on the general theme of the requirements that localities impose on private developers as preconditions for building residential units. The role of government as regulator has become an increasingly problematic one for the private-development community. For many in that community, the issue of making new development affordable – perhaps not to low-income people but to people of modest income – is very much influenced by the extent to which local and state regulations ratchet up the cost of providing housing. From this perspective regulation means higher costs. Higher costs means that the window of opportunity for ownership and renting is narrowed. The dissatisfaction of the 'privates' with the public sector on the issue is well expressed by the National Association of Home Builders (1985: 85):

Just as some regulation has helped increase the quality of America's homes, it has also contributed to problems of housing affordability ...

The rising cost of land and site improvements is the most serious manifestation of the high cost of government regulation. In recent years only the cost of mortgage finance has increased more rapidly than that of a developed lot. In 1949, land and improvements comprised 11 percent of the price of a new single-family home: by 1982, it accounted for 24 percent.

In many of the nation's communities, developers looking at the housing development process increasingly find themselves involved in a complex set of negotiations with various boards and municipal officials. The name of the game from the developers' perspective is to maximize units built at as high a price as possible. From the public's perspective the task is both to decrease the number of units that developers are building and to make some of those units affordable by people of moderate, if not low, income.

From the perspective of low-income housing production, the critical issue becomes the way in which 'the publics' and the 'privates' negotiate the regulatory and requirement hoops: the trade-offs that are made and the ingenuity with which each side crafts its case. Local regulation becomes the basis for negotiation with developers in which regulatory barriers are lowered in exchange for low- or moderate-income units. The regulation/negotiation process, or 'reg/neg,' becomes a necessary element of the development process in which private developers must become expert in order to survive the local political environment and thus to construct housing that can turn a sufficient profit to keep them in the business (see Wheeler 1988).

When discussing 'the privates' and their attitude towards the low-income issue, and their interaction with the public and the third sectors, it is important not to focus solely on new housing production. Taken in the aggregate, new production by the private sector is the least likely source of low-income housing, particularly if there is no internal or external subsidy involved. New housing is by definition more costly than the existing stock, specifically the older existing stock. Despite repeated efforts to lower sale prices of housing (and some real success in lowering the actual cost of the physical shell), new production remains expensive. Making it affordable for moderate-income people without subsidy is itself a significant challenge; making it financially viable for those with very limited income is even more difficult.

It is important to point out that there is a major issue in the United States about the possibility of home ownership for moderate-income people, particularly for young first-time buyers. Home-ownership rates in the United States had increased steadily for thirty-five years prior to 1980. From 1980 through 1985, those rates have fallen every year for a total drop from 65.6 per cent to 64.1 per cent. Most of that decline is among people under the age of 34 (Apgar 1986: 6–7).

If private producers are a limited but important resource for low-income housing, one must look to the private owners and managers of existing market-rate housing as major actors in the process of housing low-income people. The critical issues here cluster around what incentives exist to keep owners in the business of providing housing, subsidized or otherwise, to people of low income in a rising market in which low-rent housing is filtering up.

In a buyer's market, in which there are many vacancies and little opportunity for owners to shift their investment, public devices for intervention into the private housing market can be creatively applied. Regulation and subsidy can combine to pressure owners to upgrade the physical quality of their buildings and still rent to low-income people.

Technical assistance to small owners can help them borrow funds at below-market interest rates or refinance their property so as to continue to rent to lower-income households. Subsidies are welcomed by owners who otherwise would not be able to find people to afford their upgraded units.

There is, then, a difference between the way private developers and owners of existing housing perceive the public sector that depends on the character of the market. In *hot* markets private developers are prepared to put up with increasing levels of public intervention (like regulation and low-income inclusion). The same applies to markets where because of high interest rates the only financing that works is that provided by public agencies. For example, as a public lender of below-market core money, the MHFA had a virtual monopoly on financing new private housing development in Massachusetts during the early 1980s. The market-rate interest available through private lenders was so high that units could not be brought on line at a rent that was competitive in the market. Thus, hot markets or high interest rates put private developers at a disadvantage relative to 'the publics' in terms of negotiation. Conversely, there is more likelihood that 'the privates' can be convinced to produce units for allocation to low-income households.

By way of contrast, it is harder in hot markets to keep existing private owners focused on low-income households. Higher rents mean higher-income tenants. Low vacancy rates mean that owners do not have to look to federal or state demand-side subsidies to make it possible to fill their units. It seems reasonable to hypothesize that most owners, if they knew they had a high level of consistent demand for their units, would rather rent to the market and not have to bother with public agencies and their lengthy regulations and requirements for dealing with subsidized tenants and matters of equal opportunity, income eligibility, physical standards of the unit, and so on. For an owner of property utilizing a certificate housing program, the 'friction' of doing business is worth it only when there are not better options in the private market. Conversely, from the public side the urgency to perform efficiently and to minimize red tape, bureaucracy, and regulation and to process payments in a timely manner is enhanced in a low-vacancy, booming real-estate market.

I have defined the producers or owners of housing as the actors viewing the low-income housing issues through the private-sector lens. It is important to include the financial institutions that lend money for construction, purchase, and rehabilitation as additional and critical members of the private sector. Where developers are perceived as being entrepreneurial and risk-takers, lenders are generally identified as being conservative and risk-averse. But being risk-averse does not mean that lenders are any less concerned about making money. Their conservatism, however, does mean that they are concerned about the impact of low-income people on developments they finance. That concern is of two kinds: financial and social. Lenders want to be sure that there are tenants who can pay the rent and buyers who can afford the homes that are being built. They are also conscious of the social environment created in the housing they are financing. Both concerns do not carry much sympathy for at-risk households, the most disadvantaged in the housing market.

Deep subsidies, co-insurance, letters of credit, replacement reserves, and a high percentage of owner equity can mitigate the concern of the financial community as it looks at a deal involving low-income households. But each of these 'sweeteners' requires commitments from other actors, both public and private. Low-income housing can be made enticing enough for the private financial community to participate in its development and long-term management and operation. But in the last analysis, those sweeteners end up being direct or indirect public subsidies.

The ways that private-sector housing people react to and view the low-income issue are critical for at-risk low-income households. Given their marginal economic bargaining power under the best of circumstances (a weak market), such households are clearly the most vulnerable in hot real-estate situations. Since the advent of the War on Poverty in the 1960s, the traditional inequities of the landlord/tenant contract that dominated the legal system have been mitigated. The rule of law, however equitable, does not help the low-income family in the long run if the rent moves inexorably above the family's financial resources. In the absence of rent control, a rarely utilized sanction in American cities, a rising market that does not include subsidies on either the supply or demand side spells trouble for those with the lowest incomes. If unaided by a public subsidy, or a rising income, the low-income tenant must hope that he or she is living in a flat or declining market area where the owner has no short-term option but to keep the rent at its current level.

PRIVATE/PUBLIC SYNERGY

Low-Income Housing in Massachusetts
Massachusetts is currently dealing with the issue of permanent housing

for low-income and homeless people. A case study helps to make more effective the concepts enumerated in the preceding discussion about the ways that the private sector interacts with the public and third sectors in going about the business of providing new and existing housing for people of limited income.

The Commonwealth of Massachusetts sustained an economic boom from 1981 to 1987. In 1989, the bloom is slightly off the 'Massachusetts Miracle.' The boom put unparalleled stress on the state's housing markets. Rents and prices for homes have escalated at enormous rates (38 per cent a year in 1984–6), and Massachusetts has become one of the country's most expensive residential settings. The problem of the homeless has become a profound one for the state as more and more households have found it increasingly difficult to survive in the private rental market, even though the dimensions of the problem are not as great as in cities like New York and Los Angeles.

In terms of housing production, Massachusetts has been a slow-growing state for many years. Unlike for the fast-growth areas of the country, such as Florida, Texas, and California, the state's private-development sector has not been characterized by large-scale developers operating on vast tracts of unincorporated land. The state is entirely divided into incorporated municipalities with long traditions of home rule and local decision-making. Any private developer wishing to do business must deal with the rigours of the local municipality and its regulatory procedures. In Massachusetts, untrammelled growth as a 'good thing' long ago gave way to the view that extensive residential development means a change in the quality of life, as well as costs to the community for schools, roads, and improvements.

Massachusetts has a long tradition of state involvement in housing issues. The public sector system that exists today, 'while dramatically enhanced during the current Dukakis Administration, represents a long tradition of commitment by the legislature and the executive branches to an active state role in insuring affordable housing for the Commonwealth's citizens ... not only for low income families, the elderly and the handicapped, but also the increasingly urgent affordability concerns of the middle income residents of the Commonwealth' (Executive Office of Communities and Development 1983: 2).

In spring 1985, Governor Michael Dukakis created the Massachusetts Housing Partnership (MHP) to focus attention on the problem of housing for low-income as well as moderate-income households. The partnership has a board of some thirty-five housing notables from across the state representing the public, private, and third sectors. The board meets on a quarterly basis to review the process of housing in the state and to pass on policy issues. The real heart of the partnership process lies at the municipal level and the relationship between the partners there and the state funding programs made available to partnership communities. An MHP publication (idem, no date) gives a vivid sense of the degree to which a partnership relationship among the three sectors is the core of the initiative.

In the development of housing the functions and needs of the public and private sectors intertwine. There are many actors: in the public sector these include agencies and programs at the federal, state and local levels; in the private sector, they include a myriad of developers and builders.

In the production of housing, at the state level, the Executive Office of Communities and Development has responsibility for the conceptualization, development and implementation of programs to construct public and private housing for rental and homeownership. Many of the housing programs are implemented at the state level by the Massachusetts Housing Finance Agency and at the local level, by local authorities. Locally elected officials in conjunction with local planning and development staffs are also involved in the housing development process.

The private sector is also a very active participant in the housing development process, through developers, builders, lenders, architects and engineers, real estate brokers and attorneys. The neighborhood itself is frequently involved in the housing development process, through a locally initiated, non-profit community development corporation.

The Massachusetts Housing Partnership has produced a framework that encourages communities to form local partnerships – groups of individuals representing local government, local bankers, builders and business people, consumer and housing advocates and other capable, interested citizens. These local partnerships are then challenged to develop an agenda for the development of affordable housing in their communities.

Massachusetts has developed an exhaustive array of programs – subsidy, technical assistance, long-term financing – which local partnerships can draw on as they go about the task of setting up and implementing a local partnership. At present there are over one hundred active partnership efforts in the state, with many others under consideration. Budget and fiscal problems have clouded this picture in 1989. But for the most part, these housing programs have survived if not intact at least without deep cuts. Affordable housing remains a state-wide concern, even in trying times.

Massachusetts is as close as a state in the United States is likely to get to a 'comprehensive approach' to the housing issue (see chapter 4). Economic pressure, an active governor, a supportive legislature, a flush state budget, and enormous pressure at the local level for affordable housing have produced a situation in which the housing issue is given the kind of paramount attention it was given nationally in the late 1960s, the high-point period of national concern for a comprehensive approach. It is clear that the Massachusetts Housing Partnership is an innovative mechanism for creating affordable housing, but what is its significance for connecting the private sector to low-income housing issues in general and to the plight of the homeless or at-risk households specifically?

The MHP concept extends and promotes the low-income private-sector nexus in several ways. Foremost is the extent to which the concept of the local partnership per se – the coming together of representatives from all three sectors, public, private, and third – lies at the heart of the whole enterprise. The central argument for such three-way 'bonding' is that (given the complexity of local development politics in Massachusetts) without such joint efforts the development process will be stalled in trying to get through the hurdles of the local zoning, permit, and approval processes. Particularly if that development is to focus on housing for low-income people or people with special needs, the way must be prepared politically, through the works of the local partnership, to overcome local opposition and conflict. The 'reg/neg' concept becomes the process through which developers, both private and third sector, work their way through the municipal political process; and the local MHP is the vehicle through which the procedure is formalized.

The negotiating process provided by a local MHP sets the context for private-sector involvement in the production of housing for the most disadvantaged in two ways. The first way is directly through the State Housing Assistance Rental Program (SHARP), a private multi-family rental housing program initiated in 1983 by the Dukakis administration; it subsidizes the interest rate of mortgages provided by the Massachusetts Housing Finance Agency (MHFA) down to 5 per cent. In addition to providing a 'moderate' subsidy through its interest reduction, the program requires that the sponsor provide 25 per cent of the units for low-income tenants. The state then guarantees the back-up subsidy to ensure that the 25 per cent low-income rental can be met. Over the course of the last four years the program has been enormously successful. Ten thousand SHARP units have been built or are in the pipeline: over 25 per cent are for low-income tenants.

The private-development community has been very much involved with SHARP. The majority of the units are being produced by private sponsors. The Massachusetts Housing Partnership provides the local context through which SHARP developments are filtered. A community that can evaluate a development proposal in the context of an overall housing plan is in a better position to negotiate intelligently than if it is simply reacting to the market. Conversely, private developers who are in an MHP project gain a degree of legitimacy that helps them negotiate their way through the local approval process.

I do not mean to overstate the significance of either SHARP or the MHP for housing the most disadvantaged. We are talking about 25 per cent of the total number of units and those units are not directly allocated to homeless families per se. But MHFA does require that 3 per cent of the units in any SHARP be available to those with mental disabilities and the 25 per cent does ensure that there is some production of new units dedicated for the life of the mortgage to poor households. Although SHARP is billed primarily as a production program for affordable units, it represents a structured mechanism for direct private-sector involvement in creating new low-income units.

The Massachusetts Housing Partnership also provides the mechanism through which housing for special-needs groups, generally sponsored by the third sector and social-service providers, can be negotiated through the community. The second way in which the MHP sets the context for the involvement of the private sector in low-income housing issues is more indirect. The state has a variety of programs for special-needs groups, people with mental and physical handicaps, and low-income households. In general these projects are sponsored by either public-sector agencies or the third sector. But representatives of the private sector who are active participants in a local MHP partnership can lend their considerable political weight to the process of negotiating such projects through a local approval process that is fraught with political and technical barriers. They can also provide technical assistance. The involvement of local contractors and builders and the creative role often played by the local financial community are also important if low-income housing is to be built. These are roles that involve actors from the private sector.

In its ideal form, a local partnership provides a setting in which the private sector, even when it is not directly involved in the production of housing for the most disadvantaged, can be a supportive instrumental actor. The partnership can ensure that the needs of the poor are not overlooked in the local evolution of an affordable housing plan and the specific developments to implement that plan.

The Existing Stock
In Massachusetts, as in every other state, most low-income people live in private unsubsidized rental housing. Although the commonwealth has worked aggressively during the past half-decade to develop new public housing and privately subsidized housing for people of low income, the fact remains that two-thirds of the Aid to Families with Dependent Children (AFDC) households, some 66,000, reside in unsubsidized private rental housing (Grollman 1987: 17). The critical agenda for these households, then, is how to keep them in their units in the face of a rising market and how to find ways of subsidizing a sufficient number of those private units to keep low-income households in them even when market rent soars above that which a family on welfare can afford. The gap between what the average welfare grant can purchase in the private rental market and rent levels has widened over the past decade and a half. It is estimated that the cost in Massachusetts of housing for a family totally dependent on welfare rose four times faster than the rate of increase of AFDC income during the period 1970 to 1985. The Massachusetts housing market is an extreme example of a seller's market. As demand for units rises, rents rise accordingly. Owners who had traditionally rented to low-income households see the possibilities of shifting their orientation and aiming for higher-income tenants; in a rising market, landlords have fewer and fewer reasons to stay in the business of renting to low-income people. What combination of public carrots and sticks can be used to keep these owners focused on the low-income end of the rental business?

The state and local public sectors have taken on this challenge in a variety of ways in Massachusetts. Their experience is instructive in making explicit the opportunities available for self-interested private-sector landlords and creative public-sector officials. Three state agencies – the Department of Public Welfare (DPW), the Executive Office of

Communities and Development (EOCD), and the Department of Social Services (DSS) – have been working to combine the 'regulation, support, and subsidy functions' so as to keep private landlords involved in housing welfare, i.e., in housing low-income families.

To make the example explicit, let us look in detail at how the 'synergistic' process works in one housing market in the state. The example is, perhaps, the most successful one of public/private co-operation around the homeless issue in Massachusetts. It makes clear the elements of a successful strategy and the roles that must be played by actors in the public, private, and non-profit sectors to bring about that success.

In a study of homeless prevention in Massachusetts, Lisa Grollman (1987) explored the interaction between state agencies and private landlords. She was concerned to discover what kept the landlords involved and the dynamic between them and the agencies. One of her case studies was of Fitchburg, a working-class city in central Massachusetts that has become a model example of how the public and private can come to terms with the homeless issue. 'As of the middle of January 1987, the problem of homelessness among welfare families had been nearly eliminated ... This progress is largely the result of a variety of public and private agencies and landlords whose efforts were coordinated by the Fitchburg Department of Social Services (DSS) office' (ibid.: 35). The *Boston Globe* (17 January 1987) described the situation in Fitchburg: 'The at-least temporary end to one of the state's worst family homelessness problems was the result of a dynamic social worker, a sympathetic bureaucrat and a network of private landlords and public service workers determined to lick the problem.'

The key person in the system is a social-service worker, Anne DeMartino, who has figured out how to get and keep private landlords engaged in the low-income housing business. The story paints a vivid picture of the interactive personal relationship between private landlords and public bureaucrats necessary to keep 'the privates' engaged. The relationship shows how creative use of the regulatory, support, and subsidy roles of government can pull in rather than push away the private sector.

This social-service worker who has become expert on issues of housing markets has recruited an 'ever increasing supply of landlords willing to rent to welfare families by appealing to the landlords business interest as well as their moral concerns. Landlords have discovered that though DeMartino is a human services worker, she is also a business woman.' DeMartino states: 'We treat our clients as people and we treat our landlords like people, and it turns out they have hearts just like everybody else' (Grollman 1987: 48). To discover why DeMartino was so successful in holding onto private landlords, Grollman interviewed five landlords in the Fitchburg area, including one who owned 248 units and rented half to welfare families and another who owned three units and rented only to welfare families.

Grollman found that although all five landlords 'displayed a sense of compassion for welfare families,' the primary reason for renting to welfare families was profit: 'Their money,' one of the landlords stated, 'is as green as anybody else's.'

What DeMartino has done, with much help from various other public agencies, is to make welfare clients as competitive in the private market as non-welfare tenants. She has managed to 'package' all the welfare aids, including '(1) finder's fees amounting to an additional month's rent for landlords accepting clients from homeless shelters, (2) Emergency Assistance for the first month's rent security deposit and back rent protective payments[6] to ensure a continuous rent stream' (Grollman 1987: 50).

In addition to providing a package of financial enticements to the private sector and guaranteeing a rent stream, DeMartino assists landlords in going after 'additional financial reimbursements from public programs such as apartment deleading, weatherization, and rehabilitation.' Beyond packaging financial and programmatic resources, she 'makes a commitment to the landlord to mediate any problems which might result' from taking welfare tenants (ibid.: 52). This willingness to intervene when trouble arises is the key to DeMartino's success and she clearly has special talents for mediating between landlords and tenants. DeMartino is also flexible on issues of code enforcement and physical standards of the buildings in which her clients reside. Although concerned with the issue, she is not bound to enforce those standards as are other public agencies involved in lending money and providing subsidy for rental housing.

Grollman's study was one of several undertaken to get a better understanding of the degree to which a more aggressive stance on the part of the local welfare office could help in homeless prevention. The exploration led to the conclusion that even in the 'hot' housing markets of Massachusetts there was space for a public/private partnership of the kind that Anne DeMartino developed so successfully.

The Fitchburg example did not draw heavily on leased housing units, i.e., units paid for by either state or federal funds for which the tenant's rent is reduced to 25 per cent of income and the difference between fair market rent and that 25 per cent is paid for by the public housing authority. Other parts of the state with higher rent levels require a heavy dose of subsidized units to allow low-income tenants to stay on in private housing. But the same kind of sensitive role played by DeMartino in using the 'privates' and mediating between them and the AFDC tenants is necessary in these situations.

Particularly when 'situational' homeless – households with social or psychological issues to work through – are involved, there is a need for help from the social-service agencies of the kind that DeMartino was providing in Fitchburg. Any program focused on enticing the private sector into housing homeless families through subsidies or the kinds of 'financial aids' utilized by DeMartino must recognize that for many of these households the issue is more than shelter. If they expect the private landlords to keep in the business, the public actors must be prepared to stand behind the social needs of the tenants when the going gets rough. When the clientele includes the chronically mentally ill, service demands become even more compelling. The role of the private-sector landlord is limited unless services are built in from the start and the landlord can look to experts in the mental-health field to deal with the problems that will inevitably arise.

In the arenas of creating and maintaining housing production and the existing stock, Massachusetts is not singular. Many other states are exhibiting energy and imagination in finding ways of bringing the public, private, and non-profit sectors together around the low-income housing issue, which has once again become an important national issue. The vividness of the homeless problem has helped push it to the forefront of the media. National legislation was passed by the Congress in 1987 focusing on the plight of households in the street. President Bush has presented himself as a staunch supporter of 'full funding' for that legislation. Department of Housing and Urban Development Secretary Kemp has put homelessness at the top of his priority list.

The seven lean years of the Reagan administration's federal housing agenda have taken a toll, yet many valuable lessons about how to craft programs at the state and local level have been learned during this period. Public/private partnerships in which there is a genuine negotiation between equals is an element in this learning process. The critical challenge is how to scale up the kinds of effort represented by the

Massachusetts experience. How do we structure national legislation to ensure that the public and the private sectors stretch themselves to find ways of making the most of scarce resources and mutual opportunities? That challenge lies ahead and we can only hope that the partnership mode of dealing with the low-income housing issue is sufficiently institutionalized to provide the basis for the work of the emerging national housing agenda.

Clearly, there is a need for public subsidy, in most instances, to bridge the gap between effective market demand and housing need; that reality has and always will be with us. More critical, however, is how to ensure that scarce public resources are utilized in the most efficient, economic, and equitable way to close the gap. The central argument of this paper is that the private sector has an important role in this effort. The successful participation of the private sector in the low-income housing challenge requires, however, an enlightened and creative view of self-interest and a willingness to refocus the lens through which the housing market and the profit margin is perceived. That willingness to participate requires an enlightened attitude on the part of the 'publics' as well. The absence of enlightened self-interest on both sides will force society to look elsewhere – to the third sector or the public sector alone – for remedy.

History indicates that, in the United States, when the low-income housing issue gets framed as the sole responsibility of the public sector, isolation and polarization result. There is a limited tradition for using the third sector. But to build on the tradition of the mixed economy is to look to a public/private partnership. That at least is where we seem to be laying our bets at present. The next five years will tell us to what extent we have been backing the right strategy.

NOTES

1 See Friedman, *Government and Slum Housing* (1968) for a detailed discussion of this concept, particularly chapter II.
2 Figures used are US dollars.
3 See 'Childhood without a Home' by Kathleen Hirsch (1986) for a graphic presentation of the debate and the arguments posed on both sides.
4 This is an expression coined by Wurster (1957) in her seminal article entitled 'The Dreary Deadlock of Public Housing.'
5 In a Massachusetts program to house the mentally ill in the community that brought together private landlords and social services, we discovered that

a motivating force behind certain private landlords' involvement was their own personal experience: someone in their family had mental illness. These private sponsors were actively seeking to generate a profit while meeting a social objective about which they had strong personal feelings.

6 Protective payment is a process whereby the tenant's rent is paid directly by the Welfare Department to the landlord. In situations in which the rent constitutes a majority of the welfare cheque, this direct payment ensures that the landlord is guaranteed rent. The practice is a controversial one among welfare advocates. Some argue that the procedure by which the tenant is cut out of the loop is a violation of individual rights. There is no question, however, that from the landlord's point of view, the guaranteed cheque makes a world of difference in calculating whether or not to take a welfare tenant.

REFERENCES

Apgar, William. 1986. 'Homeownership and Housing Affordability in the United States, 1963–1985.' Working paper. Cambridge: Harvard-MIT Joint Center for Housing Studies

Bassuk, Ellen. 1984. 'The Homeless Problem.' *Scientific American*, July

– 1985. 'The Feminization of Homelessness: Homeless Families in Boston Shelters.' Address given at Shelter Inc., Cambridge, MA, June

Executive Office of Communities and Development. 1983. 'The Massachusetts Housing System.' Photocopy

– No date. 'The Massachusetts Housing Partnership Guide to Producing Affordable Housing'

Friedman, Lawrence. 1978. *Government and Slum Housing*. Chicago: Rand McNally

Grollman, Lisa R. 1987. 'Homeless Prevention of AFDC Families.' Master of City Planning thesis, Massachusetts Institute of Technology

Hirsch, Kathleen. 1986. 'Childhood without a Home.' *Boston Phoenix*, 21 January

Karlen, Neal, et al. 1986. 'Homeless Kids, Forgotten Faces.' *Newsweek*, 6 January

National Association of Home Builders. 1985. 'Housing America – The Challenges Ahead.' Washington

– 1986. 'Low and Moderate Income Housing: Progress, Problems and Prospects.' Washington

National Association of Homebuilders, National Association of Realtors, and Mortgage Bankers Association of America. 1987. 'Towards a National Housing Policy.' Washington

National Governors' Association. 1986. 'Decent and Affordable Housing for
   All: A Challenge to the States.' Washington, August
Weicher, John. 1980. *Housing: Federal Policies and Programs*. Washington: Amer-
   ican Enterprise Institute
Wheeler, Michael. 1988. 'Resolving Local Regulatory Disputes and Building
   Consensus for Affordable Housing.' MIT Housing Policy Project Working
   Paper no. 9. Cambridge: MIT Center for Real Estate Development
Wurster, Katherine Bauer. 1957. 'The Dreary Deadlock of Public Housing.'
   Architectural Forum, May

JEANNE M. WOLFE AND WILLIAM JAY

7 The Revolving Door: Third-Sector Organizations and the Homeless

The role of third-sector agencies in the provision of shelter for the homeless is not well known despite the fact that religious and charitable agencies, such as church missions and the Salvation Army, have long been on the front line in the battle against homelessness. They are the oldest welfare agencies in Canada and pre-date by far any governmental programs of social welfare. (Homelessness is not a new phenomenon in this country, as Marc Choko [1980] reminds us in his aptly titled book, *Cent ans de crise de logement*.) This chapter attempts to assess the role of third-sector organizations in the provision of aid to the homeless and to explore their probable and possible future directions.

DEFINITIONS, CLASSIFICATION, AND SCOPE

The rather clumsy phrase non-governmental organizations (NGOs) is used in many contexts to describe collectively religious orders, churches, benevolent and community associations, and self-help, co-operative, and non-profit groups (STAD 1983). In some jurisdictions they are known as non-statutory organizations (NSOs). Secular groups are also known collectively as the voluntary sector, meaning agencies that have grown up in a voluntary manner in response to some perceived need. The voluntary sector also subsumes the volunteer sector, in which workers give their time. However, there is some blurring of the lines. Many benevolent and community associations rely, at least partially, on government grants. In many cases, there is a complete symbiosis between government and NGOs. Many non-profit shelter organizations and most housing co-operatives are dependent on government funding policy, although they do not necessarily owe their existence to it because they are usually started through local initiatives. In some cases the local motor might be a municipal government.

We prefer the term 'third sector' to mean non-profit and/or co-operative agencies, although this definition, too, can lead to difficulties. All sorts of registered non-profit associations are devoted to lobbying for profit-making causes, such as business and professional institutes. Further, despite their name, many so-called volunteer or benevolent organizations employ paid staff, often professionals with appropriate qualifications. The volunteer work is done by donors, fund-raisers, members of boards of directors, and persons who give working time. Although these organizations are largely directed towards social causes, they also may provide services for all income groups such as, for example, municipally based recreation organizations, the YW/YMCAS, mental health associations, and golden-age clubs. In the same vein, many co-operatives, particularly production co-operatives in agriculture, fisheries, construction, and manufacturing, evidently hope to make a profit for the benefit of their members. To avoid confusion, this chapter uses this varied terminology to describe organizations with the social objective of helping the poor or deprived.

The third sector can also be described negatively as non-market and non-government. 'Exchange' characterizes the market sector and 'authority' the government sector (Douglas 1983). The activities of these two sectors are widely reported and documented, but those of the third sector receive scant attention even though they permeate our society.

A great number of voluntary agencies are involved to some degree in housing issues, even though this was not their original or intended mission. For instance, associations set up to aid people with mental or physical handicaps usually began as medical support groups providing family encouragement, training, social outlets, and specialized equipment. Adapted housing became perceived as a need only later in their evolution.

The amazing number, diversity, and variety of organizations make classification and generalization rather hazardous. There are two major approaches to classification, neither of them totally satisfactory. The first one groups third-sector organizations according to the characteristics of their primary clientele, while the second one bases classification on organizations' management styles and funding sources. Both are offered as a guide to better illustrate the complexity of the subject and to demonstrate the enormous range of activities undertaken by the third sector.

The first approach groups agencies according to the social problems they were originally intended to address. This, of course, is in line with the contemporary understanding that the homeless and those with housing difficulties are not a homogeneous group and that solutions to homelessness must address all the problems that people face and not simply the demand model for housing. The list includes emergency-shelter providers who supply beds for vagrants, itinerants, and bag-ladies, and hostels for homeless juveniles; and agencies that aid former prisoners and parolees, deinstitutionalized psychiatric patients, people with physical handicaps, the chronically sick, battered women, native people, refugees, and low-skilled immigrants. Each of these groups has particular needs; most require special facilities or support services. A few examples serve to indicate the range.

The *deinstitutionalized* face rejection problems on all fronts. The John Howard and Elizabeth Fry societies aid ex-prisoners, and various groups under the umbrella of the Canadian Mental Health Association have a hand in finding and running half-way houses or group homes for former psychiatric patients (Maass 1986). The housing of transitional people is rendered especially difficult by the not-in-my-backyard (NIMBY) syndrome, that is, the resistance of property owners to the establishment of half-way houses in their neighbourhoods, partly out of fear that the residents may be dangerous, and partly out of fear of diminished property values (Dufour 1988).

Victims of *domestic strife* need emergency shelter, often in the middle of the night, and they need anonymity for fear of reprisals. Government agencies close at five o'clock. Many referrals are made by police at all hours of day and night. Associations working with battered women usually run hostels for immediate succour and shelter for women and children, but as these people begin to recover from their trauma, finding a permanent home at reasonable cost becomes a major hurdle to establishing a new and stable life.

People with *physical handicaps* and the *fragile elderly* need specially adapted homes built to help accommodate their disabilities. This means housing custom-designed for wheelchair use or mobile beds, sympa-thetically designed bathrooms and fittings, appropriately scaled kitch-ens, houses without obstacles like doorsills and steps to trip over. Stories of individuals with some handicap trapped forever in one room that lacks special facilities make sensational journalism, but unfortu-nately these circumstances are much more common than reported. A review of fifteen special-client projects in Toronto showed nine special-needs types and came to the conclusion that 'each project is a unique situation in itself' (CMHC 1983a: 7).

Immigrants, and especially *refugees*, often arrive in Canada almost penniless and unable to speak either official language. Most large cities have community cultural associations that help take care of people of their own ethnic group by providing translation services, helping with paperwork and clothing, and especially finding low-cost accommodation. There are always difficulties: 'NGO's will help as much as they can, but they are often low on funds' (CEIAC 1985: 12). It is ironic that the groups most in need of help are from countries from which there has not been much migration historically, so consequently the community organizations that theoretically could provide the most aid are fledgling ones, struggling to get organized and generally without funds.

The second approach to the classification of third-sector agencies is through an examination of their management and funding. Religious organizations are found in every community in Canada and are usually grouped according to denomination and ethno-linguistic origin (Millet 1971). Each has its own unique management system. Voluntary, secular agencies, also defined as organizations in which sponsorship and leadership are not governmental, can be grouped into at least three types according to their management and degree of autonomy (Armitage 1975: 212). These are:

1. Quasi non-governmental agencies, privately incorporated but depending mostly, if not entirely, on government funding. Management normally includes some government representation. They are usually organizations that existed before general welfare programs were invented, and they were integrated into governmental social-service delivery systems as these evolved. Examples include the Children's Aid societies, and Red Cross blood banks.

2. Private service agencies, managed by a self-perpetuating board of trustees and often having a paid professional staff. A private service agency is legitimized by the utility of its program rather than by its status as the representative organ of defined groups of citizens. Financing may come partly from government grants or contracts, partly from user fees, from United Way funding, or from other fund-raising efforts. Examples are settlement houses, the YM/YWCA, Community Resource Organization Program (CROP) groups, and, more recently, groups running homes for battered women, runaway juveniles, or victims of AIDS.

3. Totally voluntary organizations and self-help groups, created by action taken by private citizens of their own volition and outside the

initiative and authority of government. Funding is from members, user fees, and fund-raising drives. Examples include churches, Alcoholics Anonymous, community recreation groups, and MUMS (Mothers United for Metro Shelter). In all three groups can be found advocates and activists for those with housing problems.

Despite the rash of contemporary concern, little is known about the homeless who seek the aid of churches and charitable social-service agencies. This is partly because most clients wish to preserve anonymity, partly because many agencies are too busy to keep records, and finally because there is no common gathering of data. A little more is known about the residents of non-profit housing corporations and co-operatives because these depend to a much greater extent on government mortgage guarantees and rent subsidies, which involve a certain amount of bookkeeping, auditing, and recording. Similarly, little has been written about the role of the third sector in providing housing even though it has always taken the lead in times of emergency and is the first to take initiative in the face of new crises.

Published research on special-needs groups – for example, the case histories of residents of a given hostel, or the evaluation of low-income housing co-ops, or the outreach activities of one church – do not give us many clues from which to generalize. Such studies represent only a tiny fraction of the difficulties of people with problems and their sources of aid; and they provide a rather random sample from which to draw a general portrait of the characteristics of the third sector. Our subject, thus, is hard to systematize and cover comprehensively. This chapter necessarily draws from fragmentary evidence: personal experience, a sample of agency reports, journalistic accounts, and scattered research papers.

Homelessness is generally described in terms of a continuum, with 'sleeping rough' at one end to having problems in finding appropriate, affordable, long-term accommodation at the other (Brandon 1974: 5). In between there is 'an extensive grey area' ranging from hostels, hotels, temporary accommodation, sleeping on friends' floors, to insecure rented accommodation and perilously mortgaged property (Watson and Austerberry 1986: 9). The nearer to the 'sleeping rough' end of the continuum that the definition of homelessness is made, the smaller appears the problem. It is inevitable that political policy-makers veer towards the narrowest definition, while social workers and housing advocates tend toward a wider interpretation, with some risk to credibility in both cases.

Church and voluntary agencies provide help all along this continuum: soup kitchens for those of no fixed address, food banks for those with an address and no money left over for sustenance, emergency shelter for the distressed and dispossessed, hostels that provide impersonal dormitory accommodation, special-purpose residences for persons half-way between institutional and community life, specially equipped residences for the people with handicaps or elderly citizens, and co-operative developments providing decent, affordable, and personalized housing with security of tenure.

ORIGINS AND EVOLUTION OF THIRD-SECTOR AGENCIES

The earliest social agency of the European colony in Canada was the Roman Catholic church, which, in addition to saving souls and 'bringing light to the heathen,' assumed responsibility for the sick and aged, orphans, foundlings, 'fallen women,' paupers, and lunatics (Lapointe-Roy 1987). As other waves of immigrants and other churches became established, they followed suit. Nineteenth-century industrialization and rapid urbanization led to squalid living conditions for the working poor. Almost every city experienced major fires resulting in massive homelessness, and rampant infectious diseases such as typhus, cholera, diphtheria, and tuberculosis left many children orphaned and widows destitute. By the middle of the nineteenth century the antecedents of the major voluntary welfare organizations were beginning to be formed, usually based directly on English or American models. Examples are the Ladies Benevolent Association (Montreal 1815), the Montreal City Mission (1854), the Toronto Children's Aid Society (1891), the Red Cross (1896), and the Victorian Order of Nurses (VON) (1897). The St Vincent de Paul Society (1848) was modelled on that of France; the Salvation Army, founded in 'darkest England' by Charles Booth in 1865 to aid the most destitute, was brought to Canada in 1882.

Although the best-known response of church and voluntary agencies in the field of housing has been their work in providing shelter for the most visibly destitute, many third-sector agencies have long provided specialized services for the other groups. For example, the YM/YWCA has long provided safe and healthy lodgings for young people away from home in the big city for the first time. Problems that seem to be new have been recognized for years by certain groups. For example, the 115-year-old Montreal YWCA provided the city's first free day-care and fitness classes for women. In 1895, it established the first shelter for homeless women, almost a century before the declaration of the International Year of Shelter for the Homeless.

By the turn of the century, limited municipal responsibility had developed for the poor and the indigent, but most aid for the unfortunate continued to come from benevolent associations, which were rapidly increasing in number as the plight of the poor became more and more evident. The multiplicity of welfare organizations in most large cities led astute observers to note that some wily beneficiaries were able to do quite well by signing up with several different agencies. In Victorian times, one might note, it was commonly held that the poor were usually responsible for their own misfortunes and that these were attributable to their shiftless and lazy ways. This view was not shared by the National Council of Women, the enduring federation of women's clubs founded by Lady Aberdeen in 1897, whose membership included most of the early charitable organizations and was responsible for founding others, such as the VON (Strong-Boag 1976).

The perceived need to co-ordinate the work of voluntary organizations, coupled with the development of 'scientific' social work, led to the formation of a 'Charity Organization Society' (COS) in each major city. This was a federation of organizations that initially kept registers of beneficiaries to avoid duplicating aid. Later the COS started co-ordinated fund-raising drives and many other joint activities. This was a model imported from the United States to Canada. An example is the Montreal COS, which was established in 1900 under the chairmanship of Sir George Drummond but was largely run by ladies of influence (Shepherd 1957).

Meanwhile the growth of what are today the major voluntary welfare organizations continued apace, often through the banding together or federation of local groups. Examples include the Toronto Family Service Agency (1914), the Canadian Mental Health Association (1918), the Canadian National Institute for the Blind (1918), and the Canadian Welfare Council (1920), later to become Canadian Council on Social Development.

The Charity Organization Societies gradually evolved into social-planning councils with the fund-raising activities being funnelled into community chests (united funds), later to become the Red Feather (1921), and still later to fuse with the Catholic and Jewish social-service federations to become the United Way or Centraide (1974). Social-planning councils were first organized with the double role of identifying needs and of suggesting ways in which needs might be served by member agencies. This was seen as an essential role, both for planning fund-raising activities and in fund allocation procedures. Most metropolitan areas have had, and some still have, a social-planning council.

After the Second World War, government involvement in social welfare and housing gradually assumed major proportions. The purview of social-planning councils broadened, but the lack of any mandate for government service planning left them in an advisory, evaluative, or advocacy role. Research departments had been added to many larger councils, and in the 1960s their activities expanded to include the preparation of briefs dealing with poverty, urban development, housing, and urban renewal, espousing such strategies as community development as taken up by the Company of Young Canadians and Opportunities for Youth programs. Some cities, recognizing the value of such activities, even established their own municipal social-planning departments; examples are Halifax and Vancouver.

By the late 1960s it was recognized that the welfare state was well and truly established, and the major issue that seemed to face the allocation committees of United Funds was what useful supplementary functions the philanthropic organizations might fulfil. For example, the Vancouver Chest and Council's Priorities Study (1964) and the Winnipeg Social Audit (1971) addressed these questions and generally came to the conclusion that they should supplement government activities by (a) helping organizations not receiving government aid such as YM/YWCAs, neighbourhood houses, and the like; (b) supporting agencies that were working to improve government services; and (c) financing new services for emerging problems and unserved populations (Buchbinder 1971).

The promise of reasonable standards of living for all Canadians was beginning to fade as early as the late 1960s (see chapter 4). An initial enthusiasm for community development in the early part of the decade was dampened by the failure of society to deliver what it had seemed to promise (Ley 1973). Housing and urban development became burning issues. Inner-city neighbourhoods were being destroyed by massive redevelopment schemes and careless highway building, and low-income housing was disappearing at an alarming rate. The federal government's Hellyer Report (Canada 1969) on housing and Lithwick Report (1970) on urban problems were commissioned in response to this crisis (see chapter 5), as was the Legault Report (1976) in Quebec. The dimensions of rehabilitation needs for low-income housing across Canada were clearly laid out by Dennis and Fish (1972), and government action became a necessity.

In 1973, in recognition of the problems of inner-city areas, the federal government introduced the Neighbourhood Improvement Program (NIP) and Residential Rehabilitation Programs (RRAP) through Canada Mortgage and Housing Corporation (CMHC). A full explanation of the functioning of these and other federal government programs is given in chapter 5; the important point in relation to the third sector is the spin-off effects these programs had on local populations.

Also in 1973, CMHC provided new encouragement to the development of the co-operative housing sector. This was done by providing funds for the start-up of local technical resource groups under the Community Resource Organization Program (CROP); such groups were to work in aiding community groups to establish non-profit housing co-operatives. The 1973 co-op funding program provided 10 per cent capital grants and 90 per cent low-interest, long-amortization loans. CMHC directly financed approximately 7800 co-operative housing units under the National Housing Act (NHA) Section 34.18 between 1973 and 1978.

In 1979, this approach was modified. The government introduced a new co-operative program under Section 56.1 of the NHA. Private mortgage loans for 100 per cent of accepted capital costs, insured by CMHC, replaced direct CMHC loans. The loans were contracted at market interest rates with amortization periods of up to thirty-five years. CMHC pays each project an operating grant to bridge the gap between the project's economic housing charge or break-even rent, and the market rent. In addition, CMHC provides each co-op with a pool of geared-to-income assistance, enabling it to reduce the charges for up to a maximum of 25 per cent of the number of its low-income households. This new co-operative program, with its imposed philosophy of social mix, essentially replaced the old public housing program. One of the aims of this approach was to encourage community acceptance of social housing and another was to make the available money go further. The federal government assisted more than 33,000 co-operative units under this program (CHF 1985: 2).

Meanwhile, local non-profit groups dedicated to saving their neighbourhood and improving the housing situation started to proliferate in all major cities. For instance, a conference organized by La Fédération des Unions de Familles in Montreal in 1977 attracted sixty-three different citizen groups concerned with housing issues and these were representative of the francophone sector only (Simoneau 1977). One of the most startling revelations publicized at the meeting was that between 1957 and 1974, 23,234 housing units had been demolished in the City of Montreal, equivalent to 6.4 per cent of the total stock of 1974. Needless to add, most of these demolitions were in low-income inner-city areas, and although many units may have been in poor condition, the rents were modest (Simoneau 1977: 55–6).

Similar realizations and reactions were becoming evident in most Canadian cities, and it is during this period of the late 1970s and early 1980s that numerous new non-governmental organizations devoted entirely to housing advocacy were born. Third-sector organizations of this new generation vary enormously in composition and objectives. Some focus on neighbourhood preservation and combating potential developers; others fight for tenants' rights or the maintenance of rooming-houses; and still others struggle to gain control over their own living conditions through the formation of non-profit groups or housing co-operatives, either to build new houses or to purchase and renovate existing buildings.

Initatives such as these were fuelled by shifts in government policy, at both the federal and provincial levels. The introduction of Neighbourhood Improvement Programs by CMHC in the early 1970s had given a raison d'être for citizens' groups in designated areas, and in some areas not so fortunate as to be named, contestatory groups emerged. Similarly, the evolution of the CMHC co-operative housing program stimulated the formation of many non-profit groups whether or not they were successful in obtaining government funding. The financial aid offered to embryonic CROP groups facilitated their start-up and resulted in the useful building up of technical expertise for non-profit associations.

At the same time, it also became evident that not only were persistent problems being neglected, but that many of society's emerging problems were not being appropriately addressed by the welfare state. The feminist movement, the increasing number of women in the work-force, and the increasing number of single-parent families (usually female-headed) have all led to greater awareness of the problems of the feminine condition (Ross 1982; Cohen 1984). These developments have led to the formation of a number of organizations to help neglected women. Using Montreal as an example: the establishment of many women's refuges is recent; for instance Chez Doris was founded in 1977, Maison Marguerite in the same year, and Auberge Madeleine in 1983.

Meanwhile, the federal government again changed its social housing program. In 1986 it entered into a series of agreements with each of the provinces for the provision of housing to what is defined as the 'core needy,' those families or individuals that spend more than 30 per cent of their income on shelter. It was argued that the old NHA Section 56.1 did not do enough for the most impoverished. Costs are to be split approximately 60:30 between the federal and provincial governments. At the same time, federal support for co-operative housing has diminished. In 1988 the federal government sponsored only 2900 new units, down from nearly 3600 in 1967 and from a peak of 6500 in 1982 (CHF 1989). Provincial governments have sponsored a total of about 5000 co-op units to date.

The overall size and importance of the third sector in housing and housing-related issues today is impossible to gauge with any accuracy. Most hostels are run by church missions but a few such as the Dernier recours in Montreal are municipal. These are estimated to provide a total of 8000 beds nation-wide (CCSD 1987). 'Non-profits' may be municipal or non-governmental. In terms of permanent housing units, all social housing in Canada makes up about 3 per cent of the national stock, and the approximately 60,000 co-operative housing units underwritten by CMHC are less than 1 per cent. Because CMHC data group all social housing together, precise figures are hard to obtain.

It is extremely difficult to piece together the pattern of third-sector activity (CCSD 1980; Ross 1983; Robichaud 1985). The problem is further complicated by the fact that many agencies deliver government-funded services, and many other agencies do not report or do not fall into any category invented by Statistics Canada. Some organizations rely heavily on volunteer work, which is difficult to quantify (Statistics Canada 1980). In fact, the invisibility of volunteer work is a whole hidden field of economics that needs to be explored in detail, but has received almost no attention in Canada. Some attempts have been made in the United States by the Urban Institute (Disney et al. 1984), but the results are not transferable to the Canadian scene because of the vast differences in the delivery of social services, particularly health care. Some of the fragments that are known are noted below.

Special residential facilities for the aged and the young are provided by all three sectors: government, the non-profit, and the private sector. Voluntary organizations provide 23 per cent of the total places for the elderly and 35 per cent for children in Canada (SPCMT 1984). A recent Ontario government survey shows the great variety of support services, both governmental and non-profit, used by elderly residents of social housing (Denton et al. 1986, 1987), but does not quantify their worth.

We have no similar information on specialized housing for people with handicaps.

The Co-operative Housing Federation (CHF) of Canada has almost 1400 member co-ops, totalling nearly 60,000 dwelling units, and housing something like 200,000 people (CHF 1989: 4). It is estimated that there are probably at least another 1000 units of co-operative low-income housing funded by churches or foundations. The effect of self-help – or the supply effect of the renovation of housing through informal barter, reciprocal aid, and group effort described by Krohn et al. (1977) as 'the other economy' – is impossible to gauge. Statistics Canada has examined the unrecorded economy but paid no attention to housing (Berger 1986).

Martin (1985: xiv), one of the few observers to look at the whole of the voluntary sector, has estimated that Canada has close to 50,000 'humanistics organizations' (i.e., people-serving: they may range from stamp-collecting clubs, to symphony orchestra supporters, to groups trying to establish homes for the homeless). He estimates that together such groups handle nearly one-third of the country's national income. (This evidently includes all government funding to voluntary groups.) He points out that well over half the 47,000 charitable organizations registered in Canada could be classified as welfare related (Martin 1985: 15), but there is no specific information on housing.

Total funds raised by the United Way and Centraide in Canada amounted to $184 million in 116 local campaigns in 1988 (Centraide, Montreal), but this is only a fraction of private giving. Figures for church and foundation funds used for housing and related purposes have never been estimated separately. Statistics Canada (1981) estimates that the volunteer sector involves 2.7 million people. In terms of person-hours worked and the funds or services-in-kind allocated to the not-for-profit sector, volunteerism represents $6 billion a year or over 1 per cent of the GNP (Ross 1983). Again, initiatives to do with housing are not mentioned separately. (A recent survey made by Statistics Canada and the Secretary of State on the nature of volunteer work is to be published in October 1989.)

EVALUATION OF THE STRENGTHS AND WEAKNESSES OF
THE THIRD SECTOR

Advocates of non-governmental organizations cite their many advantages in the provision of socially responsive housing (Manchee and

Drover 1981). These include the claim that such NGOs originate from local initiatives, understand client needs, have democratic structures, can provide special-purpose housing, and, if appropriate funding is available, can respond rapidly to perceived needs. These organizations are basic forces in community development; they are ideal vehicles for people to gain social and economic skills, to develop local expertise in management, finance, building, and construction; and they are able to take advocacy positions when needed. Workers in small organizations know their clientele and, if necessary, can protect the anonymity of persons sheltered and minimize bureaucratic procedures. In addition to providing basic housing, non-profit housing groups are committed to developing a style of management that involves the residents, thus benefiting their individual sense of self-worth and increasing pride of possession, leading to a sense of social responsibility.

In contrast, critics of NGOs point out that they are usually poorly funded, may offer substandard services, may be ineptly managed by amateurs, are too few in number to have much effect on the national scene, and are directed only to target groups, thus not serving the population at large. Other critics go even further, suggesting that NGOs are another nail in the coffin of comprehensive social services, that they suffer from a lack of co-ordination both between themselves and with government, and that they are not accountable to the public.

Between these competing claims, it is extremely difficult to form any definitive opinions. Because of the number and diversity of agencies, and their widely varying functions and geographical distribution, a comprehensive appraisal is impossible. However, we can look at some of the forms of shelter provided according to five criteria: clients' needs, responsiveness to perceived societal needs, management, efficiency, and complementarity to government programs.

Life in emergency shelters and hostels is clearly dreadful; although they obviously fill a need, building more hostels or dormitory accommodation is not a long-term solution (Imbimbo and Pfeffer 1987). This view has been recognized for a long time. Whitney (1970: 73), in discussing a skid row, called for 'a team approach focusing on rehabilitation efforts and not sheer physical maintenance.' Street people need transition housing as well as life-skills and job-skills training.

Many of those involved in establishing non-profit housing projects have worked with people who live in hostels and emergency shelters, and so are especially sensitive to the inadequacies of this kind of accommodation (TUUW 1987). They recognize the limitations of short-term solutions for their clientele and, for the most part, they are working towards more permanent housing solutions, coupled with the provision of support services (Single Displaced Persons' Project 1983).

Residents of half-way houses and group homes seem to be reasonably satisfied with them. This acceptance, of course, may well be because the alternatives are too appalling to consider. Senior-citizens homes vary from the decrepit to the splendid. Physical conditions seem to be less important than individual autonomy and the preservation of personal dignity. Most client surveys of non-profit housing and co-operatives have indicated high levels of satisfaction, significantly higher than with previous residences (Serge 1981; Hulchanski 1983). This attitude is understandable, especially in those projects where client participation has been part of the development process. The problem is that there is simply not enough of this kind of housing: the waiting-lists are enormous. Another criticism has been that such housing does not serve the most needy or hard-to-house people (CMHC 1983b).

The responsiveness of third-sector initiatives to perceived societal needs historically has been their raison d'être. For instance, the impetus for the establishment of homes for battered women or, even more recently, hospices for people with AIDS came first from concerned citizens and charitable agencies. However, even though the third sector may spearhead initiatives, it is not able to support permanent or comprehensive solutions to widespread crises because of the present situation of discretionary short-term public funding.

Management and operation of non-governmental organizations are marked by an extraordinarily high degree of commitment, which often distinguishes them from both the government and private sector. People sitting on boards of directors, fund-raisers, housing managers, social-work professionals, and workers have a strong belief in the usefulness of their jobs and in the help they are providing. A fair number work on a volunteer basis, and many derive much personal fulfilment from doing community work. There are also negative aspects to this work. Ungrateful, untruthful, quarrelsome, or substance-addicted residents can try the patience of the Sisters of Mercy. A common problem is worker burn-out, seen for instance in community resource organizations, group-home managers, and the staff of shelters for battered women.

Funding is always scarce (Hamel 1983), and many managers spend enormous amounts of time writing grant proposals, lobbying foundations, and grubbing around for money. Many groups stretch their resources by laying off employees who then go on unemployment insurance while continuing to work. United Fund allocations to worthwhile embryonic NGOs may be only $15,000 for a half-time executive director, but that person may well work full-time and more. In fact, in many senses, the third sector may itself be trapped in a culture of poverty.

Another problem related to financing is that NGOs are often competing with each other for government grants, or United Way or foundation funding. This competition is very divisive for the sector as a whole and undoubtedly reduces its potential force. Recent moves to shift some housing programs to the provinces have created a climate of uncertainty. Revised programs always have slightly different criteria and priorities, and agencies often have trouble adjusting.

In terms of efficiency, NGOs are hard to evaluate. Because of the factors already mentioned, and in terms of services for money, many NGOs are probably much more efficient than any other kind of organization, whether governmental or private. Large agencies have sometimes been charged with conspicuous spending, but stories of profligacy and waste in the other sectors abound, too. Recent evaluations of the CMHC-funded non-profit co-operative housing program came to opposing conclusions; and it becomes difficult to judge whether the assessments were pragmatic or ideological (Woods Gordon 1981; CMHC 1983b, Hulchanski and Patterson 1984; Poulton 1984).

The final criterion, the degree of complementarity or conflict with government programs, is becoming easier to assess as governments reduce their social programs (Leman 1980). Demands are being put on the third sector and volunteers to fill the gaps that remain (Carter 1975). The problem with this approach is that NGOs that are entirely dependent on government funding will, in fact, be controlled by government, because only those that are willing to fall in with government policy will be financed. The much-touted independence of action will be lost. It will be recalled that programs such as the Company of Young Canadians and Opportunities for Youth were cancelled when they became too critical of government (McGraw 1978).

THE FUTURE

In the immediate future there will be an increase in the leadership role and the number of NGOs in the field of housing. Evidence of these increases is already apparent. In the same way that charities formed into federations at the beginning of the century, so housing advocacy groups are forming networks that will become more widespread and powerful in the coming years.

On the national level the Urban Core Support Network (UCSN) has, since 1974, been bringing together groups and individuals working with single low-income individuals, sharing analyses, developing new strategies, and providing mutual support to workers who constantly face burn-out. Recently it has developed a specific interest group, the Housing Network Project (HNP), for groups working on alternative housing for street people (emphasizing facilitative management and social support) and participating in decision making with residents (HNP 1986). In various major cities there are similar networks, most of which are affiliated with UCSN and HNP. These include Toronto's Single Displaced Persons' Project and the Supportive Housing Coalition (1981), Montreal's Réseau d'aide aux personnes seules et itinérantes (1987), Vancouver's Downtown Eastside Residents' Association, and Halifax's 'Housing for People' Coalition.

Co-operative groups similarly are becoming much more cohesive. There are now eighteen regional federations of housing co-operatives in Canada. For example, much energy has been spent in establishing the Fédération des coopératives d'habitation de l'île de Montréal (FECHIM), which has sixty-seven member co-ops. FECHIM has set up a consolidated fund, totalling about $500,000, which it hopes to build up for use in starting future projects, as well as for use as leverage for mortgage borrowing. Meanwhile, a provincial confederation is being incorporated that brings together the five regional federations of Quebec, Montreal, Sherbrooke, the Outaouais, and Monteregie. All are members of the CHF (Co-operative Housing Foundation) founded much earlier. Several Montreal non-profit housing groups have similarly formed the Fédération des OSBL en habitation de Montréal (FOHM) to pursue similar steps with respect to their work. Other groups, more generally concerned with questions of social justice, are either organizing housing committees, such as the Assembly of First Nations, or are lobbying for improved housing programs, such as the National Association of Friendship Centres and the Native Women's Association of Canada. The National Anti-Poverty Organization, founded in 1970 as an umbrella for poor people's associations, is an especially well-organized and vociferous advocacy group.

At the same time, some of the older church and voluntary agencies, which have joined the Housing Network Project of the Urban Core

Support Network, have begun to change their focus. Instead of concentrating on emergency shelters, which they recognize as a temporary stopgap measure, they are putting their energies into building or converting buildings to apartments because security of tenure in a place of one's own helps overcome social pathology (Bosworth et al. 1983). For example, a former United Church community building in downtown Montreal (Macdonald House) has recently been recycled into twenty-nine units of long-term supportive housing for hard-to-house single low-income people. The Fred Victor mission in Toronto is doing similar work, as is Christ Church and the Ecuhomes Corporation.

The devolution of social housing programs towards the provinces in 1986 meant long delays in organizing new programs. The effect of these changes on the third sector has been great. Some observers see the future of private non-profits as bleak: for instance, in the Halifax urban area, new starts in 1986–7 were negligible.

The reduction of federal support for co-op social housing has already been noted. Although some of the slack has been taken up by the provinces, the CHF and other advocacy groups are asking for a target of 5000 units per year – a very modest aim in view of the magnitude of the housing problem (CHF 1989). Meanwhile the sixty or so community resource groups that have grown up and honed their expertise over the years do not have sufficient work to keep themselves going and an alarming number of them are closing down.

Despite these mixed messages, it seems likely that the third sector will continue to play an important role in housing and housing advocacy. We are witnessing today an unusual conjunction of interest between local community activists and neo-conservative governments (Wineman 1984; and chapter 4). The 'localists' see that putting housing into the hands of NGOs gives all the advantages of community development and neighbourhood power to small groups of people. The federal and provincial governments, pleading unmanageable deficits, have promised to trim the costs of social programs and a too-large bureaucracy, and are cutting back wherever they can. A cynical explanation of the new localism could be that governments are exploiting the cheap labour of the third sector and divesting themselves of political responsibility if things go wrong.

The larger problem of NGOs involved in housing is how to preserve their autonomy. Since well before Confederation their watch-dog and advocacy roles have often been at the cutting edge of societal change.

How are they now to strike the appropriate balance between providing service to the population while providing a source of criticism of statutory welfare services? When, in practice, does a watch-dog become a lap-dog?

PUBLIC-POLICY CHANGES THAT COULD ENHANCE THE ROLE OF THE THIRD SECTOR

The war against homelessness must evidently be fought on all fronts and by all sectors. Kaufman (1984) has suggested a continuum of services that are needed within any community, as depicted in fig. 7.1. Emergency services are necessary for those with nowhere else to go. However, these should only be regarded as a temporary measure while the victims of homelessness are aided in transitional housing, where they are provided with a full range of medical and social services, and with supportive training. This assistance will enable them to gain sufficient personal autonomy to move on to the third stage: permanent housing with appropriate support and welfare services.

The third sector evidently plays an important role in all three phases: emergency shelter, transitional accommodation, and permanent housing. However, as Oberlander and Fallick (1987) have pointed out, solutions demand the participation of and new partnerships between the various actors involved in the production of housing. For example, in Chicago, private/public/non-governmental joint ventures are becoming important (Przeworski and Fredrickson 1980). Trust Incorporated, a non-profit group made up of United Way agencies, foundations, banks, and private corporations, puts great emphasis on neighbourhood or community development. It recognizes that constituency-based community organizations, that is, those serving a defined territory, have a major role to play in improving the housing environment through both social- and economic-development projects. Such organizations can bring together local merchants, financial institutions, landlords, employers, and various government agencies to develop projects that respond to local conditions. A Canadian example is the Core Area Initiative in Winnipeg.

It is well known in the housing field that programs invented by senior levels of government like CMHC or provincial housing ministries rarely dovetail neatly with those provided by health and social-welfare departments, and that municipal policy has to fit in with these regardless of the particular context. Locally based initiatives have then

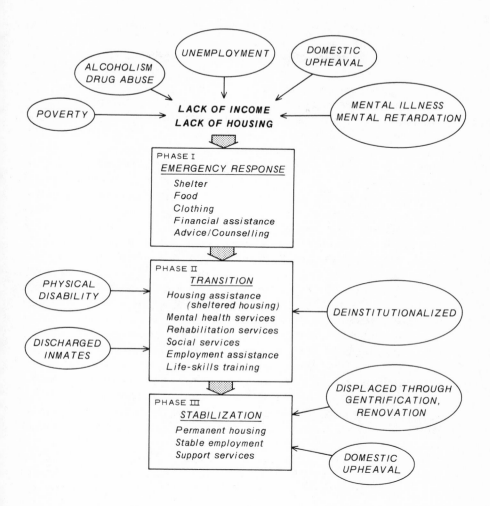

Figure 7.1
Homelessness: the continuum of services needed.
SOURCE: after Kaufman 1984

to adjust as best they can, and their projects are often unevenly distributed and uncoordinated.

The promise of neighbourhood agencies in relation to housing problems is in the emergence of partnerships among community organizations, government, and the private sector. The private sector brings an essential ingredient, capital investment, along with business know-how; government provides infrastructure, grants, guaranteed loans, and social assistance; and the community group brings local knowledge, neighbourhood insights, energy, and if strong enough, community support. The community group can act as the catalyst or manager for a variety of housing projects, using associated support services and avoiding the fragmentation of present delivery systems (Bratt 1986; MacLeod 1986).

Up to now, funding and public support for neighbourhood or community-development groups has been slight; public and private agencies have been much more inclined to finance single-mission-oriented non-profit organizations that have clearly defined and easily understood objectives. As the role of broad-based neighbourhood-focused organizations, which treat housing as an integral part of a package of necessary social services, becomes recognized as a responsive solution, this funding approach will have to change.

The prognosis for increased direct government participation in the provision of affordable housing for low-income Canadians is not encouraging. At best there is interest in some form of housing allowance scheme (see chapter 4). However, as critics have pointed out, this approach risks putting up rents, resulting in the transfer of money to landlords and no improvement in the adequacy and affordability of housing.

Several Canadian municipalities make provision for dedicating municipally developed housing units to non-profit groups. Toronto's City Home and Montreal's Société d'habitation et de développement urbain are two examples. There are, however, drawbacks. The most obvious is that such housing authorities are large scale and bureaucratic and lack responsiveness to client needs. Further, unlike in projects developed by the non-profit sector, there has not been user or advocate input at the design stage, and consequently problems peculiar to special-needs groups are not anticipated. The failure of top-down municipal enterprise has been most visibly evident in earlier slum-clearance projects such as Regent Park in Toronto or the Jeanne-Mance scheme in Montreal. Such deficiencies could be overcome through a political will to forge a collaborative partnership with the third sector.

Another interesting approach is one taken by certain Scandinavian countries where government encourages private developers to provide suitable housing for all population groups, irrespective of income or a special-needs category. For example, in Sweden, not only the issuing of construction permits but also the mandate for reintegrating psychiatric patients into their home community is primarily a municipal responsibility. Because the local psychiatric hospital facility has an intimate firsthand knowledge of the housing needs of its patients, it can fairly accurately project the need for additional community accommodation; and the psychiatric authorities are adequately funded to provide such housing. In this climate, the Swedish practice is to require private builders, as part of the procedure for acquiring a building permit, to collaborate with the social sector in assuming that a reasonable portion of new housing is constructed and made available to those usually viewed as a state responsibility. Negotiations, including adequate financial compensation to builders, are thus carried out in a mutually satisfying manner. Such an approach in Canada could lead to an effective partnership between government resources and the third sector.

Under the present circumstances, for the voluntary sector to improve its role in the provision of housing, it needs increased funding, as well as guaranteed and continuing funding for groups with a good track record so that energies are not lost in perpetually making applications and lobbying for grants. This approach requires four changes in granting policies, whether from public or non-governmental agencies: (1) clear, consistent rules for eligibility; (2) a move from discretionary to sustained grants; (3) an adequate level of funding in terms of price per unit of housing to allow for both independent living and social management; and (4) the recognition of a variety of solutions to housing delivery mechanisms.

Robichaud (1985), studying provincial government policies and voluntarism, found that much of the funding from government is considered discretionary or non-statutory because governments often perceive non-profit groups to be unreliable and lacking in continuity. In contrast, voluntary-sector workers maintain that their services are much more reliable than the grant-payment structure and procedure of governments. A very small proportion of public housing money is spent through voluntary agencies, but there is a great reluctance to support initiatives until, under very difficult conditions, the voluntary sector has dramatically demonstrated the need. The case has been made for shelters for battered women, but it now is being presented for housing for victims of AIDS.

Technical problems in financing also require adjustment. For instance, in the co-operative and social housing sector, fluctuating mortgage rates and the formulas for loan repayments make long-range budgeting difficult. The CHF (1985) proposed a very sensible scheme for price-level-adjusted mortgage financing, which was adopted by CMHC in 1988. Clearly, other financial vehicles, such as reverse mortgages, capitalization of mortgage payments, and the setting up of land-banks and their use for collateral, need to be explored further.

In a similar vein, although money is often forthcoming for operating costs for agency services, for example, for homes for battered women, funds covering capital costs are much harder to amass. Most such agencies occupy rental property and their permanence is insecure, and good locations are often lost to gentrification or urban redevelopment schemes.

Another problem in acquiring funding is paperwork. The number of forms to be filled in to apply for government money and the bureaucratic permissions that are needed to get projects started are unnecessarily complicated and cause excessive lead-time preparation. In some cases this preparation is so long that it has led to lost opportunities for the purchase of buildings for renovation or of land for building. The application procedure needs complete streamlining by all levels of government.

A worrisome aspect about government funding is that it provides the means for controlling non-statutory organizations, which can be done directly through the selection of projects to be funded. Groups whose objectives are out of line with those of the state will be refused (Lawrence 1983: 23). Institutionalizing partnerships with other sectors carries the same dangers. A similar restriction applies to voluntary associations receiving money from United Way or Centraide funds. It is understood that in no way must groups appear to be political for fear of jeopardizing fund-raising campaigns by alienating donors.

All of this analysis suggests that third-sector groups that take radical positions should develop sources of funding other than government. In Montreal, churches have sometimes helped. For instance, in the Centre-Sud district, Interloge has received front-end money for building purchases for non-profit groups. Credit union and union funds are also being made available for socially responsible housing. In Quebec, Les caisses populaires Desjardins has taken a lead role in providing mortgage money and in developing co-operative housing projects for lower-income workers. The Fonds de solidarité of the Quebec Federation of Labour also takes an active interest in housing.

The growing co-operative movement is vigorously exploring other sources of funding by setting up consolidated funds and foundations, so that it can capitalize on its own momentum. FECHIM has started such a fund, and there is a good chance it will succeed. The CHF already has a co-op assistance fund (to help co-ops in temporary difficulty) and a risk-underwriting fund, neither of which has suffered a loss so far. It has also established a charitable foundation, 'Rooftops,' which provides housing aid to non-governmental organizations both in Canada and in the third world. The co-operative movement should look more closely at the possibility of establishing limited-equity housing co-ops, that is, co-operatives in which the members make a down payment, which provides the project with sufficient start-up funds to get under way. Although this idea may be distasteful to purists, two or three thousand dollars down payment, repayable upon withdrawal from the co-op, could provide sufficient funds for a project to begin and could help house those with 'moderate' housing problems. Such schemes, assuming a reasonably robust membership, could also include a sweat-equity component.

In Surrey, British Columbia, two experiments have been tried with equity co-ops for senior citizens. Members purchase shares equal to at least 20 per cent of the cost of their unit and pay monthly operating and mortgage charges. If they leave the unit, shares are redeemed at cost. Such resident-funded housing co-ops require no government subsidies.

Self-help has long been a driving idea in many third-sector organizations, particularly those involved with health (Romeder 1982). In the housing field, the most well known projects in Canada are those accomplished through the work of Father Tomkins and the Antigonish movement in Nova Scotia in the 1930s, when miners and working-class people banded together to build houses. The problems with adopting this idea today are fairly severe. First, the people most in need of housing are the least able, physically and mentally, to assume responsibility for demanding work; they have enough trouble running their lives without extra responsibility. Second, a fair amount of capital is still required and lending institutions are nervous about keen amateurs. Nevertheless, given appropriate technical aid, it is a possibility to be explored. The Affordable Cost Housing Group at McGill University is developing prototypes of houses that could be finished by their owners with a considerable saving in cost.

The co-operative and non-profit housing movements must also move beyond the provision of shelter, into the social- and economic-support systems that are necessary for a good living environment. These initiatives should include land-banking and community social and economic development (CHF 1982; Hulchanski 1983; Wolfe 1985). Hulchanski (1983: 36) has shown how the potential of much social housing investment over the last fifty years has been lost on short-term solutions that assist only the overall supply of housing: examples are assisted-rental programs and rental-construction loan programs. He strongly proposes that community land-banks be set up to purchase, lease, and manage land for housing purposes. By this means, land would be withdrawn from the market and the benefits of public expenditure would be enduring. Controlled by a community trust, the land would be made available to non-profits, co-operatives, or other institutions interested in developing social housing. One such example is Milton Park in Montreal, where the land is jointly owned by all the twenty-six non-profits and co-ops, while the buildings are owned by the individual groups.

Further economic- and social-support systems can be developed through grass-roots community development. An example is The Third Way/La troisième voie, a Montreal group working in the Plateau area. Here, eleven community associations have gotten together and, with help from the Laidlaw Foundation, the Quebec government, the City of Montreal, the local caisses populaires, and some local benefactors, have set up a revolving fund to finance community projects. This is a new venture, so the results are hard to predict, but it seems likely that socially useful projects such as housing and day-care centres will be undertaken. Borrowing from the fund will be at modest rates, and returns will be ploughed back into the community.

Some observers go much further, and suggest that the only way in which shelter problems will be solved is through basic structural changes in society, including the 'decommodification' of housing (Hartman 1983). Although not advocating total societal change, the aim of the social co-op and non-profit movement is to remove housing from the market for low-income groups and thus avoid cost and rent escalation. However, it has not been successful in persuading private-sector advocates that it is no threat to their well-being, and could gain much respect by clearly explaining its relationship with the market sector.

Such an explanation should point out that of the five elements of housing production – (1) land purchase and preparation, (2) materials and construction, (3) mortgage financing, (4) project management, and (5) rent or profit from sales – the first four are carried out under normal market-economy conditions, regardless of the future tenure form or occupants of the property. It is only the fifth element, profit from rents or subsequent market transactions, that is denied to the private sector.

Competition between non-profits and for-profits has started to be seen as a problem in the entrepreneur-conscious United States (United Way of America 1987). Small businesses have charged that third-sector agencies delivering services in competition with private firms have an unfair advantage because of tax exemptions and the like. Non-profits, in contrast, charge that market-economy companies are moving into areas that have traditionally been the place of the voluntary sector, and then are crying 'unfair.' Engaging in income-generating enterprises has become one way in which the third-sector has been responding to public-sector funding cut-backs. It is evident that as the third sector grows, it will have to be careful to preserve its human-services image, because it is vulnerable to possible ill-conceived legislation and regulation designed to curb abuses.

Voluntary action in Canada has a venerable tradition. It is incredibly diverse, and it is impossible to catch more than its essence here. The formal voluntary sector is only one aspect of the voluntary tradition. The sector is embedded in and interacts with a complex of informal organizations rooted in mutual self-help in local communities. Current momentum is high. The voluntary sector will continue to grow in the future for four reasons. First, because it is encouraged by government policy, part of the rolling back of the state and the reduction of public expenditures. Second, because it represents to some extent a nostalgia for a vision of ordered community life as was manifest prior to the establishment of the welfare state – an order, which, incidentally, any survivor of the 1930s will insist was largely imaginary. Third, because it has appeal for the neo-anarchists and the new 'localists' who are disillusioned with large-scale government policies that do not respond to local needs (Ross and Usher 1986; MacLeod 1986). And finally, because participants in the third sector find satisfaction in their work. For many young people the setting up of a NGO has been a form of job-creation program for themselves. For many retirees – and their numbers are growing – volunteer or non-profit work is seen as a socially useful and fulfilling way of redeploying their energies and expertise (Smith et al. 1972).

The expansion of the role of the third sector in the provision of housing requires two major thrusts. The first depends on the establishment of lasting partnerships within the non-profit sector and with the government and private sectors. The second depends on recognizing, and persuading the other sectors to recognize, that community-based social- and economic-development programs offer the most promise for the sensitive provision of housing, including a complete range of supportive services and facilities. Through these means the third sector will continue its role of service to the population at large.

REFERENCES

Armitage, Andrew. 1975. *Social Welfare in Canada: Ideals and Realities*. Toronto: McClelland and Stewart
Berger, Seymour. 1986. 'The Unrecorded Economy: Concepts, Approach and Preliminary Estimates for Canada 1981.' *Canadian Statistical Review*. April: vi–xxvi
Bosworth, Bill, et al. 1983. *The Case for Long-Term, Supportive Housing*. Toronto: Participants in the Single Displaced Persons' Project. Mimeo
Brandon, D. 1974. *Guidelines to Research in Homelessness*. London, Eng.: Christian Action
Bratt, Rachel G. 1986. 'Community Based Housing Programs: Overview, Assessment, and Agenda for the Future.' *Journal of Planning Education and Research* 5, no. 3 (Spring): 164 – 77
Buchbinder, Howard. 1971. 'The Toronto Social Planning Council and the United Community Fund.' In *Social Space: Canadian Perspectives*, ed. D.I. Davies and Kathleen Herman. Toronto: New Press
Canada. 1969. *Report of The Task Force on Housing and Urban Development* (Hellyer Report). Ottawa
Carter, Novia. 1975. *Volunteers: The Untapped Potential*. Ottawa: Canadian Council on Social Development
CCSD 1980. (Canadian Council on Social Development). *Directory of Canadian Welfare Services, 1980*. Ottawa
– 1987. *National Survey on Homelessness in Canada*. Ottawa
CEIAC (Canada Employment and Advisory Immigration Council). 1985. *Services to Refugee Claimants*. Ottawa
CHF (Cooperative Housing Foundation). 1982. *Co-op Futures Project*. 5 vols. Toronto: York University, Cooperative Future Directions Project
– 1985. *A Proposal for a Co-operative Housing Program Based on Price-Level Adjusted Mortgage Financing*. Ottawa

- 1989. *From the Rooftops* 16:1 (January)
Choko, Marc. 1980. *Cent ans de crise de logement à Montréal*. Montreal: Editions Albert St Martin
CMHC (Canada Mortgage and Housing Corporation). 1983a. *The Private Non-Profit Housing Program*. Ottawa
- 1983b. *Section 56.1 Non-Profit and Cooperative Housing Program Evaluation*. Ottawa
Cohen, Leah. 1984. *Small Expectations: Society's Betrayal of Older Women*. Toronto: McClelland and Stewart
Dennis, Michael; and Fish, Susan. 1972. *Programs in Search of a Policy: Low Income Housing in Canada*. Toronto: Hakkert
Denton, Margaret A.; Davis, Christine K.; and Nussey, Brenda J. 1986, 1987. *Patterns of Support: The Use of Support Services among Senior Citizen Public Housing Tenants in Ontario*. 2 vols. Toronto: Ontario Ministry of Housing
Disney, Diane M.; Kimmich, Madeleine H.; and Musselwhite, James C. 1984. *Partners in Public Service: Government and the Non-profit Sector in Rhode Island*. Washington, DC: The Urban Institute
Douglas, James. 1983. *Why Charity? The Case for a Third Sector*. Beverly Hills: Sage
Dufour, Lise. 1988. 'La désinstitutionalisation et la réintegration sociale: Rêve ou réalité?' *Municipalité*, février: 2–4
Hamel, Pierre. 1983. 'Crise de la redistribution étatique et financement des organisations populaires.' *Revue international d'action communautaire* 10/50 (Automne): 63–77
Hartman, Chester, ed. 1983. *America's Housing Crisis: What Is to Be Done?* Boston: Routledge and Kegan Paul for The Institute for Policy Studies
Hellyer Task Force. 1969. *Report of the Federal Task Force on Housing and Urban Development*. Paul Hellyer, chairman. Ottawa: Information Centre
Hulchanski, J. David. 1983. 'Shelter Allowances and Canadian Housing Policy: A Review and Exploration.' Manuscript prepared for the CHF
- ed. 1983. *Managing Land for Housing: The Experience of Housing Co-operatives in British Columbia*. Vancouver: University of British Columbia, Centre for Human Settlements
Hulchanski, David; and Patterson, Jeffrey. 1984. 'Two Commentaries on CMHC's Evaluation of its 56.1 Housing Programs. Is It an Evaluation?' *Plan Canada* 24.1 (June): 28–31
Imbimbo, Josephine; and Pfeffer, Rachel. 1987. 'Reflections of Home: Women in Shelters.' *Women and Environments* 10, no. 1: 14–15
Kaufman, Nancy K. 1984. 'Homelessness: A Comprehensive Policy Approach.' *Urban and Social Change Review* 17, no. 1: 21–6

Krohn, Roger; Fleming, Berkley; and Manzer, Marilyn. 1977. *The Other Economy: The Internal Logic of Local Rental Housing.* Toronto: Peter Martin

Lapointe-Roi, Huguette. 1987. *Charité – bien ordonné: Le premier réseau de lutte contre la pauvreté à Montréal au 19e siècle.* Montreal: Boréal

Lawrence, Roger, 1983. 'Voluntary Action: A Stalking Horse for the Right?' *Critical Social Policy* 2, no. 3: 14–30

Legault Report. 1976. Groupe de Travail sur L'Habitation. *Rapport: Habiter au Québec.* Montreal: Quebec Government Printers

Leman, Christopher. 1980. *The Collapse of Welfare Reform: Political Institutions, Policy, and the Poor in Canada and the United States.* Cambridge, MA: MIT

Ley, David, ed. 1973. *Community Participation and the Spatial Order of the City.* BC Geographical Series no. 19. Vancouver: Tantalus Research

Lithwick, Harvey. 1970. *Urban Canada: Problems and Prospects.* Ottawa: Central Mortgage and Housing Corporation

Maass, Barbara. 1986. *A Report on the Housing Needs of Psychiatrically Disabled Individuals in Ottawa-Carleton.* Ottawa: Ottawa-Carleton Branch of the Canadian Mental Health Association

McGraw, Donald. 1978. *Le développement des Groupes populaires à Montréal, 1963–1973.* Montreal: Editions Albert St Martin

MacLeod, Greg. 1986. *New Age Business: Community Corporations that Work.* Ottawa: CCSD

Manchee, Rod; and Drover, Glenn. 1981. *Mutual Housing: An Alternative to Homeownership.* Ottawa: Centre for Policy Alternatives

Martin, Samuel A. 1985. *An Essential Grace: Funding Canada's Health Care, Education, Welfare, Religion and Culture.* Toronto: McClelland and Stewart

Millet, David. 1971. 'Religion as a Source of Perpetuation of Ethnic Identity.' In *Social Space: Canadian Perspectives,* ed. D.I. Davies and Kathleen Herman. Toronto: New Press

Oberlander, H. Peter; and Fallick, Arthur L. 1987. *Shelter or Homes? A Contribution to the Search for Solutions to Homelessness in Canada.* Vancouver: University of British Columbia, Centre for Human Settlements

Poulton, Michael. 1984. 'Two Commentaries on CMHC's Evaluation of Its 56.1 Housing Programs: An Indictment of the 56.1 Program.' *Plan Canada* 24.1 (June): 32–6

Przeworski, Joanne Fox; and Fredrickson, J. William, eds. 1980. *Stimulating Joint Urban Ventures: Community Organizations and Organized Philanthropy.* Chicago: Trust Inc.

Réseau d'aide. 1987. 'Document de reflexion sur la situation actuelle des Sans-Abri à Montréal.' MS préparé par les membres du comité Année

Internationale du Logement des Sans-abri, invité par Le Réseau d'aide aux personnes seules et intinérantes de Montréal, Inc.

Robichaud, Jean-Bernard. 1985. *Voluntary Action: Provincial Policies and Practices*. Ottawa: CCSD

Romeder, Jean-Marie. 1982. *Self-Help Groups in Canada*. Ottawa: Health and Welfare Canada

Ross, Aileen D. 1982. *The Lost and the Lonely: Homeless Women in Montreal*. Montreal: Canadian Human Rights Foundation

Ross, David P. 1983. *Some Financial and Economic Dimensions of Registered Charities and Volunteer Activity in Canada*. Ottawa: Secretary of State, Social Trends Analysis Directorate, Policy Coordination Analysis and Management Branch

Ross, David P.; and Usher, Peter J. 1986. *From the Roots Up: Economic Development as if Community Mattered*. Ottawa: CCSD

Serge, Luba. 1981. *Assessment of Organization of Third Sector Groups: Milton Parc*. Ottawa: CMHC

Shepherd, William F. 1957. 'Genesis of the Montreal Council of Social Agencies.' MSW thesis, McGill University

Simoneau, Jean, ed. 1977. *Avant de se retrouver tout nu dans la rue: Le problème de logement*. Montreal: Editions Parti PMS

Single Displaced Persons' Project. 1983. *The Case for Long-Term Supportive Housing*. Toronto

Smith, David Horton; Reddy, Richard D., and Baldwin, Burt R., eds. 1972. *Voluntary Action Research: 1972*. Voluntary Action Research Series of the Center for a Voluntary Society [Washington, DC]. Lexington, MA: D.C. Heath

SPCMT (Social Planning Council of Metropolitan Toronto). 1984. *Caring for Profit: The Commercialization of Human Services in Ontario*. Toronto

STAD (Social Trends Analysis Directorate). 1983. *The Development of a Typology of the Voluntary Sector in Canada*. Ottawa: Secretary of State

Statistics Canada. 1980. *An Overview of Volunteer Workers in Canada*. Cat. no. 71-530 (occasional). Ottawa

– 1981. 'An Overview of Volunteer Workers in Canada.' *The Labour Force*. Cat. no. 71-001 (May): 77–113

Strong-Boag, Veronica. 1976. *The Parliament of Women: The National Council of Women of Canada 1893–1929*. Ottawa: National Museums of Man

Supportive Housing Coalition. 1981. *Community Housing for Consumers of Mental Health Services in Metropolitan Toronto*. Toronto: SHC

TUUW (Toronto Union of Unemployed Workers). 1987. 'Inquiry into the Effects of Homelessness on Health.' Toronto. Mimeo

United Way of America. 1987. *Trend Intelligence Program: Seven Trends for*

Strategic Planning. Washington: United Way of America, Strategic Planning Division

Watson, Sophie; and Austerberry, Helen. 1986. *Housing and Homelessness: A Feminist Perspective*. London: Routledge and Kegan Paul

Whitney, Keith. 1970. 'Skid Row.' In *The Underside of Toronto*, ed. W.E. Mann. Toronto: McClelland and Stewart

Wineman, Steven. 1984. *The Politics of Human Services: Radical Alternatives to the Welfare State*. Montreal: Black Rose

Wolfe, Jeanne M. 1985. 'Some Present and Future Aspects of Housing and the Third Sector.' In *The Metropolis: Proceedings of a Conference in Honour of Hans Blumenfeld*, ed. John R. Hitchcock, Anne McMaster, and Judy Kjellberg. Toronto: University of Toronto, Department of Geography, and Centre for Urban and Community Studies

Woods Gordon. 1981. *Evaluative Study of Non-Profit and Cooperative Housing in Ontario*. Report prepared for CMHC and Ministry of Housing of Ontario

TOM CARTER AND ANN McAFEE

8 The Municipal Role in Housing the Homeless and Poor

Local governments are keenly aware of housing needs. Employees in a number of municipal departments and agencies, and often local politicians, have almost daily contact with people facing housing difficulties. This 'grass-roots' relationship with housing need is not present to the same extent for provincial and particularly federal officials. Although municipalities are often placed in the best position to gauge housing need, the Canadian Constitution does not give them the direct responsibility for housing. As well, the Constitution limits their ability to generate sufficient revenue to implement effective and on-going programs capable of addressing the needs of lower-income households. Rose (1980: 185) has pointed out that municipalities, even with the best of goodwill and motivations, cannot be expected to fulfil all the roles and responsibilities required to respond to housing need. Nevertheless, when community needs are not met, pressure is placed first on local government officials to respond, so municipalities do tackle housing problems – though often with inappropriate tools and inadequate funds.

This chapter reviews the municipal role in housing; actions initiated by municipalities to assist the lowest-income households – those whose needs for adequate and affordable basic shelter are not being met by the housing market – are identified and discussed. Examples are drawn primarily from those larger Canadian cities most active in addressing unmet housing needs, but the discussion of problems and initiatives is applicable in a general sense to all municipalities. Local initiatives in the United States and Britain and their applicability to the Canadian situation are also discussed.

The role that municipalities have assumed in the provision of social housing is discussed first, with emphasis on municipal authority and responsibilities, the changing role of municipalities and their changing relationships with other levels of government, models of municipal involvement, and the constraints municipalities face. Second, the tools available to local governments to help address housing needs are identified and recent municipal housing initiatives are assessed for lessons that can be learned and applied on a wider basis. Finally, the municipal role is redefined with a view to directions that might be taken in the future.

THE MUNICIPAL ROLE IN HOUSING THE POOR

Municipal Authority and Responsibilities

The British North America (BNA) Act of 1867 was designed at a time when many of the social programs, including social housing, that are taken for granted today were not issues that were given any degree of public attention. Welfare of any sort was largely left to philanthropic individuals, church organizations, or the provision of minimal relief at the municipal level. As a result the responsibilities for social housing were not clearly defined in the BNA Act. As well, Alexis de Tocqueville pointed out that in a federal state it is always difficult to determine, with any degree of accuracy, the share of authority each level of government has or will obtain (see Birch 1955: 3). Section 91 of the BNA Act, however, gives the power to control fiscal policy, and the spending power it provides, to the federal government, along with the power to make payments to individuals, institutions, and other levels of government. The federal government also claims the right to attach conditions to the way this money is spent. Under Section 92, however, implementation of many of the programs funded by federal fiscal power falls under the provincial jurisdiction. A more detailed description of the federal and provincial roles in housing is provided in chapter 5. Municipalities, in contrast, are really creatures of the province under the terms of the BNA Act. As such they are not designated any formal housing responsibilities, although traditionally they have played a role in providing welfare since before the turn of the century. It is within these rather confusing parameters of authority that municipalities act out their role in social housing.

The powers of the BNA Act, however vague, have been translated into various responses to housing need. Senior governments have used their broader powers and fiscal resources to provide both supply- and demand-side incentives, but local governments have seldom had the necessary combination of legislative authority and fiscal resources, or, in some cases, the political will, to offer the same level of extensive housing incentives. The provinces, however, have delegated to municipalities the authority to regulate the use of land through zoning and development by-laws and to establish building quality standards, subject in some cases to appeal and direction from senior governments, and the power to collect taxes and own land and to assist the poor.

Within this sphere of authority, municipalities have assumed a wide range of housing responsibilities varying from land-use regulations to cost sharing of social housing programs with the senior levels of government, and in a few cases, to implementing their own programs. Most municipal actions, however, are regulatory in nature and are designed to ensure that safety standards are met, infrastructure and community services are provided, and the operations of the market are controlled to the extent that housing is appropriately located relative to other land uses. Although these regulatory actions and other aspects of local government may not carry the significance and strength of the spending power available to the two senior levels of government, municipalities can play a prominent role in the provision of housing for the needy and many do.

Traditionally, however, municipalities have not used their powers extensively. Instead, they have focused on lobbying senior governments to respond to housing problems or engaged in actions to support provincial or federal initiatives by facilitating zoning changes and providing land, municipal infrastructure, and services. A brief overview of the recent history of municipal involvement in housing illustrates a constantly changing relationship between municipalities and the two senior levels of government. Although the tools available to municipalities have not changed significantly over time, the use of these tools has varied with changing relationships between the various levels of government and the private sector.

Intergovernmental Relationships: The Changing Role of Municipalities
Prior to 1964, the federal government played a strong and controlling role in the development of publicly provided housing (Rose 1980: 83). Since then, amendments to the National Housing Act (NHA), the need for federal fiscal restraint, and growing provincial constraints on federal control and leadership have weakened federal control of policy develop-

ment and federal involvement in the delivery and administration of social housing programs. As the federal role has declined the opportunity has existed for expansion of provincial and municipal initiatives.

In 1964 the NHA was amended to increase municipal participation through authorization of loans to municipal non-profit corporations for the construction or purchase of low-rental housing. At the same time the definition of 'public housing' was amended to include municipal ownership. The assumption at the time was that local governments would assume much more responsibility for low-income housing with municipal housing agencies undertaking the work (Canada, Parliament 1964: 3717; Dennis and Fish 1972: 14). The Ontario government, however, upset such an idea by announcing that Ontario municipalities would not be allowed to take advantage of such legislation and that the provisions of the NHA would continue to operate on a federal/provincial basis as opposed to more direct federal involvement with municipalities (Dennis and Fish 1972: 146). Most provinces over the next few years set up provincial housing corporations to ensure this status quo was maintained.

In 1973, however, additional amendments to the NHA further strengthened the potential for municipal involvement in social housing. Added incentives were made available to co-operative and non-profit groups including municipal 'non-profits.' Several municipal non-profits were soon formed to take advantage of this legislation and emerged as active participants along with private non-profits and co-operatives in policy formation, delivery, and management of housing. However, despite these legislative changes that favoured more municipal involvement, most local governments continued to lobby for, and contribute land and limited funds to, social housing built by the senior levels of government; the municipalities assumed little responsibility for delivery and management themselves. In the early 1970s, most of the approximately 200,000 public housing units built after 1949 were still managed by provincial housing corporations (Cogan and Darke 1983).

In the late 1970s, an era of federal accommodation of provincial attempts to obtain more control of a variety of social-policy initiatives as well as continued erosion of the federal government's fiscal position prompted further amendments to the NHA. These amendments again reduced the federal role and 'disentangled' the delivery of social housing. Under these amendments it was anticipated that 'federal authorities would withdraw from the planning and regulation of public housing programs and likely the community services programs such as neighbourhood improvement and residential rehabilitation ... Municipalities and provinces would play a larger role in the administration of programs while the federal government limited itself to a broader role of financing' (Toronto 1978: 127).

As responsibility for social housing became decentralized, the activities of municipal planning and housing departments diversified. By the end of the decade Maass (1980) found that most larger cities had completed housing needs studies and a survey by CMHC confirmed that the majority of municipalities had adopted a formal social housing policy by the late 1970s (Burchinshaw, Jeu, and Spurr 1985). In some cities the mandate of departments whose activities previously focused primarily on physical planning (e.g., land-use regulation) expanded to incorporate social housing planning. More often, new departments of social planning or housing were formed to manage housing initiatives (Egan 1977).

The impetus for a more active municipal role in housing in the 1970s could frequently be attributed to reformist councils elected on a platform of improving the overall quality of city life and the conditions of low-income households. The provision of affordable housing is both a direct and a highly visible action, so it lends itself to a role in political campaigns. Though, as Rose (1980: 128) observes of the Toronto experience, the assumption of a direct active role in the housing field by cities was not achieved without serious administrative, organizational, and financial difficulties, resulting, in large measure, from the complexities of intergovernmental legislation, the public/private housing-sector relationship that cities had to deal with, and the fiscal demands of programs to accommodate low-income groups.

The gradual reduction of the federal role in the provision of social housing continued in the 1980s and current federal policy is epitomized by the following basic principles:

- a desire to devolve federal responsibility to the private sector, the provinces, and non-profit organizations including municipal 'non-profits';
- federal disengagement from programs that were housing related but did not directly produce additional or improved units;
- an intent to re-target social housing assistance to ensure only the most needy are recipients; and
- an intent to limit any direct federal role to one concerned with weakness or failure in the housing market. (Canada, Minister of Supply and Services 1986: 9–14)

These principles send a very clear message. There will be continued federal involvement, but a high degree of flexibility permitting an expanded provincial and municipal role (see chapter 5). They also send a very clear message that the federal government is not prepared to engage in the multi-faceted programming that is required to respond to housing need in many situations. Instead, provinces and municipalities find themselves having to respond to those program requirements.

In summary, changes since 1964 have witnessed legislative amendments to the NHA that provide more flexibility for municipalities to participate in social housing initiatives, and the recent federal move toward disentanglement encourages local involvement at both the provincial and municipal level, although a stronger municipal role is still viewed with some hostility by the provinces. In addition, in several municipalities the political will to address housing concerns appears to have emerged. Municipal social housing initiatives in Canada are designed to meet two very basic goals: to ensure increased municipal control over the type, location, and social composition of assisted-housing initiatives targeted toward low- and moderate-income groups; and, accordingly, to increase the availability of housing for these same groups (Ontario Welfare Council 1977: 7). These are very worthwhile goals but they are rarely the end result municipalities try to achieve. There are other broader and more basic reasons for municipal involvement in the provision of social housing, reasons that are strongly associated with identification of need and delivery of services.

Housing problems vary from region to region, city to city, neighbourhood to neighbourhood. Accordingly, locally devised programs are often most appropriate (Daly 1988: 1). Municipalities have long recognized this fact and it is one of the primary reasons for local involvement. As well, few housing problems can be solved by a housing-only solution. Multi-faceted programming, an arena in which the federal government is reducing its role, is required and often includes educational, employment support, health, and counselling components. Local governments are usually in the best position to identify such needs and to organize and deliver the appropriate services. Therefore, municipalities have become involved because they are best able to identify the diversity of needs and deliver the variety of services required by those in need of housing assistance.

Certainly the rationale for involvement has not weakened. There continues to be a substantial number of households in inadequate and unaffordable housing and the number of homeless continues to grow.

The pressure from residents for local governments to address housing needs is certainly as strong as, if not stronger than, it was in the 1960s and 1970s. The rationale for municipal involvement is there and, combined with the regulatory environment and changing intergovernmental relationships, provides municipalities with considerable strength to address housing problems.

Municipal Involvement in Social Housing: Models of Scope and Process
Despite the commonality of tools with which to address social housing needs, not all municipalities are equally active in the provision of social housing. The reasons cities have assumed different roles in the provision of social housing can be traced to varying degrees of affluence, different local development patterns, levels of need, and political climates. Broadly speaking, there are three models of city involvement in social housing: reactor, facilitator, and comprehensive developer.

In the *reactor model* social housing is initiated by the senior levels of government or by various private non-profit and co-operative groups. The city processes applications, adjudicates between land uses, and inspects to ensure that adequate standards are maintained. This model occurs in jurisdictions where the local government is unable, unwilling, or concludes that it is unnecessary to assume an active role in the provision of affordable housing.

In the *facilitator model* the city continues to respond to the initiatives of others, but with the added dimension of actively facilitating non-market housing through the provision of land and/or subsidies, supporting or even initiating rezoning applications, expediting permit processing, and lobbying with senior governments for funds if the sponsors are private non-profits or co-operatives. This model is applicable where a local authority has limited funds to allocate to social housing or where community private non-profit groups and resource organizations are active. When a city assumes a facilitator role, social housing responsibilities generally are added to the mandate of an existing city department as has occurred in cities such as Vancouver prior to 1989 and Regina (Carter and Badiuk 1987: 4–8).

Concerned that indirect action through the non-market and private sector is not providing the necessary stock of affordable housing prompts some municipalities to play a more direct role by creating civic housing departments. In this *comprehensive developer* model the city adds site design, project implementation, and ongoing management to the previously listed activities. In this model a municipality has direct control of social housing initiatives. It also assumes the highest level of potential risk by providing ongoing subsidies if rents and senior government subsidies are insufficient to cover costs. Social housing initiatives can be delivered through a new department, as occurred in Toronto, or by expanding the role of an existing department, as occurred in Ottawa. Actual design, development, and project management can be assumed by municipal staff or contracted out, the latter occurring most frequently (ibid.).

A discussion of municipalities typical of each model illustrates how the defined roles in housing, the organizational structures, the initiatives, and the processes of delivery vary with the model type. The Winnipeg approach typifies the reactor model, Vancouver the facilitator, and Toronto the comprehensive developer model. All three cities took the necessary step in the 1970s to prepare well-documented housing needs studies (Burchinshaw, Jeu, and Spurr 1985). All three cities appear to have had the political will to address social housing needs. Here the similarity ends and the processes and initiatives under which social housing units have been delivered are very different.

In Toronto a municipal non-profit housing corporation was incorporated in 1974 and was in full operation as a separate civic housing department by 1975. Its aim was 'to develop new housing for low and moderate income people and acquire and renovate existing housing in the city' (Toronto 1976). Several responsibilities were given to the corporation that provided it with a broad and effective mandate to deliver housing initiatives. These responsibilities included

- *research* to identify annual housing production targets, demonstrate housing need, and develop new responses to housing the poor;
- *land acquisition* for the purpose of increasing the supply of land in public ownership for assisted housing sites;
- *construction* of assisted housing with an emphasis on rental units;
- *purchase and renovation* of existing housing for low and moderate income households;
- *property management* of assisted housing;
- *coordination* of non-profit housing activities; and
- *program and policy coordination* between the city and senior governments. (Toronto 1976)

The city department has, at present, a large permanent staff responsible for developing, on average, 400–500 units a year and managing the growing housing portfolio. It is headed by a commissioner who, in the early years, directed five divisions: Intergovernmental Cooperation and Research, Planning, Development, Property Management, and Administration. The department has been involved in a broad range of housing initiatives including St Lawrence Square, a half-billion-dollar sixty-seven acre comprehensive residential and commercial development that will eventually provide 7000 units, up to 50 per cent under the non-profit program and many designed for the homeless; new scattered site projects; acquisition and rehabilitation of existing rooming-houses and older apartments to provide non-profit rental units; conversion of non-residential buildings to housing; and partnerships with the private sector to provide affordable housing in exchange for density bonuses.

Expectations that senior government programs would provide the necessary funds to implement local housing initiatives proved optimistic. The department has been able to recover some, but not all, of its administrative costs, so it has taken the ultimate potential risk in providing ongoing subsidies. In 1980, largely in response to accumulated deficits, the department was reorganized, resulting in fewer on-site project offices, tighter budget controls, and more efficient management techniques, including computerization of waiting-lists, vacancy lists, and tenant rent-reporting systems. However, the basic organizational structure remains, with municipal housing being delivered by a civic department that plays the role of a comprehensive developer as opposed to facilitating or reacting to initiatives by others.

By contrast, the City of Vancouver instituted, abandoned, and then reinstituted the civic department model. In 1975, Vancouver created the Vancouver Municipal Non-Profit Housing Corporation, with the intention of assuming a comprehensive developer role and the explicit objective of housing families and low-income singles in the city's 'skid row' area. Where Toronto established a comprehensive housing planning and production bureaucracy within a department of housing, Vancouver hired a director of housing in the expectation that he would call on the services of staff in the existing Planning, Property Acquisition, Finance, Law, Engineering, and Social Planning departments. The director resigned in frustration within a year.

In retrospect, his problems stemmed from an inappropriate administrative structure and an erroneous analysis of the non-market sector in Vancouver. The administrative structure established separated policy, planning, and production functions, which were not entirely at the disposal of the director. In addition, the absence of adopted housing goals made co-ordination within the city difficult, thus exacerbating co-ordination difficulties with the two senior levels of government. A comprehensive developer role is most effective when the reason that housing needs are not being met is either the absence of third-sector sponsors or their inability to meet existing needs. Neither was the case in Vancouver during the mid 1970s. Problems in Vancouver were a shortage of suitable sites and the high cost of land. In creating the Vancouver Municipal Non-Profit Housing Corporation, Vancouver added another developer to compete with established non-profit groups for land and funds – in effect duplicating existing capabilities rather than alleviating problems.

After the demise of the housing corporation, policy planning and program delivery initiatives were allocated to existing departments. Special short-term development groups were hired to project-manage larger sites such as the seventy-acre city-owned False Creek area. City staff assisted non-profit and co-operative resource groups to acquire sites, get funds from senior governments, and move expeditiously through the development process. The process proved to be effective, and on an annual basis, the number of units assisted during the late 1970s was comparable to the production of the Toronto housing corporation. A social housing strategy was adopted in the 1980s that incorporated this particular approach (Vancouver 1979).

Vancouver, like Toronto, found that an active role – even as a facilitator – in municipal non-profit housing was not without cost. To ensure non-profit sponsors could build within federally established maximum unit prices, Vancouver leased land at less than full market recovery. Between 1978 and 1982, a period of rapid price rises, the city contributed some $16.5 million in forgone revenues toward social housing. Even with this subsidy contribution, and without additional support from all three levels of government (which was not forthcoming), rents for social housing units were not affordable by the lowest-income households.

In Winnipeg during the 1970s the two most pressing housing problems were affordability and the large portion of the stock in poor condition. Some 23 per cent of the inner-city stock required major repair; and a housing crisis existed, particularly for single parents and elderly singles (McKee et al. 1975: 8). Neither the private nor public sector, including other non-profits, was able to meet the needs for low-cost housing. Faced with this situation, Winnipeg City Council established the Winnipeg Housing Rehabilitation Corporation (WHRC) in 1977, with a mandate to address the housing crisis for persons of limited income and the upgrading of the residential stock in the inner city.

The WHRC was established as an autonomous legal entity by City Council with sole powers to enter into financial and other legal agreements. City Council's ability to influence the objectives, policies, and activities of WHRC rested mainly on its powers of appointment to the WHRC Board of Directors and whether the city adopted ancillary policies that facilitated or inhibited WHRC activities. WHRC was designed to be a small organization (the staff complement has never exceeded six) on the understanding that the use of contract professionals would be encouraged and assistance would be forthcoming from staff in appropriate city departments (Newman 1986: 5).

The WHRC appeared to start out with a strong mandate reinforced by a $1,000,000 revolving fund cost shared 50:50 by the province and the city (personal interview with WHRC general manager 1988). However, from the very beginning, the organization has had difficulties. To begin with there was no strong endorsement from City Council. The council vote to create the organization was a tie and only the mayor's tie-breaking vote in favour of WHRC allowed the organization to proceed. In addition, assistance from city staff has been minimal and the city only provides an annual operating grant of $30,000. The city has also never adopted a social housing policy or strategy to support WHRC initiatives.

After more than ten years of operation, the WHRC portfolio contains less than 400 units and the organization is almost entirely dependent on an annual allocation of approximately fifty units from the federal 56.1 non-profit budget. Basically, the WHRC has to line up for federal/provincial budget allocations as would any private non-profit group; and the city, playing the role of reactor, treats project proposals from WHRC as it would proposals from private non-profits (ibid.).

During the 1970s many other larger Canadian urban municipalities took a more active role in social housing initiatives. By 1981 thirteen of the major metropolitan areas had operational municipal non-profit corporations and since then over 100 more have been established, many of them in much smaller centres (Carter and Badiuk 1987: 4). However, the processes of delivery vary substantially. Very few municipalities have adopted the Toronto comprehensive developer role. Most have selected the Vancouver facilitator role and many, like Winnipeg, tend to react as opposed to initiating. Although there does not appear to have been any systematic evaluation of the comparative effectiveness of various municipal delivery mechanisms, several observations can be made. First, there is no one process that appears to work for all cities. The process must fit the resources and local situation, as Vancouver discovered. Second, as experience in Winnipeg demonstrates, unless there is substantial political will backed up by a strong municipal social housing policy, even the best-planned initiatives will be difficult to deliver. Finally, with very few exceptions, municipalities that have selected more active roles have found it is necessary to contribute extensive operating capital, maintain ongoing subsidies, and use their regulatory authority to provide special concessions to deliver affordable housing.

Common Constraints Faced by Municipalities
Regardless of the delivery model chosen, it is clear from the annual reports of municipal housing authorities and from a joint statement issued by the Federation of Canadian Municipalities in 1984 that local authorities face many common problems in ensuring a stock of adequate and affordable housing (Federation 1984). They face these problems within a legislative context that lacks clarity as the discussion of roles and responsibilities suggests. Municipalities have no clearly defined mandate within existing legislation and there is no legislation demanding that they play a direct and active role. When they do take the initiative it is often regarded with concern, if not hostility, by the provinces; and they face the problem of obtaining an adequate amount and continuity of funding from senior governments. Such funding as is available from these sources is seldom viewed by local authorities as sufficient in terms of the number of units or the depth of subsidy per unit to address the very needy. As well, for cities to undertake responsible social housing planning, either three-year to five-year funding agreements are required or a three-year notice to change or terminate programs is necessary for municipalities to complete transactions. There is an enormous loss of momentum and credibility if cities encourage social housing only to find programs alter or funds are inadequate to house low-income households.

The amount of funds some municipalities have contributed to social housing suggests that, by and large, cities are willing to cost-share social initiatives. However, many cities suggest that their limited tax base makes it difficult to generate sufficient revenues for social initiatives. The minister of State for Urban Affairs, André Ouellet, pointed to the significance of the taxation dilemma facing local government in an address in May 1977.

Property tax can be a serious constraint on municipal governments ... It is these variations in property tax burdens, caused by differences in the tax capacities of municipalities and in the ability of Canadians to pay property taxes ... which I think serve to reduce the ability of certain municipal governments to raise the revenues necessary to provide adequate levels of public services.

If a municipality levies a residential property tax at above average rates, the cost of shelter services will be higher in the community relative to the price in other communities. If a community levies a higher than average non-residential property tax, investments in factory buildings and other assets subject to property tax will be less profitable than elsewhere. (Ouellet 1977: 5–6)

The tax base is a valid concern but the municipal shortage of funds may be as much an aversion to raising taxes in general as it is a problem with the base. Property taxes are especially unpopular. Citizens do not always appreciate the relationship between increases in taxes and the increasing cost of services, particularly if the level and standard of services does not improve appreciably. Many people also view property taxes as regressive. Ouellet's argument, however, is valid even if one substitutes sales taxes or income taxes. Local taxes should not and cannot be used to effect income redistribution because taxpayers will flee to municipalities having lower taxes.

Even if local governments could be expected to take the lead in providing housing subsidies through increased taxation powers, they may not allocate substantially more funds to social housing. Rose (1980: 185) points out that 'legislators in municipal government tend to be self-made men and women, small business men and a few members of the professions. They are generally quite conservative in their views towards the poor and those who require assistance or subsidization in any aspect of their living conditions such as the provision of housing accommodation.' Political reluctance is certainly a factor in funding. However, housing need can vary substantially from one municipality to the next; and if municipalities had the primary responsibility for housing subsidies, people and businesses might move from high-need, high-tax areas and the needy would move to high-benefit areas. This possibility does not absolve municipalities of the responsibility for addressing need, but it does clearly suggest that fiscal responsibility for housing must remain a priority of the senior levels of government because of the broader tax base they command.

Funding difficulties faced by municipalities, as well as other levels of government, are further aggravated by a succession of problems outside the housing sector, ranging from concern about the carrying costs of public debt to general economic downturns. These changing conditions have forced governments, including municipalities, to reconsider the resources available for social programs. Faced with scarce resources, cities have turned to a variety of public and private programs to provide accommodation for those in core need.

HOUSING PROGRAMS IMPLEMENTED BY LOCAL AUTHORITIES: THE SEARCH FOR EFFECTIVE AND EFFICIENT MECHANISMS

Actions to improve the quality of life of households can be delivered through a variety of income and social-service supports. When actions are taken through the housing sector they can either be directed toward the housing stock (supply side) or to households (demand side). Examples of a variety of action areas toward which municipal programs can be targeted are shown in table 8.1. In some areas, incentives (carrots) can be offered to encourage the provision of housing. In other areas, controlling actions (sticks) can be implemented through a municipality's regulatory authority to encourage the provision of affordable housing by the private sector, the public sector, or through some combination of private- and public-sector initiatives. Municipalities have tried a variety of approaches, some with more success than others, but few have provided assistance to those most in need.

Facilitating Social Housing through Better Information: The Local Lobby as a Social Housing Tool
One of the least-costly initiatives undertaken by cities is to estimate unmet housing need and use the data as a basis for lobbying senior governments for implementation funds. Maass (1980), when reviewing housing-needs studies in ten Canadian cities, found that there were three reasons housing-needs studies were done: to define the extent of need and hence target actions, to ensure the relevance of programs to local needs, and to foster action to alleviate housing need.

Housing-needs studies typically use cross-tabulations from census data. Broad estimates of need are obtained by user group, income, shelter costs, tenure, land type, and condition of the housing stock. However, there are serious limitations to the use of census data to estimate the numbers of core needy. Those with the most serious housing problems are those without shelter and persons in temporary or hotel accommodation – neither of which are identified as households

TABLE 8.1
Supply- and demand-side action areas

Supply-side action areas
(Programs can be directed to the producers)

CARROTS[a]	STICKS[b]
Reduce the price of housing	*Maintain the stock of lower-priced housing*
– inner city and suburban land banks	– conversion control
– reduce red tape, expedite housing	– demolition control
– reduce service standards	– inclusionary ordinances
Increase supply	*Quality and design control*
– servicing loans	– maintenance and occupancy by-laws
– 'bonus' zoning	– lodging-house by-laws
– transfer of development rights	– zoning by-laws
– ensure zoning provides adequate sites to meet current and projected demand	
– revise zoning/codes to allow for more efficient use of the existing stock	
– co-ordinate project reviews to speed up process	
– provide market/needs data	

Demand-side action areas
(Programs can be directed to the consumers)

CARROTS[a]	STICKS[b]
Reduce the cost of housing	*Increase opportunities*
– property-tax deferral	– anti-discrimination legislation
Increase income	*Transfer of funds*
– educational/employment opportunities	– development levies
Improve liveability	
– home-care services	
– child-care services	
– rental registry services	

---

[a]Carrots: funds to encourage an action to occur
[b]Sticks: regulations, controls to discourage certain actions

in the census. At best, these people are tabulated as collective households and it is likely that many are not recorded by the census. However, this is precisely the point where municipalities can play a role. Some municipalities augment census data with information from social-assistance and disability files, annual surveys, or housing registry records. Vancouver, for example, undertakes an annual survey of rooming-houses and residential hotels in the downtown district to estimate the low-income population and to obtain demographic, income, and housing-stock characteristics.

Maass does not calculate the cost/benefit of housing-needs studies, but if the Vancouver experience is at all typical, a housing-needs study, done in 1979 at a cost of $70,000 (Maass 1980) resulted in a special allocation of 1000 social housing units from the federal government. The potential subsidy implications over thirty-five years exceed $100 million. A similar study undertaken by Regina in 1985 at a cost of $50,000 resulted in an increased annual allocation of family public housing and was at least in part responsible for a 40-unit project for the homeless (Regina 1986: 8–10).

Some cities have found innovative ways to make a case for housing the homeless without detailed needs data. In 1979, health officers in the Vancouver skid-row area, faced with the frustration of finding nightly accommodation for hard-to-house persons with psychiatric illnesses, documented the costs of this service and compared them to the rents required to provide permanent accommodation (Beggs 1979). The documented benefits were sufficient to stimulate the building of several new hostel projects.

Although many cities have an estimate of housing need, some have been more effective than others in using this information to obtain social housing assistance. In some cities, the findings are ignored or shelved with such comments as: 'We do not believe the figures are correct' or 'We do not know what the proposed actions will cost.' By contrast, in other cities the needs studies have been used by politicians to justify civic action or stimulate action by senior levels of government. A successful housing-needs study is one that provides sufficient quality information to convince senior administrators and political leaders of its veracity and permits the politicians to decide to what extent resources should be allocated to alleviate housing need (Maass 1980: iii). The actions of several mayors illustrate the value of such work. In 1973 Mayor David Crombie said in his inaugural speech to the City of Toronto Council: 'It's time for Toronto to get back into the housing business.' Subsequent mayors, such as John Sewell, ran on a platform that included improving housing. During the early 1970s Alderman (later mayor) Michael Harcourt was elected on a platform of improving housing conditions in Vancouver's 'skid row.' These politicians commissioned numerous reports on housing needs (Toronto 1980). More important, they used the information to lobby senior governments successfully for social housing funds.

An Advocacy and Educational Role for Municipalities
Municipalities are often portrayed as weak when it comes to ability to respond to housing need; as the discussion has indicated, there is some justification for this view, particularly in the arena of fiscal policy. However, the reluctance of municipalities to become more involved in low-income housing initiatives is often as much a response to community resistance as it is a result of limited funding ability.

Community acceptance of low-income public housing has been mixed. Projects for senior citizens are generally welcome, but large developments for families and special-needs facilities are not. Fears of declining property values, inferior design, strain on community services, adverse socio-economic mixes, and establishing precedents for building higher densities in lower-density areas are among the objections raised by residents. However, a Vancouver study found fears of declining property values and adverse socio-economic impacts as a result of nearby smaller social housing developments to be largely unfounded (French, Morrison, and McAfee 1986). Nevertheless, to reduce community resistance, public housing is often located in areas of low desirability. Another study by the City of Vancouver showed that 20 per cent of public housing was not located within easy access of public transit or shops. Only 50 per cent of all projects were located within five blocks of park or recreational facilities; 40 per cent were located near to, or within audible distance of, major traffic corridors or railway tracks; and 6 per cent were located on the fringe of industrial areas (McAfee 1979).

Nearly every major city in Canada can document several incidents where projects have been stopped or placed in less than adequate surroundings because of the reaction of resident groups. Often this public reaction is not justified. Combating or prevailing in the face of unjustified community resistance can be a very effective role for municipalities and could increase significantly the number of social housing initiatives that proceed. A few mayors, as previously indicated, have been very supportive of social housing and defended construction of projects for the very low income population, but a more positive attitude and stronger advocacy role on the part of all municipalities is required.

Canadian municipalities could well take lessons from the actions of major British cities in this area. Locally funded Housing Aid Centres operated by non-profit organizations are located in many major urban areas in Britain. Two such examples are the centre in London and the one for the boroughs of Kensington, Chelsea, and Westminster (Daly 1988: 19, II-1 to II-7). Established in the early 1970s, these centres offer essential advocacy and information services to homeless people so they will know how to deal with and utilize housing and other social-service bureaucracies. Specifically, the centres provide advice to tenants on a variety of housing problems ranging from repairs to racial harassment, legal issues, negotiations with landlords, referrals to other housing agencies, and other crisis situations. These centres also work to focus national attention on housing and related issues by lobbying higher levels of government, conducting research, and publishing the findings. They may also undertake much of the work necessary to encourage fundamental changes in law and administrative practices.

Local governments provide funding because they feel the centres, operated as they are by non-profit organizations, can provide these services at a cost lower than the local government itself could, particularly as a considerable self-help component is built into the operations. Similar centres funded by Canadian municipalities, with a knowledge of the variety of needs that exist at a local level and access to the many local services, could provide a valuable advocacy and educational role. They could also provide the co-ordination so often lacking at the local level and could contribute to the multi-faceted approach that is often required. Chapter 7 contains a more detailed discussion of the role of NGOs and non-profit organizations.

Municipal Subsidies to Social Housing
A number of variations can be discussed under the heading of municipal subsidies to housing. Some municipalities have contributed direct funding in the form of up-front grants or ongoing subsidies; others have provided assistance in the form of forgone revenue such as writing down the cost of land; and still others have adopted a cash-in-kind approach by offering the expertise and assistance of municipal staff to non-profits or other levels of government. There are no national estimates of the municipal contributions to social housing but examples from a number of municipalities across Canada suggest contributions are clearly substantial.

In capital grants, for example, the small urban municipality of Regina contributed $324,000 in fiscal year 1986/7. This represented the city's 5 per cent share of capital costs of family public housing built under the Section 40 Public Housing Program. In addition, during the last five fiscal years, Regina contributed $1.5 million in ongoing subsidies on just over 700 units of public housing for seniors and families. These subsidies continue for the life of the projects in the portfolio (Carter and Badiuk 1987: 24). With respect to forgone revenue, Vancouver provides an excellent example of municipal commitment. Between 1978 and 1982 the city allocated $16.5 million in forgone revenues to social housing through land sold at less than market value. An additional $17.6 million was spent between 1982 and 1986. In Winnipeg, residential lots taken back on default of taxes, condemned units, and other municipal property have been provided to accommodate infill housing at prices that are far below market value (Institute of Urban Studies 1987: 88). Similar land write-offs have occurred in Toronto and Halifax.

Although lower land costs certainly provide assistance that substantially lowers the cost of social housing and allows very low income groups to be assisted, these costs often create problems for the municipality over the longer term. Winnipeg, for example, has virtually run out of inner-city lots suitable for infill housing; selling the supply it had at less than market value has weakened the city's ability to purchase new sites. The result is higher overall program costs, which in turn have reduced the number of very low income people assisted (ibid.: 89). Vancouver solved this problem by switching from a sale to a leasehold program. Under the leasehold system, non-profit groups, which did not have the resources to purchase the land outright, were leased land at a value estimated to be equivalent to the market value of a forty-year lease (Wilson 1984: 28–33). The city retained ownership of the property, thereby listing the site as an asset to improve the city's credit rating and borrowing capacity. Long leaseholds are probably only applicable where there is a relative shortage of land, but the successful development of the leasehold system in such prime residential areas as False Creek is indicative of the value of the approach (Wilson 1984).

Calgary, Ottawa, Toronto, and Halifax are all examples of municipalities that offer cash-in-kind assistance in the provision of social housing (Carter and Badiuk 1987: 30). This service varies from the time contributed by planning staff to develop policy and identify housing needs, to contributions to project development by site planners, architects, and legal staff. As well, one cannot ignore the time spent by senior city executives and politicians in liaison with private and non-profit sponsors of housing and lobbying senior levels of government. Although the dollar value of such contributions is perhaps not as substantial as land write-offs or direct subsidies to housing programs, these actions often help initiate projects and are instrumental in getting them through municipal bureaucracy and red tape.

Many municipalities channel a considerable amount of their subsidy contribution, in whatever form, through locally established municipal non-profit housing agencies. The structure and operation of municipal non-profits was discussed earlier, using examples of the organizations in Winnipeg, Vancouver, and Toronto. The lesson to be learned is that municipal non-profits, although they have been successful in providing housing accommodation, still rely on senior governments and other community-based organizations to provide substantial funding. Nowhere is this demonstrated more clearly than in the provision of hostel accommodation. Municipal non-profits have difficulty balancing their books because their subsidies are limited under federal and provincial programs – and hostel tenants typically have no resources other than basic social assistance, so the flexibility to raise rents is very limited. If subsidies are insufficient, as is generally the case, local governments have to step in with additional subsidies or plead their case to higher levels of government.

The most successful local developments appear to involve at least two and sometimes three levels of government and in some cases community non-profit organizations. Costs of the Winnipeg Main Street Project Hostel (including meals) are borne by the municipality, the province, and the United Way. Similarly, in Vancouver, the St James Powell Place, a transition house annually providing emergency shelter for more than a thousand women and children, was funded by the federal government, on land provided by the city, and is assisted by an annual operating grant of $304,000 from the provincial government. The Salvation Army Hostel in Regina receives subsidies from the federal and provincial governments but the capital to build the project came from the Salvation Army, which also provides a considerable portion of the required operating revenue.

Despite what appear to be substantial contributions, municipalities still find that subsidies are insufficient to accommodate the lowest-income households. When subsidies are insufficient to ensure acceptable rent-to-income ratios for lower-income groups, municipalities are faced with the difficult choice of housing low-income people at higher and perhaps unacceptable rent-to-income ratios or assisting those less in need. The Greater Vancouver Housing Corporation faced this choice during the early 1980s. It chose to leave the choice to lower-income households. As a result, 40 per cent of assisted families were paying in excess of 30 per cent of income to rent (11 per cent paid over 50 per cent of income). However, such an approach tends to be an exception, and generally only a portion of municipal funds spent on housing is directed to improving living conditions of the very low income households and the homeless. Similarly, only a portion of social housing units in housing sponsored by all levels of government are directed to those most in need. A study by CMHC (1983) indicated that only 37 per cent of all social housing built between 1979 and 1982 assisted people with incomes in the lowest quintile. Studies by the City of Vancouver (McAfee 1983) also demonstrate that the proportion of low-income households varies for different types of social housing. Generally, public housing, seniors' and disabled non-profit housing, and municipal family housing are well targeted toward lower-income households. Units managed by co-operatives, however, are less likely to be targeted toward the most needy.

It is also impossible to tell how many of those assisted are truly homeless. Overall, only 12 per cent of Vancouver's assisted units are specifically directed toward housing people who previously lived in temporary, hotel, or rooming-house accommodation. Approximately 35 per cent (5000) of Toronto's City Home units are occupied by single people, not all of whom are in core need or homeless. Regina provides approximately 100 units for the homeless or 4 per cent of a total portfolio of approximately 2700 social housing units targeted at low- and moderate-income people (Regina Planning Department and Bairstow 1985: 41–9; Saskatchewan 1988: 32). In Winnipeg there are 497 emergency housing spaces and 851 longer-term spaces in a total portfolio of over 16,000 units (Manitoba 1987: 89–91), but only the emergency spaces can be credited with providing accommodation for the true homeless. The point is that not all housing is targeted toward low-income households and even less of it accommodates the homeless. The current program-subsidy arrangements in which municipalities are involved are not always sufficient to accommodate the most needy.

Maintaining and Upgrading the Stock of Affordable Housing
The more highly publicized municipal housing initiatives have been directed to new units. This presents the paradox of placing the lowest-income households in the newest and most expensive accommo-

dation. Less attention has been directed to 'saving' and improving the quality and affordability of existing rental stock. Prior to the 1970s, private rooming-houses, boarding-houses, and residential hotels provided a substantial stock of low-priced accommodation. However, demolition, upgrading to meet safety standards, and a renewed interest by higher-income people in living in the inner city have resulted in the loss of many low-priced rooms. Bairstow (1986), in a study of homelessness in Ontario, stated that 'the rise of homelessness in major cities in Ontario is directly correlated to the loss of rooming house units. City of Toronto planners estimate that the City has lost 1,700 rooming house units per year in the past few years through demolition and conversion to higher use.'

Because municipalities have a prominent role in the regulatory environment, addressing the preservation of the existing stock is an area in which they can have a positive effect. Municipal initiatives in the Canadian context do exist but they are limited in number. Jacks Hotel in Vancouver, the Main Street Hostel, Prairie Horizons Co-operative, and the Warwick Apartments in Winnipeg, Fred Victor Mission plus several other buildings in Toronto, as well as several projects in Montreal are all examples of older buildings that have been purchased and renovated with varying degrees of municipal assistance (Daly 1988: 1-12 to 1-19; Carter and Badiuk 1987: 25).

However successful these specific projects have been, they are not part of an extensive overall municipal strategy to maintain this form of low-cost housing for the very low income group. Two examples, one in Britain and one in the United States, demonstrate a more extensive policy commitment. In several major urban centres in Britain short-life public buildings have been saved from demolition and allocated to local organizations along with sufficient cash to renovate and repair the structures to a point where they are habitable. Although the building's life may still be limited, the short-term accommodation it provides is still considered cheaper than providing bed and breakfast accommodation. As well, it provides a base from which to co-ordinate other services (Bailey 1977). In the United States, Cincinnati City Council made preservation of 1300 single-room occupancy (sros) old hotel units a priority in its downtown plan. The plan also included commitments to replace lost sros with low-rent units and to make residents displaced by development anywhere in the central business district eligible for relocation benefits (Schwab 1986: 25).

However, preserving the existing stock often means implementing fire, safety and maintenance, and occupancy by-laws, all of which can be a double-edged sword. These regulations can be used to improve the stock but to obtain compliance the city often has to enforce closure on private owners. Units are lost, some permanently; but even if upgrading occurs when they are ready for occupancy, rents may exceed the resident's ability to pay. There are occasions when upgrading is ruled out on humanitarian grounds. In a recent court case in New York, the judge ruled that the City Housing Department could not evict tenants from obvious fire-traps because such actions would result in the tenants ending up either on the street or in shelters, a fate considered worse than the inadequate housing (Bairstow 1986: 11). In Ontario a procedure is being developed to measure the technical merit, costs, benefits, and levels of safety and risk inherent in many building-code requirements to help guide municipalities in their actions.

As well as protecting and enhancing the existing stock, municipalities should consider using the regulatory environment to provide protection to tenants. The application of 'just-cause' eviction ordinances to protect tenant rights and help provide security of tenure has been followed by local governments in the United States. For example, such ordinances used in Washington, DC, have been successful in providing a time frame within which negotiations between the tenant and the landlord can result in conciliation (Hombs and Snyder 1982). Eviction is often avoided, thus preventing the short-term housing crises that so often lead to homelessness. Such intervention can be far less costly in both economic and social terms than homelessness itself.

Canadian municipalities do not have the same authority to deal with eviction issues because these issues often fall under provincial jurisdiction. However, under maintenance and occupancy by-laws, many municipalities can decide not to enforce closure and evict people unless alternative accommodation is available in the city for occupants (City of Winnipeg Act, Clause 649[2]). Consideration should be given to enhancing local authority to deal with a broader range of issues, like those defined in the Washington just-cause ordinances, or to pressuring provincial jurisdictions to be more active in this arena.

Municipal Strategies to Encourage Private-Sector Provision of Affordable Housing
There is a temptation for cities faced with demands for housing

assistance and limited funds to search for 'costless' solutions. Some municipalities have turned to land-use planning powers (real or imagined) to encourage or require the private sector to house the poor. Generally, zoning-based strategies, especially those that rely on the imposition of regulatory powers to require the private sector to provide affordable housing, have not provided many units. Therefore, municipalities have looked toward partnerships with the private sector in the search to accommodate those most in need.

Maintaining Affordable Housing through Downzoning
During the 1970s, concern that the urban-renewal approach of the previous decade had resulted in substantial displacement of lower-income households in inner-city residential areas prompted the introduction of the Neighbourhood Improvement Program (NIP). Cities, because they were instrumental in project planning and delivery, initiated neighbourhood preservation projects under the program. A companion program, the Residential Rehabilitation Assistance Program (RRAP), was introduced at the same time, with the objective of improving the housing stock. The program provided grants and low-interest loans to low-income home owners and owners of older rental apartments. Funding under these programs, however, was not sufficient to maintain the older stock of affordable housing. Recent surveys show very little reduction in the percentage of dwellings needing major repair since the 1970s, and there are still substantially more dwellings that require upgrading in older residential areas of the inner city than in suburban areas (CMHC 1987: 2, 7).

Recognizing these problems, cities such as Winnipeg, Vancouver, and Toronto have tried to maintain affordable housing through downzoning and associated conversion, and through demolition controls. Again, however, evidence suggests that success in maintaining housing opportunities for low-income households has been limited. Prior to downzoning, inner-city areas provided modest accommodation in older buildings owned by absentee landlords who were awaiting the appropriate time to demolish and rebuild. As development opportunities were reduced, through downzoning and development controls, investors sold the units and looked for alternative investments. In many areas of the cities, higher-income households were now able to afford inner-city locations and moved in, gentrifying the area. A more complete discussion of gentrification and loss of housing stock is included in chapter 3. The net result, whether accomplished by the bulldozer or 'white painter,' has been to reduce the stock of affordable housing. In 1982 the Vancouver Planning Department surveyed almost a thousand households living in downzoned neighbourhood-improvement districts. They found that stabilized zoning policies and an improved environment had contributed to private upgrading of the housing stock. Newer residents were less likely to have children and more likely to be in a higher-income bracket than their longer-term neighbours. The poor and the renter had been priced out (McAfee 1982).

The conclusion to be drawn is that rezoning strategies in attractive inner-city residential areas can retain the physical but not the social character of the area. Studies in Toronto (Schwab 1986: 24–7) and Winnipeg (Lyon 1986) came to similar conclusions. Private upgrading of central-city stock, assisted by public downzoning actions, has emerged as the primary threat to central-city housing stock and tenants in many Canadian cities in the 1980s (Patterson 1989).

Providing Affordable Housing by Making More Efficient Use of Existing Stock

One of the least used, though potentially most effective, ways to increase the stock of affordable housing is to permit conversion of single-family houses to include a secondary suite. Walker (1986) documented significant amounts of unused housing potential in Ottawa that could be tapped by home sharing, conversion, granny cottages, and additions. However, she also noted that property standards and building codes had to be co-ordinated to support such initiatives or their requirements could preclude taking advantage of zoning opportunities that encouraged conversions and additions.

In Ontario the Ministry of Housing offers a convert-to-rent program of interest-free loans to create hostel-type units for single persons and to add units in single-family homes. The major road-block to this and similar programs is municipal zoning regulations, usually vigorously supported by existing residents, who wish to prevent the construction of new rooming-house and secondary-suite accommodation. Nevertheless, where the demand exists, conversions are occurring illegally. In Vancouver many existing single-family houses are illegally converted to include a suite, and new single-family homes are designed for easy (illegal) conversion to include one or more suites at a later date. Municipalities should review and rationalize the appropriate regulations to ensure that this process can occur. It would be naïve to suggest, however, that regulations could be revised without raising the ire of some of the existing residents.

Requiring or Encouraging the Private Sector to Provide Affordable Housing through Zoning Regulations and Zoning Bonuses

A more complete discussion of the private-sector role in providing housing for the homeless and poor is contained in chapter 6, but a discussion of the municipal role in encouraging or requiring private-sector participation is appropriate here. To involve and encourage the private sector, municipalities have often turned to inclusionary zoning, generally defined as the use of zoning to include rather than exclude the poor. Inclusionary programs require or encourage developers to provide low- and moderate-income housing. Programs range from mandatory to voluntary inclusion and from those without much in the way of incentives for the developer to the more commonly used programs that utilize density bonuses. Variations of zoning-incentive programs originally developed in San Francisco, Boston, New York, and Toronto have been adopted by many larger Canadian and American cities (Howard 1985).

Programs are designed either to preserve existing affordable housing or to add new units. Within these two categories the types of programs are similar – conversion control, demolition control, and inclusionary housing – although each city has a somewhat different approach and programs vary in strength. Programs are also in a constant state of change as cities refine and adjust to keep abreast of legal challenges and evaluations of program success. The trend is toward the use of inclusionary programs, often attached to commercial rather than residential developments, because most cities have far more office than residential growth. These are then known as office/housing linkage programs. The argument is that increasing office growth means more employees, who, in turn, place greater demands on city housing and city services: the developer should be prepared to contribute and respond to this demand. In American cities, where environmental-impact statements are often the basis of planning action, this rationale is sometimes expanded from housing in general to affordable housing because increased housing demand can lead to rising prices. Therefore, cities develop programs to link the office development not only to housing supply in general, but also to affordable housing specifically.

Inclusionary programs are usually linked to some form of incentives.

In San Francisco, all major office developers are required to provide housing, but each low-income unit is worth more housing 'credits' than a moderate-income unit. In Seattle, under a Housing Bonus Program for offices, the maximum density for office development can only be achieved by providing affordable housing. However, if incentives are insufficient, the market will not respond. In several cities a zoning schedule has been created with an additional bonus density in exchange for affordable housing. Few units have been built, largely because the bonus density is not a sufficient subsidy to encourage developers to take on the added negotiation and ongoing management required for the social housing units. Rather than providing an ongoing inclusionary program, the City of Toronto negotiates increased density with developers on a site-by-site basis in exchange for affordable housing. This program, although limited in scope, has provided more housing than the standard-schedule approach attempted in many other cities.

Most cities offer alternatives to the developer to building units on-site under inclusionary programs. Off-site construction, pay-in-lieu, rehabilitation, and donation of other property for housing purposes are particularly suitable alternatives for small sites. Such approaches are especially useful if developers are building in areas where services are insufficient for a residential population. They are also appropriate when there is uncertainty that a particular subsidy program for new housing construction will be available in the future to provide the additional subsidies required. Some cities (Seattle, San Francisco) have designed their inclusionary zoning to provide results regardless of whether senior government programs exist or not, although they also link the inclusionary zoning with subsidies when available. Toronto relies more heavily on receiving senior government subsidies. In either case, the developer's contribution makes limited government subsidies go farther, and where inclusionary units are coupled with a program such as rent supplements, even more very low income households can be accommodated. In general, the cities that have adopted inclusionary programs have done so for similar reasons: to replace or supplement decreasing government subsidies. The cities in which the programs have been most successful are those with a buoyant economy, where growth in the business sector is sufficiently strong to support compensatory programs.

Inclusionary programs have been more successful in the United States than in Canada, in part reflecting differences in legislation and financial tools. The US cities often derive legal and other support for their housing programs from environmental-impact legislation. Environmental-impact statements are required for large projects and incorporate displacement as one of the categories that must be addressed. Study results are then used to set conditions for development. Furthermore, citizen groups can appeal to the courts, thus creating costly delays that developers sometimes prefer to avoid by agreeing to inclusionary conditions. By contrast, the City of Edmonton found in the development of the Mill Woods subdivision that provisions to require developers to provide affordable housing were found by the courts to exceed the city's authority. Such provisions were judged to be inequitable in terms of who pays subsidies and who benefits from development.

It is too early to estimate how effective these programs will be in providing significant amounts of affordable housing, particularly for the core needy. In general, a variety of programs have been implemented, but few units, relative to need, have been provided. Only a few programs, such as the Los Angeles Single Room Occupancy Corporation, place a priority on assisting those who have difficulty obtaining housing. San Francisco's prototype office-housing linkage program generated some $23 million worth of housing, most of it for low- and moderate-income households, during the first five years of activity. But overall, most units that have been provided are to assist modest-income households into ownership in higher-income communities. Keatling (1986) concludes that only a few cities are likely to adopt linkage programs and that these programs are likely to have only a marginal effect on social problems aggravated by downtown growth; as well, the effects and legality of linkage programs are still largely unresolved. Even in the United States, when inclusionary programs (with or without subsidies) have been challenged in court, the courts have often found for the developer.

A study by the City of Vancouver (McAfee 1982) concluded that municipal programs implemented through land-use and zoning legislation were not a very effective way to stimulate the construction of modest-priced housing. Measures that require builders/owners to provide affordable rental housing without publicly funded rent-supplement assistance for the lowest-income tenants generally result in a net loss of modest-priced rental units. Various forms of subsidy programs must be combined with land-use and zoning incentives if the lowest-income group or core needy are to be effectively accommodated.

Private/Public Partnerships
To encourage private-sector involvement the emphasis has been on

zoning-based strategies that force or encourage the provision of lower-cost housing alternatives. Less effort has been spent on forging partnerships with private entrepreneurs. Municipalities, because of their role in the regulatory environment and the constant contact with private developers it generates, are in an excellent position to undertake this function. To date, however, few partnerships have been forged in the Canadian context. Considerably more activity of this nature has been initiated in the United States. In Denver, a combination of city and private money subsidized the purchase of a 21-unit building for low-income use (Schwab 1986: 26). Cleveland has formed numerous public/private housing partnerships including one that will construct a 600-unit apartment. In Portland, public/private-sector agreements have been effective in leasing, renovating, and managing residential hotel accommodation. The Portland Redevelopment Commission also operates several rehabilitation and tax-abatement programs (Martin 1987).

The fact that the number of large private companies in Canada able to invest in such initiatives is certainly lower than in the United States does not rule out similar initiatives in Canada. The private sector has been very innovative in developing housing options for the growing number of elderly; with public encouragement it may be able to turn similar talents to accommodating other lower-income groups in need of housing.

FUTURE DIRECTIONS FOR MUNICIPAL ACTIVITY

Cities have pursued a variety of directions in an attempt to ensure a stock of adequate and affordable housing and many should be commended for their action. The discussion of successful initiatives both in Canada and elsewhere suggests, however, that there is still substantial room for improvement in municipal actions. There are a number of alternative directions or a spectrum of roles and responsibilities that local governments may take to address housing problems. Lessons learned in the past can be used to improve local effectiveness in the future.

Legislative Changes to Define Local Roles and Responsibilities
One solution that should be considered is to define more clearly, and perhaps broaden, municipal responsibility in a legislative manner. Because housing was not a priority item when the BNA Act was fashioned, housing responsibilities were only implied or broadly identified. It is now time to reconsider these responsibilities.

Local governments in Britain have played an extensive role in housing for those with low income and the homeless for many years. Since 1948 they have been obliged by legislation to provide temporary accommodation for 'persons in urgent need thereof.' London, as early as 1971, began to use bed and breakfast accommodation for temporary lodging of homeless families; by 1977, pressure from local voluntary organizations resulted in the Housing Homeless Persons Act, which broadened and clearly defined the local authorities' responsibilities. Under the act, local authorities are obliged to offer temporary relief to high-priority households until more suitable long-term accommodation is obtained. Although interpretation of this act varies from council to council, and some have responded much more positively than others, there is an extensive and innovative array of programs throughout British cities. Similar legislative clarification in the Canadian context could perhaps serve the same purpose. However, unless legislation requires more responsibility from all municipalities in addressing need, it is not likely to be effective.

Redefining Partnerships with the Senior Levels of Government

Legislative changes would help to define more clearly the roles and responsibilities of municipalities, the provinces, and the federal government. But legislative changes alone cannot create the partnership approach that is required to respond to housing need. Municipalities have traditionally sought assistance from senior governments and the need for this assistance will continue. This assistance must reflect program and funding continuity to meet a diversity of needs. Municipalities can undertake certain actions that will help encourage this continuity within a partnership arrangement. These actions include ensuring that housing-needs analysis is current and identifies priorities, development of a housing strategy with realistic goals and objectives that respond to identified needs, consulting with other municipalities and sharing of information and results to formulate a national perspective that can be enunciated to senior levels of government, and mounting a continuous and effective lobby. The nature of problems and, accordingly, the range of possible solutions vary from place to place. What works in one municipality is not appropriate in another and, as a result, locally devised programs are best. Therefore, an effective municipal role at the 'table' during discussions of budgets and programs is a necessary element of the partnership.

Combatting the NIMBY Syndrome
Too often, municipalities lack the political will to address housing need and instead hide behind the commonly held perception that they are constrained by a lack of revenue of their own and from higher levels of government. Municipalities do face both funding and jurisdictional restrictions that senior levels of government do not have to contend with; although the revenue factor does place some restrictions on the potential scope of municipal actions, it does not imply a lack of tools with which to address housing problems. In many cases it is local opposition (not in my backyard [NIMBY]) that prevents more active municipal involvement, regardless of the availability of funds.

Municipalities must assume a more major role both in devising policy and programs and in carrying out or assisting others to carry out realistic programs, even in the face of local opposition. Legislative changes can define responsibilities but only strengthened political will can make the changes effective.

An Innovative Approach
Political will, partnership roles, and clearly defined responsibilities have to be combined with a more innovative approach by Canadian municipalities. There have been successful innovations in Canadian cities but these centres can also learn from activities in the United States. American cities are becoming innovative housing developers. Although they may have more legal and financial tools at their disposal, these cities have taken strong initiatives in finding innovative ways to finance social housing. They often support their housing programs with municipal funds used to provide mortgage and other assistance and raised by tax-exempt revenue bonds. The interest on municipal bonds is exempt from senior government taxes and so the cities can offer a lower interest rate. Montgomery County, Maryland, which has a successful inclusionary program, also raises its own housing funds by a tax on the sale of converted condominium units. Other cities have created housing trust funds financed, for the most part, by taxes on real-estate transactions. Their experiences are worthy of careful consideration by Canadian cities, especially with respect to their commitment to the housing issue in the face of declining federal involvement and funding. In the words of a recent New York City report, 'We must decry the federal abandonment, but we cannot afford to wait for others to come to the aid of the city' (Martin 1987).

Not all initiatives are, however, being hailed as success stories. New

York's $551.1 million real-estate tax-abatement program to generate low-income housing is being questioned. Hinds (1987:1) suggests that the generous tax-abatement program theoretically added 21,253 condominium and 42,389 rental units to the city's housing stock. In fact, he states, nobody knows how many of these apartments would have been built anyway nor is there any proof that the program actually reduced housing costs even for the affluent people who occupy most of the new units. Despite the scepticism about some approaches, initiative and innovation in the American context can serve as an example for local governments in Canada who, along with creating a stronger political stance, must become more innovative in addressing housing problems, particularly in the current atmosphere of fiscal restraint.

Establish Partnerships with the Third Sector and Private Enterprise
Canadian housing during the 1950s and 1960s focused on initiatives funded and implemented by senior governments. During the 1970s community groups and municipal agencies assumed greater responsibility for housing the poor. When the history of social housing in the 1980s and 1990s is written, the central theme may well be the search for effective public/private partnerships to meet the need for adequate and affordable housing. Although there are some Canadian examples of public/private partnerships, opportunities have not been explored in a comprehensive way.

Municipalities should encourage partnership with the private sector through legislation that permits the development of innovative joint programs like Toronto's City Home mixed-income public and private partnerships. Partnership arrangements should also be encouraged with voluntary and third-sector non-profit groups. Because ordinary public and conventional housing does not reach those with very low income, and particularly the homeless, third-sector groups have been extending their activities to the development and management of group homes and other permanent housing alternatives. Municipalities should assist both private and not-for-profit groups with financial support, expeditious permit processing, flexibility in the regulatory environment, and lobbying of senior governments in a partnership arrangement. Assuming the role of a facilitator and co-ordinator, which municipalities are well placed to do, makes municipalities very effective in a partnership approach. Partnership approaches with support from a variety of groups and agencies also can mean a higher level of assistance per unit and thus more success in meeting the needs of the very poor and the homeless.

Review and Rationalization of Zoning and Building Standards
One of the few independent actions municipalities can take is to ensure that zoning and building standards do not inadvertently discourage the provision and retention of affordable housing. Other actions include ensuring that sufficient excess zoning capacity exists so that the price of housing is not unduly bid up through land scarcity; maximizing the capacity of the existing housing stock by facilitating conversion of larger dwellings; adjusting building and zoning standards to ensure that emphasis is placed on maintaining adequate, but not unusually high, safety and design standards; and ensuring that reasons for and reasonableness of regulations are patently clear (if not, zoning becomes disrespected and disregarded, which makes it more difficult to regulate those aspects of development and land use that really matter).

A realistic regulatory environment provides the private, public, and not-for-profit sectors with stability and confidence in the development process. It can also be used to prevent the unnecessary elimination of sros that are so important in the accommodation of the poor and homeless.

Co-ordination and Educational Services
Regardless of how realistic zoning and development controls are, the regulatory environment and approval process can be a formidable barrier, particularly for non-profit and charitable groups attempting to provide affordable housing. Municipalities can assist by taking the necessary steps to channel projects or initiatives through the approval process, perhaps most effectively in a partnership arrangement. In addition, local governments should offer services similar to the housing-advice centres in Britain, providing both information and guidance to those who require housing services. There is a substantial safety net of housing and welfare benefits available to people but access to them is often restricted by the lack of knowledge of such services. Staff at advice centres could intervene as advocates for the homeless with local authorities and social-service agencies. Staff could also play a role as a 'one-stop application' agency, helping clients to deal with the maze of bureaucracy that so often has to be overcome before acquiring access to housing services. The grass-roots relationship with those providing services and those in need of such services places local governments in the best position to organize such services.

It is not possible, nor advisable, to prescribe any one role for municipalities. Diverse housing needs exist in various parts of the country and they each require different responses. Municipalities must adopt a spectrum of roles to respond to this diversity of needs, and municipal roles and responsibilities must be more clearly defined, perhaps even enhanced, to deal with the process. Local governments should be encouraged to become more innovative in actions they initiate on their own and in forming partnerships with other levels of government and the private and non-profit sectors. Municipalities have considerable knowledge of housing needs and a number of regulatory tools at their disposal that, if used wisely, can be effective in addressing such needs. But municipalities also must be prepared to make a stronger commitment, in many cases including increased funding. Even more important is a political commitment – the one ingredient required to make any role successful. Such commitment will permit the testing of new directions and the creation of new initiatives to address the current and future housing needs of low-income and homeless people.

REFERENCES

Bailey, R. 1977. *The Homeless and Empty Houses*. Harmondsworth, Eng.: Penguin Books
Bairstow, D. 1986. *Housing for Roomers, Boarders, and Lodgers: The State of Knowledge*. Toronto: Ministry of Housing.
Beggs, D.M. 1979. *Cost of Community Workers Services on Behalf of Clients with Psychiatric Illnesses, Who Are Very Difficult to House and Maintain in the Community*. Vancouver: Health Department
Birch, A. 1955. *Federalism, Finance and Social Legislation in Canada, Australia and the United States*. Oxford: Clarendon Press
Burchinshaw, M.; Jeu, D.; and Spurr, P. 1985. *Survey of Municipal Housing Policy*. Ottawa: Canada Mortgage and Housing Corporation
Canada. Minister of Supply and Services. 1986. *Housing Programs in Search of Balance*. Ottawa
CMHC (Canada Mortgage and Housing Corporation). 1983. *Section 56.1 Non-Profit and Cooperative Housing Program Evaluation*. Ottawa. November
– 1987. *A Consultation Paper on Housing Renovation*. July
Canada. Parliament. House of Commons. 1964. *Debates*. 28 May
Carter, T.; and Badiuk, E. 1987. *Feasibility Study on the Development of a Municipal Nonprofit Housing Corporation for the City of Regina*. Winnipeg: Institute of Urban Studies, University of Winnipeg
Cogan, S.; and Darke, D. 1983. *Comparative Canadian Social Housing Characteristics*. Vancouver: British Columbia Housing Management Commission

Daly, G. 1988. *A Comparative Assessment of Programs Dealing with the Homeless Population in the United States, Canada, and Britain.* Ottawa: Canada Mortgage and Housing Corporation

Dennis, M.; and Fish, S. 1972. *Programs in Search of a Policy: Low Income Housing in Canada.* Toronto: Hakkert

Egan, M. 1977. 'Social Planning in Vancouver.' *Plan Canada* 17: 118–26

Federation of Canadian Municipalities. 1984. 'Position Paper on the Future of Social Housing.' Ottawa. December

French, P.; Morrison, G.; and McAfee, A. 1986. *New Neighbours: How Single-Family Residents Feel about Higher Density Housing.* Vancouver: City Planning Department

Hinds, M. 1987. 'A Tax Subsidy That Cost $551 Million.' *The New York Times,* 29 March, section 8

Hombs, M.E.; and Snyder, M. 1982, *Homelessness In America.* Washington, DC: Community for Creative Non Violence

Howard, R. 1985. *Affordable Housing Programs and Applicability to Vancouver.* Vancouver: City Planning Department

Institute of Urban Studies. 1987. *Manitoba Land Policy Report.* Winnipeg: University of Winnipeg. June

Keatling, W.D. 1986. 'Linking Downtown Development to Broader Community Goals,' *Urban Innovation,* Spring: 133–41

Lyon, D. 1986. 'Neighbourhood Improvement Program Evaluation.' *Institute of Urban Studies Newsletter,* no. 17, April. Winnipeg

Maass, B. 1980. 'The Theory and Practice of Conducting Local Housing Needs Studies: A Framework for the Assessment of Housing Need in Canadian Cities.' MA thesis, University of British Columbia Planning School

McAfee, R.A. 1979. *Understanding Vancouver's Housing.* Vancouver: City Planning Department

– 1982. *Provision of Affordable Rental Housing by the Private Sector.* Vancouver: City Planning Department

– 1983. *Who Lives in Non-Market Housing: An Evaluation of the City of Vancouver Social Housing Program.* Vancouver: City Planning Department

McKee, C., et al. 1975. *Housing: Inner City Type Older Areas.* Report no. 67. Winnipeg: Institute of Urban Studies, University of Winnipeg

Manitoba. Department of Housing. 1987. *Reaching Out for Help: Manitoba's Homeless in 1987.* Prepared by Bairstow and Associates Consulting Ltd. Winnipeg. December

Martin, S.O. 1987. 'Housing '87.' *Planning* 1 (Spring): 27–34

Newman, L.H. 1986. *Municipal Non-Profit Housing: Winnipeg Housing Rehabilitation Corporation.* Occasional Paper no. 13. Winnipeg: Institute of Urban Studies, University of Winnipeg

262 Tom Carter and Ann McAfee

Ontario Welfare Council. 1977. *Municipal Action in Non Profit Housing*. Toronto

Ouellet, A. 1977. 'Remarks by the Minister of State for Urban Affairs to the Annual Meeting of the Federation of Canadian Municipalities.' Toronto, 18 May

Patterson, J. 1989. 'Housing and Community Development Policies.' In *Housing Progress in Canada since 1945*, ed. J. Miron. Ottawa: Canada Mortgage and Housing Corporation

Regina. 1986. *Regina Social Housing Strategy: Long Term Housing Requirements*. Planning Department. August

Regina Planning Department and Bairstow and Associates Consulting Ltd. 1985. *The City Of Regina Housing Study*. City of Regina. July

Rose, A. 1980. *Canadian Housing Policies: 1935–1980*. Toronto: Butterworths

Saskatchewan Housing Corporation. 1988. *Fifteen Years of Service*. Regina. June

Schwab, J. 1986. 'Sheltering the Homeless.' *Planning* 2, no. 4: 24–7

Toronto. 1976. *Housing Policy Review 1976*. Toronto: City Housing Department

– 1978. *On Target: Program Review 1977 and Housing Strategy to 1980*. Toronto: City Housing Department

– 1980. *City of Toronto Housing Strategy for the 1980s*. Toronto: City Housing Department

Vancouver. City Planning Department. 1979. *Understanding Vancouver Housing: Defining a Housing Policy*. January

Walker, N. 1986. 'Needed: Municipal Action to Tap Hidden Housing Potential.' *Canadian Housing* 3, no. 3 (Fall): 25–7

Wilson, D.J. 1984. 'The Valuation of Pre-paid Residential Building Leases.' *The Canadian Appraiser* 28 (November): 28–33

GEORGE FALLIS AND ALEX MURRAY

9 Reflecting on the Problems and Possibilities

It is probably impossible for most of us to imagine what it means to be homeless in Canada. Even if we took the test of trying to survive on the streets for a day or a weekend or a month, we would still have the security of knowing we could and would eventually return to our homes. We would still have 'our place' in the world. To be homeless means more than to be exposed to the harsh Canadian weather. It means to be without dignity or security, to live under degrading public scrutiny, and to have no place of rest and respite. The homeless do not have 'a place' in our world in more than just a physical sense; they have no place in a more fundamental sense, including almost losing their identity as human beings. Most of us would acknowledge that decent shelter is a basic right of Canadians, yet there are many homeless people. The situation is intolerable, yet it persists.

This book reflects the approach of academic analysts to homelessness and to society's response to it. The book also tries to explore possible solutions to the problem. Early chapters placed homelessness in a broad context and considered how the recession of the 1980s, urban reform and gentrification, the breakup of the welfare-state consensus, and competition between federal and provincial governments have contributed to the problem of homelessness and shaped the response of Canadian society. During the post-war period, the federal government, through CMHC, played the dominant role in designing and financing housing programs. It is not politically possible, and in any event not likely desirable, that the future Canadian response to homelessness should be a major new housing assistance program designed and financed by the federal government. This conclusion is based in equal measure on the political reality of fiscal restraint, assessment of past housing programs, and the complex differences in the homelessness problems within cities and among individuals. The private sector, the third sector, and local government will have to take on larger roles (and recently have been doing so) and will have to seek out and develop new partnerships among all those involved with the problems. Later chapters in the book analyse the roles of the private sector, third sector, and local government and begin to explore the possibility of such new partnerships.

The purpose of these concluding remarks is to note common themes and identify critical issues discussed by the contributors to this book. Their analyses complement the writings of others – social activists, journalists, policy makers, those who work with the homeless – to further our understanding of homelessness and to develop the possibility of taking ameliorating actions.

Analysis in the book, especially in chapter 2, makes it clear that we have no firm data on the numbers of homeless, or the numbers of people along the continuum of housing problems. We do not know exactly how many people are without a roof over their heads, how many are in residential hotels or doubled up with friends, how many are basically without a fixed address, or how many are at risk of falling back into one of these positions on the continuum. What we do know is how many people use existing hostels and support services, and that these are often used beyond capacity. Of course, given the scarcity of data at any one point in time, it is even more difficult to know whether the problem is getting better or worse. Surprisingly, in this group of writings by academic social scientists, there is no cry for more and better data.

We might speculate on the reasons for this omission. Firm data would be extremely difficult and costly to gather. Because the homeless have 'no place' in our world, they are outside the system and so the system has great difficulty counting them except when they make contact with the system by using a hostel, for example. But even if we had the money to gather adequate data, it is unlikely that we would want to. Imagine the intrusion into the lives of Canadians by social scientists and civil servants that would be necessary in order to find out how many people were living outside or in hostels or doubled up, or who had been that way often in the past, or who were at risk of living that way. We would find such big-brother data collection intolerable. Finally, the absence of a demand for better data is probably indicative of a more agnostic attitude toward the possibilities of social engineering even among social scientists themselves (see chapter 4).

What does the lack of data imply about political debate and policy development? It means that the problem of homelessness will probably be easier to ignore and more difficult to come to terms with in the future. There will be those who, with great intensity, vastly overstate the dimensions of the problem, sometimes excusing rhetorical exaggerations by arguing that they are necessary to catch the public's attention. There will also be those who diminish the problem, taking strength from the fact that no evidence can prove them wrong. Our information will have to come from small case studies, probably undertaken at the city level. Chapter 8 notes the important role that housing-needs studies can play in initiating programs. Also, our information will have to come from those who operate hostels and social-service agencies. This is a somewhat new role for these groups, which have provided data before – often cloaked in rhetoric and reflecting a cry on behalf of the needy. These cries will still be required. But because of the impossibility of large-scale data collection and because of the larger role played by local government and the third sector in program delivery, hostels and agencies will have to become more involved in careful data collection and in the analysis of those data that is necessary for good policy development.

A common theme throughout the book is that there are many causes of homelessness and that to understand homelessness we must recognize that the phenomenon is inherently dynamic for individuals and in general. The problem is caused by factors beyond the control of the individual – for example, recession, unemployment, the declining stock of low-rent housing – but also by factors more directly related to a person's life, such as family breakdown, drug or alcohol abuse, psychiatric problems, or just an inability to form relationships or to hold a job. A few people are permanently homeless, but the situation is constantly changing for most people. They lose a job, eventually find one, and then lose it again. They seem to get control of their alcohol problem, then fall back. A family comes back together for a time, then breaks up again. People live with a friend for a while, spend a few days on the street, in a hostel, and then, perhaps, in a low-rent apartment that sits on the edge of downtown, awaiting demolition.

Any response to homelessness must recognize its multi-causal and dynamic nature. It is now a commonplace in many policy fields to criticize existing responses to the problem as fragmented, uncoordinated, and ad hoc, and to call for a holistic, long-run response; and such a call seems appropriate here. But how is it to be achieved? Existing income-support programs, job-training programs, housing assistance, and social services are operated relatively independently and assigned rather differently between levels of government. Existing federal/provincial structures inhibit significant consolidation and co-ordination, and if decentralizing arrangements like the Meech Lake Accord become more pervasive, they would be still more difficult to achieve. Even if such consolidation and co-ordination were possible politically, it is not entirely desirable. Few would want a huge 'Ministry of Homelessness' with responsibility for income support, housing programs, and social services. We have grown disenchanted and sceptical of large, central bureaucracies. A considerable degree of separation between the various assistance programs of society will have to exist, and some overlap, gaps, and lack of co-ordination will be inevitable. It is more important that each service provider become more cognizant of other programs and alert for counter-productive interactions. A holistic, long-run response at various levels in all of society would be more effective and satisfying than having one agency responsible for a comprehensive program. Integration and co-ordination should occur at the level of the individual rather than in the bureaucracy, particularly because of the complex dynamics of each individual case. This approach places a special responsibility on the homeless themselves, and those closest to them, to see that each individual receives comprehensive, sustained, and appropriate help. Some individuals can get this assistance for themselves, but most cannot. Local government and the third sector seem best suited to the role of matching people with available assistance and are indeed taking on this task. We must openly acknowledge the importance of this role and begin to see it not as the result of a failure of central agencies to co-ordinate, but rather as part of a creative response to the multi-causal, dynamic nature of the homelessness problem.

The consensus that sustained the welfare state in the 1950s and 1960s has broken down, but in Canada there has not been a wholesale roll-back of the state's activities in society. Emerging is what chapter 4 calls the 'mixed economy of welfare.' The early development of the welfare state tended to see society as made up of the public sector and the private sector, as divided between the state and the individual. Social assistance was in the domain of government, with little role for the private sector or for individuals. The welfare state in Canada seems to be evolving toward a more pluralistic conception, with a greater role for the third sector and for volunteer groups and with greater emphasis on individual responsibility. But the state also recognizes the inescapable need for public financial assistance to the neediest.

Perhaps one of the least understood roles in this mixed economy of welfare is that of the private sector. Of course, the private sector cannot provide emergency shelters or be the primary provider of housing for the most disadvantaged. The homeless have little income and supplying housing to them will not provide a normal rate of return. Indeed, public assistance or private charity will always be needed for this group. However, the private sector does have a part to play. It builds almost all new housing; it renovates housing; and it has tremendous expertise in real-estate finance, land development, and property management. Private landlords provide most housing to low-income Canadians. Appendix 2 identifies four possible enhanced roles for the private sector under the headings leadership, expertise, the real-estate industry, and low-rental housing. The message is that the private sector can and should be involved in responding to homelessness, not simply as a critic of the inefficiencies and regulations of government, but as a partner, acknowledging the problem and contributing to the design and execution of solutions. Chapter 6 on the private-sector role deals with the United States. It may be a surprise to many Canadians that the American private sector is much more directly involved with homelessness than is the Canadian. Perhaps the American homelessness problem is more severe and federal restraint is more significant. For whatever reason, the American experience shows the possibility of a direct and creative private-sector involvement with this issue.

Whatever new partnerships may emerge and whatever form new programs may take, the solution to homelessness will require assisted housing, income support, and social services. All these require money. Homeless people do not have enough income to meet their basic needs. Government must be the primary source of this money; given Canada's political structure and traditions, most of the money will come from the federal and provincial governments, not from local government. Moreover, it is unreasonable to expect local governments to finance redistributive programs. If one area provided a more generous program than another, taxpayers would try to move out of the generous area and possible beneficiaries would try to move in. Furthermore, local responsibility would imply that poor cities could provide only low levels of assistance, whereas richer cities would be obliged to provide higher levels.

The fact that money for assisted housing, income support, and social services will come from the upper levels of government, not from the third sector or local government, presents us with a dilemma. It is the consensus of the authors of this book that responses to homelessness must be small scale and flexible, sensitive to local housing-market conditions and to the diverse needs of homeless individuals. The third sector and local government will play a larger role in providing assistance but will not have a significantly greater responsibility to raise the funds. However, a fundamental principle of responsible government is that the agency responsible for raising the money is ultimately responsible for how it is spent. This dilemma is probably irresolvable and remains one of the constant tensions of a multi-level political system. The federal and provincial governments have lived with it since Confederation. As the third sector and local government become more involved in program delivery, this tension will increase, requiring sensitivity on the part of both the upper-level government that provides the funds, and the third-sector group or local government that is close to the problem and delivers the program.

A recurring theme in debate about homelessness is the opposition to more assisted housing at the neighbourhood level. This opposition is overt and vociferous at public meetings and has been called the not-in-my-backyard (NIMBY) syndrome. The opposition can be covert, but no less forceful, when its assumptions are codified in zoning by-laws that prohibit group homes, or basement apartments, or higher-density development. If we are to develop a more sustained social response to homelessness, this opposition will have to be confronted and overcome. Sometimes a higher level of government will have to override local control. But developing acceptance of necessary action will have to occur at the local level.

Overcoming local opposition will not be easy. The need for more assisted housing seems to be recognized, although further documentation of the need would always help. In almost all cases, assisted housing has had few negative effects on a community; careful studies of the impact on neighbourhoods (investigating both the good and the bad) should be undertaken and widely publicized. Even with such studies, however, many neighbours will continue to believe that they will be adversely affected by assisted housing nearby. As the welfare state was put in place, there was general acceptance of using taxes to finance income redistribution and social assistance. The acceptance arose in part because it was felt that redistribution complemented the market economy, making it more secure and productive, and in part because the redistribution made society more just, and the burden of the redistribution was fairly distributed through a moderately progressive tax system. Also, it was recognized that some poverty was created by the operation of the market economy itself and that some people would need special assistance if they were ever to participate in that economy. The underpinnings of a consensus in favour of assisted housing can have some parallel with the welfare-state consensus, but it is not exact.

There is growing recognition that homelessness is partly caused by the operation of the urban economy itself and partly caused by liveable cities that stimulate gentrification. Our very urban success and affluence causes problems for the poor. There is, therefore, a strong moral obligation to provide assistance. We should recognize, too, that housing assistance is a necessary complement to a vibrant urban economy that will make urban prosperity and the liveable city more secure and more likely to continue.

There is, however, a special problem with housing assistance. The money to mount the program comes from taxes levied by upper-level governments and so that burden is shared relatively fairly. But housing has a fundamentally spatial aspect: it is located in a specific place in a specific neighbourhood. If there are negative 'externalities,' the burden is not shared fairly but is borne by the immediate neighbours. To reduce this perception of unfairness, effort should be made to distribute assisted housing throughout the city. Perhaps, on an experimental basis, government could offer to buy adjacent houses in a community at market value. If property values do decline (most evidence suggests they do not), then the loss would be borne by all taxpayers (rather than the adjacent neighbours). The offer-to-buy would signal a willingness to acknowledge the perceived burden and to share it.

The special problems with housing assistance are local and, consequently, much of the leadership to create a compassionate and just city must come from the local level as well. Local governments could do much more. They have been the voice opposing assisted housing almost as often as they have been the voice of leadership. Local real-estate groups and third-sector groups also have roles to play in developing the consensus needed for a sustained response to homelessness.

The International Year of Shelter for the Homeless has brought the homeless to our attention. These people are the truly marginalized, those without identity or social connections; the picture has a raw and visceral impact. The IYSH also has given us many marvellous stories of people who have helped others back to stability and into society, into a home. There have been stories of individual social workers, civil servants, politicians, real-estate developers, and non-profit groups – in many cases sustained more by dogged faith than past or likely future success – who have tried helping the almost unhelpable.

The Canadian response to homelessness is still evolving. Reflecting on possible directions it might take leads us to think about the very basic issues that surround the question of what society owes to its least fortunate members and how this debt is to be paid. In one view, the homeless are those who have fallen through the cracks between existing programs in our welfare state. We are now engaged in plugging the cracks. There has been much rhetoric in the 1980s about better targeting of our social assistance. Some have argued that this process is simply a cover for reducing social assistance and not a vehicle for redirecting resources to the neediest. Homelessness offers a litmus test for the credibility of the targeting rhetoric: there is surely no one more needy than someone without shelter. Will the new mixed economy of welfare make special efforts to help those on the margins? The answer can only be provided years from now as social, political, and economic forces interact to shape our social policy.

If we do mount a further response, how are the limited dollars to be used? Do we help those with the best chance of escaping the dynamics of housing uncertainty (likely the episodic homeless) or do we focus on those with the greatest need (likely the chronically homeless)?

But perhaps homelessness is not so much evidence of people falling through the cracks as it is evidence of a society less willing to help. When the sorry plight of a bag-lady is portrayed on our television screens, we all sympathize. However, as her background of lost jobs, failed marriage, and running feud with the public housing authorities is reported, our sympathy wanes. Discussion begins to echo the nineteenth-century distinction between the deserving and undeserving poor. She is author of her own fate. She neither wants nor deserves help. What can be done (because the poor are always with us)? The words are seldom explicit but the sentiments are there. Again, to know how widespread is the unwillingness to help, we must wait several years.

But we would do well to continue to remind ourselves, when faced with future choices and long after the International Year of Shelter for the Homeless has passed, that a society is judged finally by how it treats its least fortunate members: and in Canada, these are the men, women, and children who are homeless.

Vienna Recommendations on Shelter and Urban Development

Prepared during the Second International Shelter Conference
Vienna, Austria, September 10–12, 1986
Coordinated by the National Association of Realtors

CO-SPONSORS:
National Association of Realtors (USA)
International Union of Building Societies and Savings Associations (IUBSSA)
International Real Estate Federation (FIABCI)

SUPPORTING SPONSORS:
National Federation of Real Estate Transactions Association (Japan)
United States League of Savings Institutions

ASSOCIATE SPONSORS:
African Union of Building Societies
Building Societies Association (UK)
Caribbean Association of Building Societies and Finance Institutions
Canadian Real Estate Association
Cooperative Housing Foundation (USA)
FIABCI-Netherlands
Interamerican Housing Union
Mortgage Bankers Association (USA)
National Association of Homebuilders (USA)
National Council of Savings Institutions (USA)

INTRODUCTION

The Second International Shelter Conference held in Vienna, Austria, September 10–12, 1986 was a private sector effort in support of the International Year of Shelter proclaimed by the General Assembly of the United Nations. The objective of the conference was to produce an authoritative private sector statement which would define the principles and action steps necessary to address the problem of shelter and urban development at the national level.

The conference brought together a coalition of senior, predominantly private sector, housing professionals from 32 countries. It was co-sponsored by 10 national and 5 international private sector associations with members in more than half the countries of the world and on every continent. Participating public organizations included: The United States Agency for International Development; the u.s. Department of Housing and Urban Development; The United Nations Commission on Human Settlements; The World Bank; The Development Assistance Council of the Organization of Economic Cooperation and Development.

The Conference produced the 'VIENNA RECOMMENDATIONS' which are set forth in this document. These recommendations were subject to intense analysis and debate prior to their presentation in the Conference Plenary by a group of housing experts drawn primarily from the private sector in the developing world. The recommendations were subsequently discussed, amended and adopted by the conference attendees acting in their individual capacities. They will now be widely circulated for formal adoption by public and private sector shelter organizations throughout the world. The VIENNA RECOMMENDATIONS are offered as a contribution of the sponsoring organizations and of the conference participants to the global policy dialogue on housing. It is hoped that they will serve as a sound general basis for an effective partnership between the public and private sectors in specific national situations where housing is a serious problem and where a sensible framework for action is desired.

THE VIENNA RECOMMENDATIONS ON SHELTER AND URBAN DEVELOPMENT
September 12, 1986

Preamble

We, the participants in The Second International Shelter Conference held in Vienna, Austria from September 10–12, 1986, associated with private sector institutions and enterprises committed to shelter and urban development in our respective countries, have prepared these recommendations on shelter and urban development as a contribution to global policy dialogue and as a basis for national action.

The Global Need for Economic Growth with Equity

World urbanization trends project that over three billion people will live in urban places by the year 2000. Over one billion persons will have been added to the urban population between 1980 and the year 2000.

This surge of urban population growth is occurring during a period of global economic crisis. High foreign debt burdens, falling commodity prices, and low and negative rates of real economic growth make the outlook bleak for many developing countries in the short and intermediate term.

New policies and approaches are required if the global objective of sustained economic growth with equity for all the world's people is to be achieved. We believe that those policies must include emphasis on urban centers and the shelter sector.

Today, more than half of the Gross National Product of the developing countries is generated in urban places. We know that there is a strong correlation between rising per capita gross national product and increasing levels of urbanization. The time has come to recognize explicitly the essential contribution urbanization can make to national economic development.

Housing and urban infrastructure are prerequisite components of efficient urbanization and direct contributors to economic growth through capital formation, employment generation, and their strong forward and backward linkages to the national economy.

The complex issues of urbanization, the provision of shelter, efficient urban management, and the need for urban productivity and job generation must now be given equal consideration with agriculture and rural development in national development strategies.

The Lessons of Experience

Our experience with shelter and urban development over the ten years since the United Nations Conference on Human Settlements in Vancouver provides the basis for future development planning. The Vancouver Action Plan introduced new and useful ideas, but failed to achieve its objectives because of the over-reliance on public sector initiatives which exceeded limited capacities; the disregard for the need to mobilize financial resources; the assumption of public initiated project-by-project approaches rather than development processes; and the failure to harness the potential of the private sector as a positive contributor to national objectives.

It is time to establish a new agenda for action to unite and guide governments, the private sector, the international donor agencies, and the rest of the international community in addressing the growing world urban development crisis and the need for economic growth with equity.

The Forging of a New Development Partnership

The cornerstone of this new action agenda is the recognition of the absolute necessity to foster cooperation between the public and private sectors and the evolution of those aspects of nation building that each can do most efficiently.

Regardless of the political and humanitarian motivations of governments, national strategies must reflect the limited capacity of the public sector to meet all of the development requirements of the people. They cannot do the job alone. All non-governmental economic and human resources must be mobilized in the development effort, including the formal private sector, the informal private sector, the non-profit private sector, private associations, cooperatives, and community groups. All have a valuable role to play in establishing an efficient and productive development strategy.

The basis for effective public private cooperation rests with the understanding and fulfillment of the responsibility incumbent on each sector. Specifically, the public sector has the responsibility to:
- ensure that macro-economic policies avoid market distortions and are conducive to economic growth through private sector initiative.
- encourage the mobilization of domestic financial resources and ensure adequate access to domestic savings by the private sector.
- support pricing policies of both public and private goods and services which permit markets to function efficiently.
- emphasize efficiency in urban management, infrastructure provision; and land policy including the provision of secure land tenure, and freedom of land title transfer.
- restrict public sector activities to those which cannot be done effectively by the private sector and the people themselves.

In turn, the private sector's responsibility to the partnership is to:
- balance the essential need for operating profits with a response to social needs of all income groups.
- mobilize investment capital for housing and urban development.
- accept prudent business risks, competitive principles and market results.
- develop entrepreneurship and innovation.

We look to the international donor community to expand its efforts in support of shelter and urban development commensurate with its importance to national economic development and the rapidly growing urban populations.

We note with appreciation the contribution of the international donor community in the past, but urge that this assistance now be more evenly directed between the public and private sectors in support of the principles of partnership enunciated here.

Specifically, we urge:

- participation in the policy dialogue and reforms advocated here in support of the public and private partnership;
- sustained support in the form of technical assistance, training, and access to capital as catalysts in responding to the shelter and urban development challenge;
- assistance in the development of efficient and viable institutions in the public and private sectors, with particular priority to housing finance institutions;
- facilitating the widespread exchange of information and research on the experience of all nations with shelter and urban development to learn from successes and avoid the failures of the past.

Finally, we urge the formation of an international private sector coalition of associations, professionals and individuals concerned with all aspects of housing and urban development to act as a forum for furthering the principles presented in this agenda.

The Action Plan Recommendations

Each nation must deal with these fundamental issues in a way which reflects its own present status of urbanization, economic development, and condition of its urban physical infrastructure. While no one prescription of urban action will be directly relevant to all nations, we believe that all nations will benefit from careful attention to the development of efficient processes and the building of viable and effective institutions.

Each nation must seek a workable model of its public private partnership which is compatible with its climate and topology, culture and political system, and natural resource endowments. However, we commend to all countries and international donors the following recommended Action Plan as they frame policy and programs for shelter and urban development.

The Management of Urban Development

With the developments that have taken place in the developing countries over the last decade the importance of Urban Management is increasingly being recognized.

Efficiently run cities are essential for economic growth.

The challenge to the practitioner, both public and private, must be to develop efficient approaches to Urban Management in the future.

The following four recommendations require attention:

RECOMMENDATION I
SHELTER AND URBAN POLICY FORMULATION

I.A   All countries should have policies affecting shelter and the urban sector. These policies must relate to the existing economic conditions, availability of resources within the public and private sector and must contribute to national development efforts.

I.B   SHELTER AND URBAN POLICY SHOULD BE AN INTEGRAL PART OF NATIONAL DEVELOPMENT STRATEGY AND SHOULD BE ADOPTED AT THE HIGHEST LEVELS OF GOVERNMENT.

I.C   Recommended principles for action:
   (i)   Efficiency criteria should guide the location of economic investments in order to achieve high rates of growth and job creation at the least cost.
   (ii)   The positive relationship between urban development and rural development and agriculture should be recognized and facilitated in policy formation.
   (iii) The private sector should be encouraged to invest in housing to reduce the demand on public resources and thereby allow the public sector to contribute more effectively to those services which the private sector cannot provide.
   (iv)   Investment choices should favor projects which achieve immediate benefits for users, in order to avoid under-utilized capital assets and accelerate cost recovery.
   (v)   The development of disadvantaged regions can best be achieved by investing in those sectors in which the region has a viable economic potential rather than supporting inherently non-economic investments through subsidies.

RECOMMENDATION II
URBAN MANAGEMENT AND PLANNING

II.A   It is recognized that countries have many competing demands on available resources, particularly for agriculture and rural development and, therefore, cannot meet urban development requirements primarily through central government investment. Urban centers need to be allowed to address their own needs for capital mobilization, management and planning through a transitional strategy that overcomes the existing weaknesses at the local level of government.

II.B PRIORITY SHOULD BE GIVEN TO IMPROVING THE CAPACITY AND EFFICIENCY OF LOCAL GOVERNMENT IN ALL ASPECTS OF URBAN MANAGEMENT, URBAN FINANCE MOBILIZATION, AND EFFECTIVE PLANNING.

II.C Recommended principles for action:
   (i) Central governments should adopt decentralization policies oriented to strengthening local government so that it can accept increasing levels of management, planning, and financial responsibility for urban development.
   (ii) Priority should be given to improving effective governmental procedures for the efficient management of urban services. Attention must be paid to:
      (a) Training programs for local government officers and staff;
      (b) Local government personnel policies; and
      (c) Career incentives and salary structures which are conducive to attracting able and qualified personnel.
   (iii) Local governments should consider the development of private sector infrastructure service delivery systems. This has been successfully accomplished in a number of countries throughout the world.
   (iv) Effective urban management requires increased citizen participation in the planning and delivery of urban services.

RECOMMENDATION III
URBAN LAND POLICIES AND PROCEDURES

III.A The availability of land at affordable prices is prerequisite for efficient urban growth. Although most urban centers have adequate vacant land resources to support development, the efficient functioning of land markets is often constrained by inappropriate public policies, inadequate tenure systems, and inefficient laws and procedures for the control, regulation, and taxation of land.

The fundamental right to secure tenure whether leasehold or freehold rights is an absolute prerequisite to the stimulation of investment in shelter and economic activity.

III.B NATIONAL LAND POLICIES SHOULD REAFFIRM THE IMPORTANCE OF SECURE LAND TENURE WHILE ENSURING THE EFFICIENT FUNCTIONING OF LAND MARKETS CONDUCIVE TO ECONOMIC DEVELOPMENT.

III.C Recommended principles for action:

(i) Nations should have in place or establish forms of secure land tenure for the people and investors which meet the tests of: creating efficiency in the land market, equity in the form of access to all groups requiring land, compatibility with the social and economic system, and the capacity for continuity over time.

(ii) The land market should be subject to efficient public procedures which are convenient and affordable to enterprises and households (particularly low-income households) to facilitate land acquisition, survey, transfer, and registration.

(iii) Governments should facilitate the supply of land for urbanization through the adoption of policies which provide incentives to develop urban land for various uses in response to effective demand.

(iv) Governments should ensure that urban land is efficiently and productively utilized through the adoption of appropriate land use standards (plot sizes, road rights-of-way, open space requirements etc.) which reduce development costs and facilitate the access to land of low-income groups.

(v) Where government action, through investment in infrastructure, has created substantial additional land value for private owners, it is appropriate to seek cost recovery of this investment.

(vi) The public sector has an obligation to manage public land holdings efficiently and effectively in the achievement of urban development objectives.

(vii) Government intervention in private land should be limited to zoning, acquisition for public purposes with just compensation and in exceptional circumstances to facilitate access to land for low-income groups.

RECOMMENDATION IV
INFRASTRUCTURE SERVICES

IV.A Most developing countries are experiencing deficits in their existing infrastructure. These deficits have severe consequences for national productivity. Countries are unable to meet the demand for services for growing populations due to the following factors:

(a) capital requirements;
(b) inappropriate high standards and technology;
(c) inadequate maintenance for existing facilities;
(d) poor cost recovery for both capital and maintenance requirements.

IV.B REALISTIC APPROACHES TO INFRASTRUCTURE PROVISION SHOULD BE SOUGHT
WHICH USE APPROPRIATE TECHNOLOGIES TO PROVIDE AFFORDABLE SERVICES
TO ALL GROUPS THEREBY FACILITATING COST RECOVERY.

IV.C Recommended Action Principles
  (i) Planning
      Planning for infrastructure investment should be multi-sectoral
      and coordinated to maximize its contribution to economic develop-
      ment, and should assure the potential for upgrading over a period
      of time.
  (ii) Investment
      Investment in infrastructure networks should be in response to
      effective demand and consistent with capital available thus providing
      immediate benefits to users and not creating underutilized capital
      assets. Wherever feasible the private sector should be encouraged to
      provide services to save scarce public sector resources.
  (iii) Technology
      Infrastructure investments should utilize appropriate technologies
      and standards in order to save costs.
  (iv) Pricing
      Pricing policies should seek full cost recovery, ensure that infrastruc-
      ture services are sufficiently priced to serve as a disincentive to waste
      and overconsumption, but can usefully include selective "cross-
      subsidy" strategies.
  (v) Implementation
      The public sector responsibilities for implementation should be
      restricted to planning and tender procedures thereby leaving respon-
      sibility for construction to the private sector. Particular attention
      should be given to the tendering process to ensure efficient and cost
      effective implementation. Overlapping of responsibilities within
      planning functions and service implementation must be avoided.
  (vi) Operations and Maintenance
      Emphasis should be placed as a matter of priority on the efficient
      operation and maintenance of the existing infrastructure networks
      even at the expense of new construction.

Housing Production and Finance

Housing finance and housing production affect different sectors of the housing market; while housing finance helps create effective demand, housing production is essentially a supply response in the housing market.

National policy in housing must necessarily keep both sectors in view when designing a comprehensive shelter policy. They are different sides of the same coin and the private sector has demonstrated its capacity to contribute to both.

Partnership and cooperation between the public and the private sectors is most needed in the area of housing production. Public sector responsibility for infrastructure provision should lead to contracting procedures that will develop the experience and capacity of small contractors. In turn, this expanded capacity can lead to increased efficiency in the production of housing, and provide for the growth of building supply firms.

The key that unlocks this process is the provision of finance. Here too, the public-private alliance has proven fruitful in many instances. The scale and experience of the public sector can be used to establish financing mechanisms that allow the demand for housing to be translated effectively into real economic activity. But, private sector institutions must become dominant. Public sector efforts should all be designed to create a system of viable private financial organizations that will support the housing and building supplies delivery system.

The following recommendations require attention:

RECOMMENDATION V
HOUSING PRODUCTION AND FINANCE

V.1   MANAGEMENT OF HOUSING DELIVERY SYSTEMS

V.1.A Shelter is recognized as a basic necessity of mankind. In spite of dire warning of huge housing deficits, the evidence is accumulating from census data that the quality of housing and the density per room is not declining worldwide and in some countries is showing improvement. These encouraging trends are being achieved not through public housing programs – which have built a small percentage of the new housing stock, nor even the formal private sector – but rather through the massive efforts of the low-income people to provide their own shelter. It is the process of private incremental self-building, that is providing approximately 80 percent of the additions to the new housing stock in some developing countries.

The documented history of public housing efforts worldwide has been generally poor (with a few exceptions). Public housing has often been over-designed, expensive, of lower quality and required massive subsidies. For the most part, it has failed to achieve acceptable levels of cost recovery from the beneficiaries (who frequently have been of higher-income levels than the initial target group). The project-by-project approach to public housing has been slow in production, costly in management time, and uncertain as to the availability of annual funding. Adequate administration, institutional and managerial capacity to build and maintain public housing in sufficient quantity does not exist nor should it be expected. In sum, the resources devoted to public housing could have been better used by private sector housing efforts. When private sector can take over the home provision role of the public authorities, it should be actively encouraged leaving the public sector to concentrate on infrastructural facilities. Even the much more successful and appropriate sites and services projects, sponsored by international donor agencies, have not overcome these basic problems.

The traditional arguments of macro-economists about shelter as an unproductive consumption good are not valid. Incremental, self-built shelter adds to the national capital stock by mobilizing investment from households which otherwise would not save or would hold their savings in unproductive assets (gold or jewelry).

Private housing provision generates employment among skilled and semi-skilled workers, and creates economic activity that will foster the development of small contractors and building supply firms. In turn, the capacity of the private sector to satisfy the need for housing at all income levels is strengthened. Moreover, the process provides incentives to increase productivity and income to households in order to obtain their own shelter and upgrade and furnish it thereby contributing to backward and forward linkages in the local economy.

A significant percentage of low-income households also use their shelter units and plots as a base for other forms of micro-enterprise in retail sales, services, and manufacturing. Marginal businesses which cannot afford to pay for separate accommodations can flourish in the informal shelter environment and meet the demands of low-income populations for affordable goods and services. In aggregate, these micro-enterprises represent a significant contribution, albeit hidden, to their national GNP.

V.1.B THE FORMAL AND INFORMAL PRIVATE SECTOR MUST BOTH BE RESPONSIBLE FOR SHELTER PROVISION. THE PUBLIC SECTOR MUST FACILITATE THIS PROCESS

BY ASSISTANCE IN THE PROVISION OF THE ESSENTIAL INPUTS OF LAND, INFRASTRUCTURE, FINANCE, BUILDING MATERIALS, AND THE ESTABLISHMENT OF A SUPPORTIVE LEGAL AND REGULATORY ENVIRONMENT.

v.1.c Recommended Action Principles:

(i) National policies should be established to shift the responsibility for housing unit production wherever possible to the private sector and divert the funds saved to the provision of land, infrastructure, and finance for low-income groups. The use of low-income settlement upgrading techniques is particularly to be commended. Such approaches should be established on an on-going programmatic basis rather than in the form of individual, isolated projects. Shelter provision through the informal sector should be recognized as a legitimate and productive contribution to national development.

(ii) National policies should be established to phase out public home building corporations. However, governments should consider using public corporations for land development and infrastructure provision in support of private contractors and home builders.

(iii) Where public sector civil servants' and workers' housing is a political priority, governments should use cash housing allowances to be spent on private housing provision rather than to attempt to provide the housing units directly.

(iv) The feasibility of selling the public housing stock to the occupants should be studied in order to convert these unproductive capital assets into investment capital for national development efforts.

(v) Governments should ensure that the legal processes for obtaining building permits, inspections, and approvals for housing are efficient and affordable to private sector developers. Special flexible procedures should be used to provide convenience to low-income self-building households to obtain legal status.

(vi) The physical standards for shelter established by law should accommodate the full range of house types to be constructed. Of particular importance in setting all standards is to ensure that they provide for the least cost technology sufficient to provide the level of performance required.

(vii) Governments should ensure that no artificial barriers to the smooth functioning of the housing market are put in place which inhibit the development and affordability of housing, impair the return to investment or otherwise act as unintended disincentives.

(viii) Housing policies should reject "rent controls" which have been proven to be disincentives to maintaining and increasing the housing stock. "Rent controls" now presently in place should be phased out over time, and should in no case be applied to new housing.

V.2 THE BUILDING MATERIALS INDUSTRY

V.2.A Experience has shown that the building materials industry will operate most efficiently when it is relatively free of government regulation and relies mainly on private sector suppliers. Where governments have attempted to establish monopolies or "control boards" over building materials, the experience has been to create inefficiencies in the distribution system, higher prices, and the development of black markets.

Each country must assess its own requirements for building materials, its available indigenous building material resources, and determine the appropriate mix between imported materials, import substitution strategies, and local production.

V.2.B NATIONAL POLICIES SHOULD ENCOURAGE THE DEVELOPMENT OF THE BUILDING MATERIALS INDUSTRY THROUGH PRIVATE SECTOR INITIATIVE WITH EMPHASIS ON MICRO-ENTERPRISES

V.2.C Recommended Action Principles:

(i) Building materials should be considered as an integral part of the shelter and human settlements development process and appropriate policies adopted to encourage production and distribution through the private sector unencumbered by regulations and controls.

(ii) Appropriate standards for the production and use of building materials should be adopted which encourage the efficient use of materials in construction, that allow the use of the least cost material which can provide an acceptable level of performance, and permit the use of "temporary" materials in low-cost housing.

(iii) Professional associations should develop unified standards of building materials so that specifications can be drawn with confidence, but quality control standards should not be set artificially high thereby raising costs.

(iv) Experimentation and finance for new building materials should be encouraged with particular emphasis on the distribution of information concerning innovation to potential users. A starting point in this regard is to analyze available world experience with building materials for application in a given country situation.

V.3 CONSTRUCTION INDUSTRY

v.3.A The success of the shelter and human settlements development effort will depend on the effectiveness and availability of a viable construction industry. Approximately one half of gross, fixed capital formation, and three to eight percent of GDP is construction output. Substantial reduction in construction costs can be achieved in most developing countries through the adoption of appropriate policies, removal of procedural constraints, encouragement of efficient management and stimulation of competition.

v.3.B THE CONSTRUCTION INDUSTRY IS A VITAL PART OF THE SHELTER AND HUMAN SETTLEMENTS DEVELOPMENT PROCESS. COMPREHENSIVE STRATEGIES FOR ITS DEVELOPMENT THROUGH THE ENCOURAGEMENT OF PRIVATE SECTOR INITIATIVE, REMOVAL OF CONSTRAINTS, THE PROVISION OF FINANCE AND IMPROVED EFFICIENCY SHOULD BE A MATTER OF NATIONAL PRIORITY.

v.3.C Recommended Action Principles:
   (i)   Government should seek to encourage a competitive private sector construction industry and as part of that effort public sector construction entities should be reshaped and held accountable for performance, without subsidies or other special treatment inherently unfair to private competitors.
   (ii)   Public sector contracting procedures should stimulate fair competition, provide performance incentives, timely award of contract, timely payment to contractors, and proper supervision.
   (iii) Labor laws and mandatory wage rates should be responsive to local labor market forces and conditions.
   (iv)   Public contracting procedures should be designed to allow the participation of smaller contractors and to ensure the widest possible competition.
   (v)   Develop organized training programs to supplement on-the-job training for the skilled labor requirements of construction.
   (vi)   Support improved access to credit for the construction industry through the education of lenders as to the specific needs, requirements, and risks of the industry.

(vii) Ensure that informal construction contractors are free from restrictive practices, are encouraged to develop, and have fair access to credit, foreign exchange, training, and building materials.

(viii) Encourage the use of least cost construction techniques compatible with performance requirements. Of particular importance is to avoid industrialized building systems unless they can be proved economically viable after rigorous analysis.

RECOMMENDATION VI
HOUSING FINANCE

VI.A The lack of housing finance resources is a major constraint to the housing market in most developing countries. While in many countries it may be necessary to protect and favor the housing finance system to foster its development, housing finance should enjoy equal priority with other national needs, have full access to national capital and savings markets, and should in no case be subject to financial repression.

The financial services necessary to support housing development include finance for land acquisition, on- and off-site infrastructure, construction, and long-term mortgages for the ultimate purchaser. The sources of these financial services are likely to involve a variety of institutions in the public and private sectors as well as informal networks. Each of these financing entities must mobilize its funds from the four main sources of gross savings: the household sector, business sector, government, or international transfers.

Housing finance policy must address the needs of all target groups and not just those of the low-income groups alone. In few countries are the finance institutions developed to the point that adequate sources of funding are mobilized and allocated effectively to support the needs of housing among all income groups. Typically, there are three-tiered housing markets: a small, well-financed, upper-income market supplied entirely by the private sector; a small subsidized market of civil servants and middle-class salaried workers supported by public sector housing activities; and, a large informal housing market serving the poor.

Housing is an important sector in all national economies. Even in economic recessions, it represents a significant percentage of annual gross domestic fixed capital formation but effective demand is very sensitive to macro-economic conditions.

In addressing housing finance issues, it is important to recognize that there is no one prescription that can be generally applied.

VI.B ALL COUNTRIES SHOULD SEEK TO DEVELOP HOUSING FINANCE POLICIES AND
INSTITUTIONS WHICH ARE INTEGRATED INTO THEIR CAPITAL MARKETS, THAT
MAXIMIZE THE MOBILIZATION OF SAVINGS, AND SEEK SOLUTIONS THAT STRESS
AFFORDABILITY, REPLICABILITY, AND COST RECOVERY.

VI.C Housing Finance Institutions and Policies

(i) The development of the housing finance sector is a joint responsibility of the government and the private sector. In this cooperation, the
contributions of the government should be made in a manner
consistent with market principles and economic efficiency. These
contributions should be done in a way that will promote the
long-term growth, development and viability of the housing finance
system, particularly its private entities.

(ii) The development of housing finance institutions should be a
national objective with the rate and scale determined by the demand
associated with increasing levels of GDP and the growth of the
capital market.

(iii) Governments should provide a regulatory climate conducive to the
establishment of private specialized housing finance institutions by
allowing them to compete effectively for savings and respond to
market demand for loan rates.

(iv) The full range of potential public/private partnerships in housing
finance institutional development should be explored. The government should support and encourage the establishment of housing
finance institutions by private groups, and, if such groups do not
emerge, the government should consider establishing the institution
itself.

(v) Newly established housing finance institutions should not be
expected to lend initially to predominantly low-income groups but,
with experience, they should be encouraged to do so. The evidence
supports the conclusion that low-income groups need not be higher
risk than other borrowers. Techniques are emerging which allow
housing finance institutions to lend to lower income groups with
acceptable transaction costs even on small loans. Such techniques
should be made available to appropriate housing finance institutions.

(vi) Established housing finance institutions should be allowed the
flexibility to conduct their business in a manner consistent with long-
term profitability. This includes the ability to develop products and
services suited to the various borrowing needs of its customers and
its own needs to raise funds; the ability to locate operations in the

neighborhoods it serves, subject to management capacity; and access to technical assistance and training.

(vii) There should be efforts to link the informal housing finance mechanisms found in most countries to the formal housing finance system.

Symposium Recommendations on the Private-Sector Role

The Canadian Real Estate Association (CREA), in conjunction with Canada Mortgage and Housing Corporation, sponsored a symposium as part of the United Nations International Year of Shelter for the Homeless (IYSH) in August 1987. Seven papers were commissioned, presented at the symposium, and discussed by an invited group of some of Canada's recognized experts in the field of housing policy. (Lists of participants at the symposium and contributors to this book follow.) The papers, together with introductory and concluding chapters by the editors, form this book. The concluding session of the symposium was devoted to discussing the potential role of the private sector in responding to homelessness. On the basis of this session and discussions throughout the symposium, the editors drew up a set of specific recommendations on the private-sector role that were delivered to the Canadian Real Estate Association and also presented at the Canadian Conference to Observe IYSH held in Ottawa in September 1987. These recommendations are reproduced as this appendix. They are presented as the editors' sense of the consensus, but were not formally endorsed by the symposium participants.

There are Canadians who are homeless or forced to live without a fixed address. This is intolerable in Canada. All three levels of government have the primary responsibility to ensure that the homeless are sheltered. This shelter does not require increased government expenditure; it can be provided through a reallocation of priorities. But the public sector should not act alone; there must be a new partnership among governments, the private sector, the third sector, and the homeless themselves. Each has a role; each has limitations; each must strive to understand and co-operate with the other. There is much creative interaction already under way among the groups, and innovative solutions are being developed. We must build on this activity and strengthen our commitments.

Any solution will have to be small in scale and flexible, responsive to local housing-market conditions and the special needs of diverse, homeless individuals. Solutions require income support, assisted housing, and social services. All these require money: the homeless simply do not have enough income to meet what all Canadians would accept as basic needs. The government must be the primary source of this money. It will not be generated by the charity of the private or non-profit sectors. The money can be found.

The basic role of the private sector is to 'balance the essential need for operating profits with a response to social need of all income groups' (Vienna Recommendations 1986, reproduced here as appendix 1).

The private sector cannot provide emergency shelters or be the primary provider of housing for the most disadvantaged. Government and the third sector must take the lead. However, the private sector builds almost all new housing; it repairs and renovates almost all existing housing; it finances most purchases; and private unsubsidized landlords supply most housing to low-income Canadians. The private sector has tremendous expertise in land development, residential construction, housing finance, the buying and selling of housing, and property management. This expertise is essential in developing new partnerships and new solutions to homelessness. Thus, the private sector can play four major roles; it can: provide leadership; provide expertise to third-sector groups and governments; construct, renovate, finance, and exchange housing; and supply low-rental housing.

Leadership: The private sector can participate with governments, the third sector, and the homeless in identifying problems and analysing their causes, developing a social commitment to respond, and designing solutions. On occasion it can take the lead. The August 1987 symposium is an example of such leadership. Private-sector associations could be vehicles for developing partnerships at the local, provincial, and national levels; for example they could initiate meetings of government, third-sector, and private-sector people. Local real-estate boards could initiate discussions about how zoning and local regulations might be modified to encourage home owners to rent out small apartments in their houses. Or the associations could be vehicles for co-ordinating data collection to present a national picture. Leadership can also be shown by combining personal commitment and symbolism. The Canadian Institute of Planners is asking all members to contribute one hour's pay per year to a homelessness fund. Private-sector organizations could do the same thing. CREA members could be asked to contribute a certain amount for every real-estate transaction during IYSH.

Expertise: Private-sector expertise in land development, construction, finance, and real-estate brokerage can be of great benefit in developing government policy and in carrying out non-profit projects. This expertise is being shared now: private-sector people often assist the third sector. But more sharing is possible. The challenge is to identify the specific needs (a task for government and the third sector) and to establish procedures for matching private-sector people with individuals or groups trying to resolve those needs. For example, the third sector has indicated needs in identifying available building sites, evaluating joint commercial/residential projects, developing schemes to let individuals help finance non-profit housing, and developing accounting and management systems. Ways can be found to provide private-sector assistance, perhaps in the same way that the private sector now lends expertise to developing countries and to charity drives such as the United Way.

Real-estate industry: The real-estate industry develops land; builds, repairs, and renovates housing; finances housing; and buys and sells houses and apartments. The industry's basic role is to perform these tasks efficiently and at a profit and to innovate and develop entrepreneurship (see also appendix 1). Obviously the private sector will have a major role in providing these services under contract to government and third-sector groups. The real-estate industry can help non-profit groups by making available housing-market data to them.

Low-rental housing: It is often forgotten that most of the low-rental housing in Canada is supplied by private-sector landlords without government assistance. Much more attention must be paid to the financial plight of the small landlord, who must maintain a profitable enterprise in order that our low-rental stock will not gradually disappear. The incomes of tenants can be supplemented with a shelter allowance; the effect of rent control and gentrification on the private low-rental stock must be assessed; cities can block lease units from private landlords; landlords can be offered assistance in dealing with problem tenants; and local governments might offer some form of rental guarantee. As well, means to encourage home owners to rent out a portion of their homes should be explored.

Canada has the resources, both public and private, to solve the problems of the homeless. The question becomes how to harness these resources. The corner-stone of any response is the recognition of the absolute necessity of fostering co-operation between the homeless and the public, private, and third sectors. With this co-operation, solutions can be found and implemented.

Symposium Participants

RICHARD ARNOTT,
Boston College,
Chestnut Hill, MA

DALE BAIRSTOW,
President,
Bairstow & Associates Consulting Ltd,
Toronto, ON

GERALD DALY,
Faculty of Environmental Studies,
York University,
North York, ON

DAVID HUMPHREY,
Advisor, Federal Affairs,
Canadian Real Estate Association,
Ottawa, ON

ROBERT LAJOIE,
Director,
Strategy Planning &
Policy Development,
Canada Mortgage and
Housing Corporation,
National Office,
Ottawa, ON

Rev. BRAD LENNON,
All Saints' Anglican Church,
Toronto, ON

HARVEY LITHWICK,
School of Public Administration,
Carleton University,
Ottawa, ON

GREG MACLEOD,
University College of Cape Breton,
Sydney, NS

DAVID MORLEY,
Faculty of Environmental Studies,
York University,
North York, ON

ROBERT H. PEDLER,
President,
Canadian Real Estate Association,
Ottawa, ON

ALLAN POAPST,
Past-President,
Canadian Real Estate Association,
Ottawa, ON

NANCY SMITH,
Councillor,
Ottawa City Hall,
Ottawa, ON

SHIRLEY TAYLOR,
Manager of Communications,

Canadian Real Estate Association,
Ottawa, ON

DAVID WALSH,
President,
Realco Property Ltd,
Toronto, ON

Contributors

KEITH G. BANTING   Professor, Department of Political Studies, Queen's University, Kingston. Formerly research co-ordinator for the Royal Commission on the Economic Union and Development Prospects for Canada. Author of many articles on federalism, the constitution, and government policy. Author of several books including *Poverty, Politics and Policy: Britain in the 1960s* and *The Welfare State and Canadian Federalism*.

TOM CARTER   Director at the Institute of Urban Studies and Associate Professor of Geography, University of Winnipeg. Formerly executive director of the Research and Policy Development Division with the Saskatchewan Housing Corporation and executive officer in charge of the Urban Economics Research Division of the National Capital Development Commission in Canberra, Australia. Worked on a wide variety of subject areas including housing demand, target groups for subsidized housing, and program development and evaluation.

GEORGE FALLIS   Associate Professor, Department of Economics and Division of Social Science, York University, Toronto; chairman, Department of Economics, York University. Formerly senior researcher at the Ontario Economic Council and Ministry of State for Urban Affairs. Author of many monographs and articles on housing economics and rent control. Has published several books including *Housing Economics* and *Housing Programs and Income Distribution in Ontario*.

WILLIAM JAY   Minister of the United Church of Canada and qualified in urban planning. Formerly executive director of the city mission, Macdonald House, in Montreal; now working in Quebec City.

LANGLEY KEYES   Professor, Department of Urban Studies and Planning, Massachusetts Institute of Technology, Cambridge, Massachusetts. Formerly head of the Department of Urban Studies and Planning, MIT, and Special Assistant for Policy Development, Executive Office of Community Development, Commonwealth of Massachusetts. Author of articles on housing policy and planning and of several books, including *The Boston Rehabilitation Program* and the *Rehabilitation Planning Game*.

ANN McAFEE   City of Vancouver Planning Department, Vancouver, British Columbia. Holds an interdisciplinary doctorate in community and regional planning, and commerce and business administration. Former scholar-in-residence at Queen's University and lecturer at the School of Community and Regional Planning, UBC. Author of numerous monographs and articles on planning and housing policy at the local level. Wrote entry on housing and housing policy in the *New Canadian Encyclopedia*.

RAMESH MISHRA   Professor, School of Social Work, Atkinson College, York University. Member of the editorial board of *Critical Social Policy* and *Journal of International and Comparative Social Welfare*. Author of many essays and articles on social policy, social administration, and the welfare state. Has published several books, including *The Welfare State in Crisis* and *Society and Social Policy: Theories and Practice of Welfare*.

ALEX MURRAY   Professor, Faculty of Environmental Studies, York University, Toronto. Member, National Coordinating Committee for Non-Governmental Organizations for IYSH in Canada. Former founder and co-ordinator of the Urban Studies Program, York University. Frequent consultant on urban design to governments, universities, and non-profit groups. Author of many monographs and books on housing issues, including *Edgeley: A Study of Housing and Human Behavior*.

JEANNE M. WOLFE   Associate Professor, School of Urban Planning, McGill University, Montreal, Quebec. Formerly Urbanist Senior, Ministère des Affaires Municipales, Quebec Government, and chair, National Board of Examiners, Canadian Institute of Planners. Member of the editorial Board of *Plan Canada* and *Environments*. Author of many essays and articles on urban design, urban planning, and social policy. Collaborator on *Rapport de la Commission d'Etude sur les municipalités*, Union des municipalités du Québec.

Index